Big Cat

Big Cat

The **Life** *of*
Baseball
Hall *of* **Famer**
Johnny Mize

JERRY GRILLO

University of Nebraska Press *Lincoln*

The University of Nebraska Press is part of a land-grant institution
with campuses and programs on the past, present, and future
homelands of the Pawnee, Ponca, Otoe-Missouria, Omaha, Dakota,
Lakota, Kaw, Cheyenne, and Arapaho Peoples, as well as those
of the relocated Ho-Chunk, Sac and Fox, and Iowa Peoples.

Library of Congress Cataloging-in-Publication Data
Names: Grillo, Jerry, 1960– author.
Title: Big Cat: the life of baseball hall of
famer Johnny Mize / Jerry Grillo.
Description: Lincoln: University of Nebraska Press, 2024. |
Includes bibliographical references and index.
Identifiers: LCCN 2023033204
ISBN 9781496235442 (hardback)
ISBN 9781496239716 (epub)
ISBN 9781496239723 (pdf)
Subjects: LCSH: Mize, Johnny, 1913–1993. | Baseball—United
States—History—20th century. | Baseball players—United States—
Biography. | BISAC: BIOGRAPHY & AUTOBIOGRAPHY /
Sports | SPORTS & RECREATION / Baseball / History
Classification: LCC GV865.M547 G75 2024 | DDC
796.357092 [B]—dc23/eng/20230719
LC record available at https://lccn.loc.gov/2023033204

Designed and set in Chaparral Pro by L. Welch.

For Anna and Tony,
my wonderful parents

CONTENTS

PREFACE   Finding Johnny Mize

On a clear blue Appalachian day in April 2022, when the Major League Baseball season was barely a week old, I marched across the heart of the Piedmont University campus in Demorest, Georgia, to measure the distance of a ninety-two-year-old home run.

Or maybe it was ninety-three years old. Some legends don't have specific dates attached, which is fine. I was only counting steps anyway.

"Home plate was right about there," said Bob Glass, the dean of libraries at Piedmont, pointing in the general direction of the Sewell Center for Teacher Education, next door to the spacious Arrendale Library, with its big painting of Johnny Mize hanging there on the wall for visitors to see as they arrive.

If you take a drone's eye view of Alumni Park—the university's lush, green commons, ringed by the Sewell Center, the library, and several academic and administrative buildings—you can see its past life as a baseball field. The shape is right there. You don't have to look very hard.

Starting in the approximate spot where the left-handed batter's box would have been, I marched northwest toward old U.S. 441 on the edge of the campus, where Mize is supposed to have hit a home run while playing college baseball as a high school kid, about fifty years before he was inducted into the National Baseball Hall of Fame.

It occurred to me while traipsing across the grass, trying to avoid the stares of students sticking to the paved paths, that Mize had hit his monster shot to the opposite field. *Of course*, I thought, remembering Mize's book, *How to Hit. He taught himself to hit straight away and developed tremendous power to all fields.*

I reached the highway in 172 steps, or about 460 feet. "Jesus, what a shot," I exclaimed out loud, forgetting that Piedmont is affiliated with the United Church of Christ.

--- --- ---

The home run was already a fading legend when I first heard about it in 1999, years after Mize's death. No one I knew had seen it. There were just stories. At the time, I was editor of the *Northeast Georgian*, a twice-weekly newspaper in rural Habersham County, where Mize had grown up. His stepdaughter, Judi Mize, called one day to pitch a story.

She invited me to visit the Mize cottage, Diamond Acre in Demorest (population of about two thousand), the 1890s-era home where Johnny grew up and later died, and where Judi would die in January 2022.

Judi is a big reason that this book exists. I'd never met Johnny Mize, but Judi reached out to me that February day, sparking my interest. She loved her father, was glad to talk about him. She truly was Daddy's girl.

"Judi had him wrapped around her finger," said her big brother, Jim Mize, Johnny's stepson. Jim didn't have it quite as easy with the old man as his pretty sister, explaining, "I was a bit of a wild child."

It was Jim who had called his little sister with the big news that she then wanted to share with me. "Go get a box of Wheaties," he said to Judi over the phone.

She hated the stuff and demanded, "Why on Earth?"

Jim was excited. "Dad is on the back of the box!"

Wheaties, the "Breakfast of Champions," had just issued a special seventy-fifth anniversary box featuring little pictures of seventy-five Wheaties champions on the back (Babe Ruth, Jackie Robinson, Arthur Ashe, Michael Jordan, and so on). Johnny Mize was on the box in 1939, the year he led the National League in home runs and batting average. Consumers were asked to select their favorites, and the top ten would have their Wheaties box rereleased on store shelves, ostensibly to the delight of collectors and lovers of bland, cold cereal.[1]

After the results were tabulated and Johnny hadn't made the cut, Judi sighed, "It would have been great to see Daddy's Wheaties cover framed on one of these walls."

Instead, the walls were covered with other photos of Mize—in action, in uniforms (Major League and U.S. Navy), in street clothes, with his wife, Marjorie. There was a whole room of Johnny stuff—the Dear John room, an upstairs porch that Marjorie had converted into a space to showcase Johnny's fan mail and other mementos.

When I first met Judi in 1999, Piedmont College (not called a university yet) was in the process of acquiring Diamond Acre from the Mize family, with the understanding that Judi could live there for the rest of her days. Part of the deal sent her father's memorabilia to Piedmont for a little Mize museum the school placed in the lobby of its new Johnny Mize Athletic Center, which opened in 2000. Piedmont got gloves, bats, balls, uniforms, cards, photos, awards, and other valuables.

During a visit to Diamond Acre after the Mize family had signed the deed over to the college, Judi pulled what looked like an old dress box from under a bed. It contained signed baseballs, some photos. "I'm holding on to these," she said, running her fingers along the baseballs. With her father's mementos gone, she still felt protective of his legacy, even his nickname. She was annoyed that the Atlanta Braves' first baseman at the time, Andrés Galarraga, also was called "Big Cat."

"Daddy was the 'Big Cat'! It's on his plaque in the Baseball Hall of Fame! How can he take Daddy's name?"

I explained that someone else had given Galarraga the nickname, just like with her father. "Besides, Galarraga's a good guy and terrific player," I said. "Johnny would probably be proud someone like him is carrying on the tradition."

Another thread links the two Big Cats besides the shared nickname. Galarraga was one of the greatest stars from Venezuela to play Major League ball. And Mize, as a young man during the winter of 1933–34, played for an All-Star team from Venezuela that was one of the greatest teams ever assembled in Latin America.

That must have been an impressionable experience for a kid from rural Northeast Georgia: living the young bachelor's life and playing ball on islands where dictators ruled at gunpoint—and playing rather well, a minority among Black and Latin players who were kings of the diamond on the islands and in the Negro Leagues. Long before Johnny Mize became the best left-handed hitter in the National League, long before he was known as the Big Cat (*the* Big Cat), newspapers and fans in Latin America were singing his praises, for the "beastly" home runs he smashed through distant palm trees on sandy beaches.[2]

But neither Judi nor I were aware of the winter-ball details when we last spoke. Her father never was much of a talker and didn't spend a lot of time reflecting or reminiscing or sharing. He wasn't the nostalgic or sentimental type.

Consequently, very little was known about this interesting and, no doubt, formative period of Mize's life, his winter in the Caribbean, when I sent my original pitch for a Johnny Mize biography to another publisher, way back in 2001. I'd already interviewed several sources, such as former ballplayers Whitey Ford, Bobby Brown, Buddy Blattner, Don Gutteridge, and Bill Werber, and writers who knew Mize, like Donald Honig, Peter Golenbock, and Bob Broeg. I sent a few chapters to the publisher. Then, to my complete shock, an offer arrived in the mail.

But very soon after that, my son, Joe, was suddenly born—a preemie, three months ahead of schedule. Life, from there, took a long series of sharp, unexpected, and educational turns, shifting my attention far away from baseball and the notion of writing a book. I had to regretfully tell the publisher that my plans for a Mize biography were on hold until further notice, preferably after the world stopped spinning.

Joe, our second child, fourteen years younger than our daughter, Samantha, was diagnosed with spastic quadriplegia cerebral palsy a few months after his birth. As I write this, he is a busy, caring, handsome twenty-two-year-old young man. And though he needs assistance with most activities of daily living, he accepts it all with grace and humor and gives back to our family as a loving and wickedly funny son, and to the community as a teacher and advocate.

He also is a big music lover and was a major inspiration for my first book, *The Music and Mythocracy of Col. Bruce Hampton: A Basically True Biography*, published in 2021. Joe reenergized and helped expand my love of music. Music is a beautiful link in the chain of family tradition because my father and I bonded over music. (Speaking of music, with a bit of digging I discovered an odd connection between Johnny Mize and the Beatles—you'll see.)

But much more than music, baseball was the major bond for me and Dad. He told stories of New York in the '30s, '40s, and '50s, sometimes as he was playing cards with various and nefarious uncles and pals. He told me about Johnny Mize. Together, we watched the Big Cat lumbering on an Atlanta baseball field, stretching the manmade fabric of an early 1970s Cardinals uniform at an old-timer's game. Stan Musial, Mickey Mantle, Yogi Berra, and a lot of immortals were on the field that day. Dad was most interested in Mize, whom he described as "a true artist with a bat in his hands." But he brought us to this particular game with the specific intention of meeting Mize's longtime friend and former teammate, Stan "the Man" Musial.

That was a surreal experience. It involved a crumpled business card that an old friend of Stan's gave Dad during a trip to Musial's hometown, Donora, Pennsylvania. (Dad was an executive with Brunswick Bowling.) We presented this card to one of the field crew, who presented it to Stan, who came loping—so help me, he loped—out of the dugout to visit with us. My brother, cousin, and I shook the Man's hand, chatted a while, got his autograph, and secured a lovely memory that we still enjoy sharing decades later.

We returned, probably levitating part of the way, to our seats twenty or so rows up, behind home plate, with our autographs and our stories. Dad sat there with a wide, "Did I deliver, or what?" smile on his face. I thought of that smile and that day thirteen short years later, when my father was near the end of his life. The last time we spoke, Dad recalled the day he introduced his boys to Stan Musial, when the great players of his generation gathered in Atlanta's saucer-shaped ballpark.

Though he lived in Brooklyn for a time, appreciated the Dodgers as well as the Giants, and visited all three classic New York ballparks in olden times, Dad was a lifelong Yankees fan. He loved Yankee Stadium most of all—the Yankee Stadium, as it was called. A Sicilian American, Dad loved Joe DiMaggio, Yogi Berra, and Phil Rizzuto, but Lou Gehrig was his all-time favorite player (as much for the movie The Pride of the Yankees as for Dad's earliest baseball memories, which involved watching Lou, the Iron Horse, in action).

But Dad's memories of Johnny Mize were special. He loved seeing the Big Cat move from the Polo Grounds to Yankees pinstripes. "They thought he was finished when he came to the Yankees from the Giants in '49," Dad said. "Then he became the best pinch hitter in baseball. Without Johnny Mize, the Yankees don't win five-straight World Series."

I always knew that I'd return to Mize. While waiting for the Bruce Hampton book to be published, I started thinking seriously again about my first love, baseball, and the legendary slugger who lived and died just a few miles from where I now live: our local legend, Johnny Mize.

I went back into the old notes, asked some new questions, and did a lot of new research. I discovered a more interesting person, a more interesting life. In the years since putting down that first manuscript, I've learned so much about this mountain man of the South, unearthed some remarkable stories about his fascinating life—his family (his relationship to two of baseball's greatest legends, Babe Ruth and Ty Cobb), his loves, his ups and downs, his life away from baseball, and of course, his career as one of the greatest hitters who ever lived.

Let me introduce you to *the* Big Cat.

Big Cat

Prologue   Crossing the River

The Big Cat stands in the October shadows of Ebbets Field, a thirty-six-ounce Louisville Slugger, Rogers Hornsby model, poised over his left shoulder. The count is two balls and one strike, with two out and the bases loaded in the top of the ninth inning in Game Three of the 1949 World Series. The score is 1–1.

Here is Johnny Mize in the twilight of his stunning baseball career, now playing for the New York Yankees, facing the Brooklyn Dodgers' hard-throwing right-hander Ralph Branca. Mize is familiar with Branca because, until late August, he'd been a New York Giant, over in the National League, playing for manager Leo Durocher in the Polo Grounds, across the Harlem River from Yankee Stadium.

But Mize didn't fit into the plans of the fast-talking, speed-loving Durocher. So, Leo sent the aging first baseman with the sluggish legs over the river to the Bronx for $40,000.

Yankees manager Casey Stengel doesn't want Mize's legs. He wants his bat, and he wants it for this precise moment.

- - -

The Big Cat stood at the podium wearing his stripes on a wide necktie, the sleeves of his tan jacket bunched on his shoulders. His impassive smile barely concealed the genuine pride and giddy relief he felt just for being here in Cooperstown, New York, for his induction—finally—to the National Baseball Hall of Fame.

It was hot and cloudy in upstate New York on August 2, 1981, but the rain held, and Johnny Mize, sixty-eight, was the center of the nation's attention again. He stood up there in front of three thousand or so people in lawn chairs, on blankets, or standing. Behind him on the stage were twenty-one other Hall of Famers, including Bob Gibson, also being inducted that day.

This was the day Mize had been looking forward to with a simmering hope, ever since quitting the game twenty-eight years earlier. He'd gone out in a blaze of fortune and glory, playing a pivotal supporting role as the Yankees' aging, dangerous hitting specialist from 1949 through 1953, as the team won a record five-straight World Series.

When he quit playing, he was tabbed as a can't-miss Hall of Famer. In December 1953, a month after Mize retired, New York's *Daily News* sports editor Jimmy Powers wrote, "Rules call for a full year's retirement before a candidate is eligible for the Hall of Fame. Johnny Mize will be on our 1955 ballot."[1]

But in 1954 the Hall of Fame extended its eligibility rule to five full years following retirement. After that, an epidemic of amnesia or pigheadedness consumed the Baseball Writers' Association of America (BBWAA), which votes on Hall of Fame inductees. Despite being one of the best hitters in his era, the Big Cat never got close on the writers' ballot.

"In their fog of stubbornness, the writers badly missed on a true legend in Johnny Mize," wrote Joe Posnanski in *The Baseball 100*. (Mize is ranked number 64.) It's one of the BBWAA's biggest misses in the history of Hall of Fame voting, Posnanski continued, "a thorough embarrassment."[2]

- - -

Mize, a thinking man's slugger, played his prime years in an era of superstars named Gehrig, DiMaggio, Foxx, Greenberg, Ott, Musial, and Williams. And he could hit with all of them.

"Mize was one of the really outstanding hitters in baseball history," declared Ted Williams. "Every place he played, from the time he started to play baseball until the time he quit, he was a premier hitter. When he ambled up to the plate, people expected big things because he made things happen. I always thought he was one of the very best."[3] Perhaps Williams saw something of himself in Mize, who was a few years older than Ted.

"Mize was like Ted Williams—all he thought about was hitting," recalled Mize's former New York Giants teammate, third baseman Bill Werber, in a 2001 interview. "When you were playing against him, if you had two strikes on him, you could never relax at third, because when he swung the bat, he hit the ball, and he was so strong. He could hit the ball to left as hard as he could hit it to right."[4]

Though he did not have Ted Williams's famous temperament, or charisma, the good-natured Mize probably shared the Splendid Splinter's defensive apathy.

"Mize didn't care about his fielding, and some of his teammates resented him for that," said author Peter Golenbock. "He was a hitter, and the older he got, the less he cared about other aspects of the game."[5]

And Mize could be peculiar, or maybe he would just say peculiar things. "He told me that he never took a drink of water in a Major League ballpark," recalled Joe Lattanzi, an athlete at Piedmont College about twenty years after Mize was and who got to know the Big Cat after Mize moved back to his hometown of Demorest, Georgia, in the 1970s. "[He told me he] would chew bubblegum and tobacco together, and he kept that wad in his mouth the whole game; [he] claimed it kept his mouth moist enough and that drinking water would dry him out."[6]

Still, others found him friendly and accommodating—neither a shy person nor a gadabout, "not antisocial but not what you'd call a social butterfly either," said Buddy Blattner, Mize's occasional New York Giants roommate, who moved on to a long career in sports broadcasting following his playing a career.[7]

Johnny might be more inclined to order room service and read the sports pages than go out with the boys, especially later in his career. "He studied those box scores—he always knew what Stan Musial and the other great hitters were doing," Blattner recalled. "And he approached hitting like a science."[8]

He could even seem placid at times—he was occasionally called "Gentle John"—and could also be a bona fide nice guy. In fact, Mize's niceness was immortalized in *Nice Guys Finish Last*, Leo Durocher's dubious but highly entertaining autobiography. Durocher claimed he conjured the famous line while managing the Brooklyn Dodgers. It happened during batting practice before a game with the New York Giants at the Polo Grounds. Leo was holding forth on the merits of his second baseman, Eddie "the Brat" Stanky, when the Giants began walking out of the dugout. Pointing to their manager, Mel Ott, and several players, including Mize, Sid Gordon, and Bobby Thomson, Durocher supposedly said, "All nice guys. They'll finish last. Nice guys. Finish last."[9]

Yankees great Tommy Henrich agreed that Big Jawn was a nice guy, and "as warm a fellow as you want to meet," he wrote in the foreword of Mize's book, *How to Hit*. Mize, Henrich wrote, "wisely offers his opinions only on subjects he is familiar with."[10]

Another Yankees teammate, Bobby Brown (also president of the American League, 1984–94), said that Mize "could be loquacious if you struck up a conversation with him, especially about baseball. He would talk at great length about hitting, and he knew what he was talking about."[11]

Author Donald Honig, who first met the Big Cat in 1974, when he interviewed him for the classic *Baseball When the Grass Was Real*, said Mize was "a formidable physical presence. Though a big man, he seemed even larger, broad and powerful," but with a deep and mellow voice, succinct and to the point.[12] "He did not ramble off into anecdotal reminiscences, as many players did," Honig added. "I found him to be highly intelligent and, in his quiet way, articulate, as well as courteous and obliging, though not a warm man. He had a sly sense of humor and watched carefully when delivering some understated quip, to see if I was getting it."

- - -

At his Hall of Fame induction, Mize spoke to the crowd in his matter-of-fact, deep southern voice, clearing the gravel from his throat periodically as he spoke—a habit he kept in old age, probably due to the cigars he'd sneak out in the shed back home in Demorest, Georgia. He greeted the mayor of Cooperstown and the commissioner of baseball, Bowie Kuhn, and most importantly, he spoke directly to the fans, many of whom were still hopping mad about the Major League Baseball players strike that had been settled just a few days earlier.

And when broadcasting veteran Jack Buck, the emcee that day, told the crowd, "Isn't it fun to think that a week from today we'll be watching the All-Star Game," he received a round of righteous boos and angry cries of: "What about the fans?" Then they booed Commissioner Kuhn too.[13]

Mize had a pacifying answer when it was his turn to speak. "Without you baseball fans, none of us would be here today," he said. That got him some big cheers, some approving whistles, and a round of hearty applause. The crowd was with him. The crowd knew his story.

"Oh, years ago writers were telling me that I'd make the Hall of Fame, so I kind of prepared a speech," he said, and he surfed the resulting wave of laughter like a toastmaster, then added with perfect deadpan timing, "but somewhere along in the twenty-eight years it got lost."

Big laughter now. Mize was comfortable. He was in good company. He introduced his wife, Marjorie, who stood up and waved, looking every bit like the gleaming woman in white standing up in the Chicago bleachers in the film version of *The Natural*. Their pretty daughter, Johnny's step-daughter, Judi, was there with her second (and soon-to-be-ex) husband, and so was the Mizes' oldest grandson, Darren Mize. Also, there was a group of friends from back home in Northeast Georgia, including Lieutenant Governor (and future U.S. senator) Zell Miller and Georgia state senator John Foster.

And up there on the stage behind Mize were guys he'd been easy with for fifty years, ballplayers from his generation, other Hall of Famers like Bob Feller, Stan Musial, Ralph Kiner, Warren Spahn, Buck Leonard, and Cool Papa Bell. Now they were all part of the same fraternity, and these men remembered Mize when he was young, back when they were all written about in sports pages from coast to coast, when newspaper sports pages and box scores were like sacred scrolls to the baseball faithful.

Mize's larger than life feats had been well documented: the only player, ever, to hit more than fifty home runs in a season and strike out fewer than fifty times; the first player to hit three home runs in a game four different times, then five times, then six times in a career—first to do it twice in a season and first to do it twice in a season *twice* (1938 and 1940), including just eight days apart (June 1938); first player to hit three homers in a game for three different teams, first to do it in both leagues; most three home run games in which his team lost. He also holds some obscure records: Mize had the most consecutive games scoring a run in the National League, and he's the only player to hit the experimental yellow ball for a home run (you'll see). Also, he's the last player to lead his league in all the extra-base hit categories at one time or another—doubles, triples, and homers. No one else since Mize—not Aaron, not Mays, not Musial, not Pujols, not Bonds, not Trout—has done that.

Mize generated ferocious power with a beautiful left-handed swing. "Nobody had a better, smoother, easier swing than John," said former teammate Don Gutteridge. "It was picture perfect."[14]

- - -

Mize was a rookie sensation, twice—first with the Cincinnati Reds during spring training in 1935, then with the St. Louis Cardinals for the entire season in 1936. It's kind of complicated. But once he was allowed to stick around in the big leagues, he quickly became a star, making headlines and giving pitchers headaches.

He struggled with injuries, held out for more money, and developed a deeper understanding of baseball's mercenary underpinnings when it came time for contract negotiations each year and when he was sold to the New York Giants just as a world war was breaking out. He played baseball on Pacific Islands during his time in the navy, his lifetime baseball statistics taking a beating from the prime seasons he missed during World War II. Then he chased Babe Ruth's single-season home run record and later finished his career as a five-time World Series champion with the Yankees.

In poetic hindsight, Mize was destined to be a great ballplayer—he was related to both Ruth and Ty Cobb. He was one of the most valuable players of his generation, a good and loyal teammate, but not a rah-rah guy. He probably carried more bats than the rest of the team combined. He could be quiet and wary, distrustful of people he didn't know, "especially those who wore a press label in their hatband, which contributed no little to the reason the door to the Baseball Hall of Fame was slammed in his face so many times," wrote Furman Bisher of the *Atlanta Constitution*.[15]

He could be gracious. He could also be critical, and sometimes he was a clubhouse lawyer. He could be friendly, and he always was self-assured. He moved with the tranquil grace of a big cat. Or he moved like a big cat stuck in two feet of mud, and his famous nickname might have come from either one of those scenarios.

Mize claimed that he got the nickname from a teammate, for his slick fielding. Bob Broeg, a longtime St. Louis sportswriter, said "it was a derisive nickname" that made fun of his plodding style around first base later in his career.

But Stan Musial may have offered the best explanation for why Mize was called the Big Cat: "Did you ever see a pitcher knock him down at the plate? Remember how he reacted when they brushed him back? He'd just lean back on his left foot, bend his body back and let the pitch go by. Then he'd lean back into the batter's box and resume his stance, as graceful as a big cat."[16]

He had other nicknames: Big Jawn, Gentle John, the Mighty Mongol. Grantland Rice called him the Demorest Demon and the Demorest Destroyer.[17] But Mize always preferred Big Cat. And the Big Cat was an unsentimental pragmatist who was proud of his past but didn't romanticize it. Baseball was a job, and though he enjoyed the work, it was still work, and he took it seriously, rolled up his sleeves, and clocked in day after day with a trunk full of Louisville Sluggers that he used to bat .300 and hit baseballs out of the park.

He was a mostly tolerant white man from an intolerant South. Specifically, Mize was from Northeast Georgia, where the cussed independent streak of local people gives this corner of Appalachia a proud regional iconoclasm.

- - -

When it was Mize's turn to enter the Cooperstown fraternity, he joined an eclectic class of new inductees. In addition to him and fellow former Cardinal Bob Gibson (elected in his first year of eligibility by the baseball writers), also being enshrined that day was Rube Foster, the great pitcher and manager who'd launched the Negro Leagues; Detroit Tigers broadcaster Ernie Harwell (like Mize, a rural Georgia native), who received the Ford C. Frick Award for broadcast excellence; and veteran baseball writer Milton Richman, who earned the J. G. Taylor Spink Award.

Johnny told the crowd that he started his professional baseball career as a pinch hitter and ended it the same way. He told the story of how he played baseball for Piedmont College while still a fifteen-year-old high school kid in Demorest, Georgia, and how the coach fixed it so that, if Mize enrolled in one college course, he'd be eligible to play college ball. "They never mentioned the subject, and I didn't either," Mize told his audience. More laughter—Musial, in dark shades, nearly shook out of his chair with it.

The mood was light, but just beneath the laughter and genuine good vibes was another layer of truth. Everyone there knew that Mize had never received the minimum number of votes from the baseball writers, had never come close. They knew that Mize had been bitter, watching other players with lesser credentials pass through the door. The fans knew that Mize had rolled off the writers' ballot, per Hall of Fame voting rules, and landed in the hands of the Veterans Committee.

Years earlier, Mize stopped wondering why the writers had forgotten him. But he made sure to thank the old-timers who had elected him, and he told his audience, "The other day I was talking with some people, and someone said, 'Don't you think going in by the Veterans Committee is going in the back door?' I said, no, just look who's on that committee. You'll see managers, general managers, ex-ballplayers, nearly all of them in the Hall of Fame. Who would you want to pick you? Now there's your peers. When they pick you, you should be very proud. In Hollywood if you get picked by your peers you receive an Oscar."

Huge applause. Big cheers for the Big Cat. An Oscar moment, and Mize had people to thank: "All the people that've been sending me letters and calling me from all over the country. They were sticking with me even when I failed. They kept on writing. I want to thank all those people and all the people who worked so hard trying to get me into the Hall of Fame."

He felt truly thankful to be there in Cooperstown and concluded that it was particularly nice to be inducted while still among the living, "because it's a lot better when you're able to smell the roses."

More cheers. And this was indeed better. This was everything Mize had wanted since leaving the game in 1953. This was Valhalla, baseball's Olympus, a lifetime honor that didn't even exist when he first left tiny Demorest in 1930 to begin his professional career, an eager, husky seventeen-year-old kid from the Appalachian foothills with astonishing power, off to see the wide world and hit home runs.

1

Hills of Habersham

I never thought too much about
being a ballplayer back then.   —Johnny Mize[1]

Thomas Anderson Mize was a big man in Flintsville, Georgia. Basically, he was *the* big man in Flintsville. The Mize clan had come down from Virginia in the eighteenth century and settled in South Carolina before moving to this spot in Northeast Georgia. But it took someone strong, with plenty of ideas and ambition, to put it on the map, someone like big Tom Mize, who built, owned, and operated the only store in that part of the state.[2]

In addition to Tom's duties as postmaster (appointed by President James K. Polk in 1847) and his proprietorship of the store (which included the occasional four-day round trip by horse-drawn wagon to bustling Athens, home of the University of Georgia, about fifty miles south), Mize also was involved in the local sports scene. Men would come from miles around on a Saturday to watch, participate in, and bet on horse racing or foot racing, wrestling, jumping competitions, cockfighting, and shooting contests.[3]

Mize was a central figure in these backwoodsy games. And whenever two men let the heat of competition boil over into anger, he facilitated bare-knuckled brawls to work it out. This no doubt inspired even more wagering, as well as thirst, which could be quenched by the whiskey Mize sold right there in his store. (In those days, every country store sold whiskey, every family had a jug on the kitchen table, and the local Baptist preacher got paid in corn liquor.)[4]

After the combatants had pummeled each other, Tom made sure they shook hands in the spirit of neighborliness and parted as friends—at least until the next Saturday.[5] Through all of this, big Tom Mize—entrepreneur, community leader, fight promoter—exhibited a strength and competitive nature that he would pass down to his more famous progeny, Ty Cobb and Johnny Mize.

Thomas and his wife, Martha, had seven children. Their fifth child, Sisely, one of four daughters, married Caleb Chitwood in 1871, and their first child, Amanda, married (and later shot to death) William Herschel Cobb. Amanda's first child, Tyrus Raymond Cobb, later known as the "Georgia Peach," was born in Narrows, Georgia, about fifteen miles west of the Flintsville township, later to be renamed Mize.

Thomas and Martha's son, Thomas Addison Mize (a Confederate casualty in the Civil War), had seven children with his wife, Sarah. Their son Francis "Frank" Mize and his wife, Emma, had one child, William Edward Mize—everyone called him Eddie.

Eddie would marry Emma Loudermilk. And their second son, who became well known as the Big Cat, became one of baseball's greatest sluggers. So, Eddie Mize and Ty Cobb shared a great-grandpa, Thomas Anderson Mize, which made the Big Cat and the Georgia Peach distant cousins.

In retrospect, Johnny seemed destined for baseball glory, being related to two of the biggest stars ever to play the game, two charter members of the Baseball Hall of Fame. In addition to his blood relationship to Cobb, Johnny was related to the Sultan of Swat, Babe Ruth.

Eddie Mize's first cousin was Claire Merritt (who knew her distant cousin Ty Cobb, through her father, James Merritt—Cobb's lawyer). An actress, she was a widow with a daughter, living in New York, when she met George Herman "Babe" Ruth. Years later when he was a ballplayer and visiting or living in New York, Johnny made it a point to see his cousins, George and Claire Ruth, in their Riverside Drive apartment.

- - -

Habersham County, like pretty much every other jurisdiction in Northeast Georgia, was carved mostly out of land that was taken from the Cherokee Nation. Created by the state of Georgia in 1818, the county was named for Revolutionary War officer and U.S. postmaster general Joseph Habersham, who lived in Savannah on the Georgia coast but had a summer home near what is now Clarkesville, the county seat since 1823.[6]

Johnny Mize's family, early settlers in the region, mostly lived off the land as farmers. And during the Civil War, some of them became soldiers. They fought for the Confederacy, which wasn't odd for southern men at the time, of course. Then again, such allegiance was not automatic in this part of Georgia, where fiercely independent mountain families who didn't own slaves also didn't care about the so-called glorious cause.[7]

In the decades following the war, rail lines linking Atlanta to northern cities were expanded in the region, bringing some economic development to Northeast Georgia.[8] The railroads made it easier to efficiently ship and receive goods and resources, and easier for tourists and summer residents to visit the mountains, spend their money, then go home—a pattern of human commotion very much in play to this day.

The Habersham towns of Clarkesville and Cornelia thrived as visitors flocked to the region to enjoy the mountains, rivers, and forests. The creation in 1889 of Demorest, about halfway between those two cities, helped feed the economic growth trickling into the region.[9]

The city began as a private enterprise called the Demorest Home, Mining & Improvement Company. Named for New York philanthropist and alcohol-prohibition guru William Jennings Demorest, this was a planned community, and the plan was to build houses, establish industries, and create employment opportunities that "would attract from various parts of the nation, people with high ideals."[10]

Most of the company-city's founders were from the North and Midwest. The high ideals they had in mind conflicted with one of the region's potential growth engines. Following the war, the agricultural landscape expanded as European immigrants began growing grapes to start a wine industry. The timing couldn't have been worse for these would-be vintners.

Demorest was founded as a temperance town at a time when the sobriety movement was expanding across the Bible Belt. In 1907 Georgia banned the production, transportation, and sale of alcoholic spirits. So, the wineries didn't happen—not then. Today, dozens of wineries are thriving in the region.

Nonetheless, even with legal prohibition, Northeast Georgia did not go thirsty. An underground moonshine economy emerged across the Blue Ridge, and it sustained industrious mountain families for generations. These people discovered early on that an efficient and cost-effective way to store (and sell) corn was in a mason jar, as liquor. Georgia's statewide prohibition lasted until 1935, and many counties (such as Habersham) remained legally dry for many decades after.

Illegal liquor was available and affordable in the hills and hollers in and around Habersham for many, many years, which proved to be regrettable for Johnny Mize's family.

- - -

Eddie was born January 12, 1881, in Banks County, about thirty miles south of Demorest, where his parents, Frank and Emma, would eventually move the family. He was working as a butcher and living with his parents when he married Emma Loudermilk, a strong-minded gal with a measured, serious manner and high cheekbones that accentuated her pretty, round face.

Emma Loudermilk was one of five children born to John and Sarah Loudermilk. She was born into a large family that is still well-known throughout Northeast Georgia. Cornelia is home to the Loudermilk Boarding House Museum, which also contains the Everything Elvis Museum, operated by artist Joni Mabe, a distant cousin of Johnny Mize. And Piedmont University's Charlie Loudermilk Field is named for an influential Atlanta businessman who donated the funds for the baseball facility.

Emma was fifteen when she married Eddie, who was twenty-seven, in June 1908. The couple's first son, William Pope Mize, was born on August 21, 1910. Johnny's older brother, Pope, would play an important role in his life early on. The two boys were each other's best friends when they were young, but they would eventually drift far apart.

"They didn't talk much. Over the course of fifty years, they didn't see each other more than ten times," noted Pope's son, Gwen Pope Mize, in a 2001 interview.[11]

On January 7, 1913, Eddie and Emma celebrated the arrival of their second son, John Robert Mize. Throughout his life he would be called, almost equally, John or Johnny. But when he was a young boy, everyone called him Skippy.

"He never walked anywhere," his mother, Emma, would recall years later, after Johnny had become a World Series hero. "He ran, or skipped, or jumped along."[12]

An energetic, apple-faced, little boy skipping along a rural village road paints an idyllic image of an old-fashioned American fantasy, invoking warm feelings of family, home, community, and Norman Rockwell. But as Leo Tolstoy famously began his novel *Anna Karenina*, "Happy families are all alike; every unhappy family is unhappy in its own way."

The Mizes were part of that second group.

"It was not a close or happy family," said Gwen Pope Mize.[13]

The reasons for the dissolution of the marriage are unclear—by 1920 Eddie and Emma had split. Eddie was living with his parents on their farm just outside of Demorest, and Emma moved to Atlanta to work at the J. M. High Company department store, a job she would keep for more than thirty years.[14]

Young Pope joined Emma in Atlanta, where he attended a military school for a time, but Johnny stayed put in Demorest with his Aunt Lizzie Loudermilk and his grandma Sarah Loudermilk, in the white house on the corner of Georgia Street and Oak Avenue, near the campus of Piedmont College—a home that Mize later named Diamond Acre.

Piedmont opened in 1897 as J. S. Green Collegiate Institute by a group of New England transplants and a Methodist minister, Rev. Charles Spence. The name was changed to Piedmont College in 1903 and to Piedmont University in 2021.[15]

While young Johnny seemed to thrive in this environment, life was not easy for Eddie Mize. For one thing, he struggled with a significant disability. According to the 1910 census and his World War I draft registration card, Eddie was deaf.

As if living with a disability wasn't hard enough in the early twentieth century, Eddie fell into an alcohol-infused existential pit, and according to Gwen Pope Mize, "Though I never knew my grandfather, the story is, the alcohol is why the family broke up, why my grandma went to work in Atlanta."[16]

Eddie and Emma never legally divorced—they separated. She kept Mize as her last name and years later would claim that she moved to Atlanta after her husband died, which was not the case but evidently made for a more acceptable narrative. Even without the divorce, Eddie essentially disappeared from his family's life. As he was growing up, Johnny didn't cross paths with his father often and rarely mentioned him.

- - -

Despite the problems between his parents, Skippy managed to enjoy a mostly carefree and active childhood in Demorest, a town of some eight hundred souls when Mize was a boy. "You know how it is when you're a kid," he told author Donald Honig. "You just go from day to day, growing up, not giving much thought to tomorrow."[17]

His family wasn't rich—he didn't know any rich people in town. Everybody had their own gardens and raised what they could, "and you had relatives around, and they all had some type of farm, so there was always food, nobody was going to starve," Mize told Honig. "Whenever somebody came to visit, they'd bring vegetables and lay them on the table. We got by."[18]

There were rivers to fish and swim in, woods to explore, plenty of game to hunt, games to play, and mules and horses to ride, bareback, fast, and hard across the gnarled terrain of Northeast Georgia (the long-term, latent effects of which would threaten Mize's baseball career years later).

Mize gravitated toward sports early on, but it wasn't baseball that first captured his interest. "I played more basketball than anything else in those days because it was easier to get up a basketball team than a baseball team," he told Honig. "In fact, I played more tennis as a kid than either baseball or basketball because it took even fewer people."[19]

He won the county singles championship two years in a row as a youth and the mixed doubles title the first year. Mize developed excellent hand-eye coordination through tennis practice. "He would talk proudly about how long he could keep a rally going while hitting a tennis ball against the barn using a broomstick," writes Joe Posnanski in his book *The Baseball 100*. "He had no doubt that led to his greatness as a hitter."[20]

Bitten by the baseball bug when he was eleven and in the fifth grade, Mize tried his hand as a catcher, "without a mask, which was very foolish—for obvious reasons," he said.[21]

Living next door to a college had its advantages for the Mize boys and their friends. Johnny recalled that when he was thirteen and about a year away from attending the local high school (Piedmont Academy, affiliated with the college), "I remember how my brother and I would stand outside the fence of the college ball field and retrieve the balls hit over the fence. For this chore, we were allowed to stand in the outfield and shag flies during the team workouts."[22]

When practice was over, Piedmont College baseball coach Harry Forester would let the local boys keep the broken bats left behind. Mize and his pals would play on the field until it was too dark to see a ball in flight.

Mize went through a dramatic growth spurt after thirteen and developed astonishing power with his homegrown, left-handed swing. By the time Johnny was fifteen, Forester wanted him to do a lot more than shag flies for the college boys.

— — —

If Johnny Mize had anything like a father figure, it was probably Forester, who was the athletics director of the Piedmont College Lions, coaching football, basketball, and baseball. He also chaired the biology department, taught a full course load, and left a lasting impression on the community. "He was one of the great people I ever knew in my whole life," recalled James Davis "Spec" Landrum, whose father was the business manager for Piedmont. Landrum spent a lot of time with the Foresters, who used to give Spec rides to school.[23]

Harry, whose middle name was Bible, also had a mighty influence on young Mize, who didn't mention his parents during his Hall of Fame speech but did talk about his old coach in a rare show of sentimentality for the Big Cat. "Harry Forester is the one who started me on the road to the Hall of Fame," Mize said. "It's too bad he is gone. But I'm sure he's looking down."

The same problem that kept the Mize boys from getting up a good sandlot game prevented them from playing high school ball. "There never seemed to be enough fellows to complete a high school team, so the high school athletes would try out for the college team," Mize said.[24]

Ultimately, he played at least three seasons of college baseball while he was a high school student and a professional ballplayer. Mize was bigger than the college-aged kids, already surpassing six feet at fifteen years old. More to the point, the coach, who supposedly played some Minor League ball, saw that Mize had a gun for an arm and hit the ball a lot harder and farther than anyone else. So, he kept at the big kid with a litany of, "Come out for the team; come out for the team." Mize finally did, delivering a base hit in his first time at bat. Soon he was in the lineup as an outfielder and first baseman.

Mize was a self-taught hitting prodigy who adapted quickly to small-college baseball. Meanwhile, he started earning some cash on the weekends playing for different semipro teams. An Atlanta industrial league team needs an outfielder? Might as well spend the weekend at Mom's place and pick up a few extra bucks. Why not? Big brother Pope was doing it. While he didn't have Johnny's eye at the plate, Pope had pop in his bat and was a star player in Atlanta's semipro leagues, and he'd briefly play pro ball in the low Minors, sometimes billed as Major League star Johnny Mize's "younger" brother.

Jack Ellard, who knew both Mize boys and later spent a long stretch as clerk of the Georgia House of Representatives, remembered, "Pope might have been as good a hitter as Johnny, but he didn't have any kind of an arm."[25]

During football season at Piedmont, a gridiron took the place of a baseball diamond. Home plate was in one end zone. Ellard, who also attended Piedmont, said, "I saw Johnny hit a baseball from home plate through the goal posts at the other end of the field and clear it with a lot of room to spare, 350 to 400 feet—many times."[26]

Between college and semipro ball, Johnny was like a gunslinger for hire, shuffling gigs for five and ten bucks a pop. One week in April 1930 is a fine example: He helped Piedmont beat Elon College in Greensboro, North Carolina, on April 24, striking the key hit and playing slick defense at first base.[27] On Saturday, April 26, he played shortstop in Atlanta, joining Pope on the Southern Spring Bed Company team, which thrashed Ruralist Press in a city league contest. Pope "lifted the first ball pitched out into Fair Street for an easy home run," reported the *Atlanta Constitution*. And Johnny "made a spectacular grab of a line drive over short."[28]

There didn't seem to be any issues with Johnny's amateur status, because the rules were lax for a small, private college like Piedmont in those days. The fact that Piedmont didn't belong to any athletic conference at the time helped keep things on the down-low. Either nobody was paying attention, or nobody cared. Even after Mize had established himself as a pro in the Cardinals chain, he played for Piedmont (in 1931 and for a short time in 1932).

Forester had a reputation as a no-nonsense college coach when it came to academics—he expected his student athletes to pass their classes and sent an unusually high number of them to medical school. But he was also realistic and saw a different kind of promise in the big kid with the sweet left-handed swing. Forester realized young Mize's future would involve a bat, not a scalpel.

- - -

Always open to the next opportunity, Mize hooked up with the Morse Brothers Lumber Company baseball team out of Helen, Georgia, about eighteen miles northwest of Demorest, in White County. The competitive league featured plenty of ringers, and the company sent a car to pick up Mize on game days.

Morse Brothers, which owned and leveled tens of thousands of acres of North Georgia forest, was based in Rochester, New York, home of a St. Louis Cardinals top Minor League team. The company president, Whiting Morse, was pals with the Rochester Red Wings' president, Warren Giles (future president of the National League). Morse and Giles served on boards and committees together in Rochester and had plenty of opportunities to talk business, baseball, or both.

Through Morse, Giles found out about the teenaged phenom in the Appalachian woods who had Cobb's batting eye and Ruth's power. It seems almost too good to be true—how appropriate that Mize was discovered swinging a heavy bat for a lumber company of all things, Northeast Georgia's own version of Paul Bunyan in spikes. Giles told the Cardinals' dynamic, talent-hungry general manager, Branch Rickey, and Rickey sent his brother Frank to scout Mize in the summer of 1930.

"He could hit a baseball harder than anyone has a right to," Frank Rickey said twenty years later. He remembered the game being played in Cornelia. (Mize claimed it was in Toccoa, about twenty miles away.) "There was a country road behind the right field fence and on the other side of that a house built on stilts," Rickey recalled. "Well, this boy hit one across the road, and on top of the tin roof of the house. Then he hit one in the tops of the tall pines behind the left field fence."[29]

Rickey offered Mize $150 a month (no bonus), and Johnny liked the idea of playing pro ball. According to Rickey, he and Johnny went home to tell Grandma Sarah and Aunt Lizzie, who were not impressed with the offer or the prospect of seventeen-year-old Johnny leaving home. They basically threw a fit, in Rickey's version of events, which could not have been a comfortable scene for him, the stranger from up north—these were big country women, close to two hundred pounds each, with faces that turned red when riled. Aunt Lizzie was ready to tear up the contract.[30]

"I was afraid for a minute his grandmother was going to do the same to me," Rickey said. And then Johnny burst into tears. According to Rickey, he sobbed, "I wanna play baseball. Grandma, I'm goin' with this man."[31]

That scene, out of character for Mize, was no doubt embellished by Rickey. Regardless, Mize was ultimately inked to a deal and would soon report to Greensboro, North Carolina, to play for one of the Cardinals' farm teams. According to Rickey, when another player from the same semipro league Mize was playing in, pitching ace Spud Chandler, heard that Johnny was going pro, he begged to go too. Rickey claimed he told Chandler that he'd come back to Georgia to see him pitch. But before that happened, Yankees scout Johnny Nee signed the hurler.[32]

In another version of the story, Nee went to Toccoa to scout Mize but saw Chandler pitch a no-hitter, forgot all about Johnny, and signed Spud. Either way, Chandler became a Yankee and was Most Valuable Player in the American League in 1943.

Many years later, Mize expressed regrets over how he broke into pro ball. For one thing, he said, "the [Cleveland] Indians got after me, but it was too late to take advantage of the better deal."[33] For another, he complained how the Cardinals had signed him. "Let me tell you about that contract I signed," Mize told Honig. "It wasn't legal. The Cardinals never knew that. I was only seventeen then—underage."[34]

Mize said Frank Rickey went to Atlanta to get his mother's signature, but his grandmother Sarah was his legal guardian. "I knew I could go to Judge Landis and explain that the original contract with the Cards wasn't binding," Mize said years later, when he was with the Yankees. "I probably could have been made a free agent."[35]

But he never did anything about it. Besides, he was eager to sign a professional baseball contract and just as eager to get out of town. "Things were pretty rough around home then," Mize would recall.[36]

Mize could not have been blamed if he felt abandoned by his parents. He was very young when they split. His mother had settled permanently in Atlanta. And Johnny rarely, if ever, saw his father. Perhaps that was a blessing. Eddie Mize's life went steadily downhill. When he died in May 1930, not yet fifty years old, he'd become so forgotten or forsaken by his family and the community that he was laid to rest in an unmarked grave.

So, Johnny made the deal, caught a northbound train, and let the past roll away with the green hills of Habersham.

2

High Drama in the Low Minors

This beat any job he could have got around
Demorest, Georgia. He was on the move,
seeing things and people, playing ball
every day and getting paid for it.   —Frank Graham[1]

Johnny drove himself home after his first full season of pro ball, 1931, a conquering hero riding triumphantly into Demorest on a September day behind the wheel of a brand-new Chevrolet, a gleaming, four-door beauty that may have surprised, perhaps even embarrassed, some of his patently modest relatives. But it most definitely delighted the local kids as he glided through town—James "Spec" Landrum most of all.[2]

So nicknamed because of the galaxy of freckles on his pale, athletic body, Landrum had just turned fourteen. His family lived about one hundred yards from the Mize home, and he looked up to Demorest's resident superstar. "He was the hero for all of us," Landrum recalled in a 2004 interview for the Kennesaw State University (KSU) Oral History Project.[3]

Landrum, who spent a long career as a college coach and athletics director, grew up in Northeast Georgia and developed a knack for fun and games. "I was a really good athlete in all sports. I could play anything," he said. And Mize liked the kid's pluck. "I was his caddy, when it came to rounding boys up or doing whatever he wanted us to do," said Landrum, whose father had played baseball with Johnny's famous distant cousin, Ty Cobb, while growing up in Royston, Georgia.[4]

In the fall of 1931, three years after Cobb had retired, Mize was swinging the big bat in the family. After a short taste of pro ball at the end of the 1930 season, he returned to the Greensboro Patriots and the Piedmont League for 1931, establishing himself as a star in the Cardinals system.

Now the big teenager was driving what was probably the fanciest and newest car in Demorest, and he wanted to show his young pals a good time. "One of the first things he did when he got home, he rounded up five kids," Landrum recalled. "He had told me to get four boys beside[s] myself, and he took us to Gainesville, Georgia, in that new car to see a movie. I've never forgotten that my whole life."[5]

- - -

Johnny Mize and Jackie Robinson share a common bond besides both being born in rural corners of Georgia and breaking into big league ball as first basemen: they both played for Clay Hopper in the Minor Leagues.

When Robinson broke the color barrier in the International League in 1946 with the Montreal Royals, a top Dodgers farm team, Hopper was the manager. A Mississippi native, Hopper infamously made a disgusting racist remark about Robinson. But he also evolved as a human being and wound up becoming one of Jackie's admirers and supporters.

Hopper played a much smaller role in Mize's first taste of the Minors in 1930. Basically, it amounted to filling out a lineup card. Mize arrived in Greensboro around the same time that Hopper, a twenty-eight-year-old outfielder, was made the team's player-manager, the Patriots' third skipper of the season.

It was early August 1930, and the Patriots were in the final month of a mediocre campaign—they finished 70-71, good for third place in the six-team Piedmont League. At seventeen, Mize joined a team that featured the usual variety of players who were either on the way up or on the way down or just passing through along the bush league backroads, like the team's thirty-three-year-old third baseman and outfielder, Jimmy Sanders, who hit .314 and had more than 2,100 hits, 400 doubles, 150 triples, and 100 homers in a seventeen-year Minor League career with fourteen teams.

And there was twenty-two-year-old Jimmy Jordan, a hard-hitting, slick-fielding second baseman from Tucapau, South Carolina, a mill village about one hundred miles east of Mize's hometown. Though Mize only spent a few weeks as Jordan's teammate in Greensboro, the two men from southern Appalachia became fast friends. Several years later, after Jordan's solid rookie season with the Brooklyn Dodgers, he played an influential role in Mize's life during a remarkable offseason in the Caribbean.

In 1930 Mize got into twelve games. Three of his six hits were doubles, and he batted .194, the last season he finished under .300 for a very long time.

The high point of the season, historically speaking, was a series in late August, when the struggling Raleigh Capitals visited Greensboro for three games. The final contest, August 28, was notable for featuring a head-to-head meeting of two of the best first basemen in baseball history during their professional infancy: Johnny Mize and Hank Greenberg.

At nineteen, Greenberg—he was still called Henry then—was nearing the end of his first season of pro ball, a big galoot from New York City playing with mostly country boys in southern towns that rarely let him forget he was Jewish. "I encountered some hostility, but I'd say much more curiosity than hostility," Greenberg wrote in his autobiography.[6]

Greenberg, a prized prospect for the Detroit Tigers, was the highest paid player in the league, drawing $500 a month.[7] He and Mize were the youngest players in the league and two of the largest. In coming decades, they would be compared by fans, journalists, and historians and ranked among the best players to ever play their position, inspiring the question, "Who was better, Greenberg or Mize?" We'll get to that later.

At this point in the race, Greenberg held the clear edge. Henry batted .314 in 122 games for the Capitals, with 19 home runs, including his last dinger of the season against Greensboro on August 28, sending a ball far over the right-field fence in War Memorial Stadium—an opposite-field clout. Johnny went hitless in the game but walked twice, and Greensboro won easily, 16–6. Mize and Greenberg wouldn't meet again in a regular season ball game until 1947, when Mize was a Giant in what might have been his greatest season, and Greenberg, at the time a Pittsburgh Pirate, was in his last year as a player, mentoring Mize's chief home run adversary, Ralph Kiner.

Following his season finale with Greensboro, Johnny packed his bags for home. Three weeks later, he was playing with big brother Pope, earning a few extra bucks for the Southern Spring Bed Company baseball team in the Atlanta League championship. In the decisive third game, Pope threw five innings of hitless relief while Johnny singled and scored a run in the 2–1 triumph over their old rivals from Ruralist Press.[8]

Johnny spent that winter playing basketball with Piedmont and with Pope in Atlanta, hunting and walking the woods, staying in shape for the next baseball season. By spring training, he was being touted as one of the players on the Greensboro roster. But first he had to finish high school and the college baseball season, which led right back to Greensboro.

- - -

When Johnny Mize hit his first home run at Greensboro's War Memorial Stadium, he wore enemy colors. Piedmont coach Harry Forester took his baseball team north to Greensboro for a pair of games against the Patriots, April 14–15. Greensboro won both games, but the college boys played like men. Johnny had two hits in each game, a double in the first and his homer in the second, an 8–7 final that Greensboro had to rally to win.[9]

About a week later, Mize returned to Greensboro for a trial at first base, and he must have impressed the brass because on June 1, after graduating from high school, he signed with the Patriots. The *Charlotte News* reported, "He played 12 games here last year but hit only .194 and can hardly compete with Neal [sic] Caldwell, Patriot first sacker, who is going good at bat and afield."[10]

Neil Caldwell was going very good for Greensboro in 1931. He was in the race for the batting title all season, finishing second at .362, with lots of extra base hits and runs batted in. Caldwell was twenty-seven and became a career Minor Leaguer, mostly in the crowded Cardinals system. That was the same age as Ripper Collins, who was having a great rookie season as first baseman with the parent club in St. Louis. There was nowhere to go but sideways for Caldwell, who mainly played first base and second base for the Patriots in 1931 and then led them to the Piedmont League pennant in 1932 as an outfielder, batting .354.

Mize would play in the outfield while Caldwell held down first base most of the season. And if Johnny had been paying attention, he would have seen the cautionary tale in Caldwell's experience—no matter how well someone played down there, advancement in the Cardinals' farm system could sometimes be measured in inches or not at all.

The most remarkable player on the Greensboro team that year was probably starting pitcher Fritz Ostermueller, twenty-four, who went on to win 114 games in a fifteen-year big league career. He'd been playing in the Cardinals chain since 1926, going back and forth between the mound and the outfield. In 1931 the versatile lefty led the Greensboro staff with a 15-9 record and batted .399 with a .616 slugging percentage.

The Patriots were now part of a larger league entering a new era: the

Piedmont League (sometimes called the Cigarette Circuit or Tobacco League) graduated from Class C to Class B status for 1931.[11] It also expanded from six teams to eight: Greensboro, Durham, Henderson, High Point, Raleigh, and Winston-Salem were now joined by Charlotte and Asheville, which were orphaned in the recent dissolution of the South Atlantic "Sally" League (a temporary victim of bank closures in the Great Depression—the league would return in 1936).[12]

Running the show for Piedmont League was the powerful Judge William G. Bramham. It was an honorary title—the only bench Bramham ever sat on was in a ballpark. He'd been president of the Piedmont League since its inception in 1920.[13] A multitasker and workaholic, he also was president of the Sally League from 1924 through 1930, the Virginia League from 1925 to 1928, and the Eastern Carolina League for two seasons, 1928–29.[14] That means during one stretch, 1924 through 1928, he was president of four different leagues. As if that weren't enough, in 1933 Bramham was elected president of the National Association of Professional Baseball Leagues (NAPBL).[15] Now baseball would have two tough-minded "judges" ruling the game—Commissioner Kenesaw Mountain Landis in the big leagues, and President Bramham for the Minor Leagues.

As the world struggled through the Depression, the business young Johnny Mize had entered was suffering through a near-catastrophic recession, as leagues around the country disappeared. When Bramham became the NAPBL president, he inherited fourteen leagues with 102 clubs.[16]

But Bramham was indefatigable—he essentially worked himself to death—and held the whole operation together. The Minors recovered, and by the time Bramham retired at the end of 1946, there were fifty-two leagues and 388 teams.[17] But toward the end, it became evident that the times had passed him by. After Branch Rickey signed Jackie Robinson to a contract in October 1945, beginning the integration of baseball, Bramham criticized the Dodger boss, complaining bitterly of "the carpet bagger stripe of the white race."[18]

- - -

Johnny Mize made his debut as a regular player on Friday night, June 5, 1931, against the visiting Durham Bulls, under the lights at War Memorial Stadium. The Minor Leagues and Negro Leagues were years ahead of

Major League Baseball in introducing night baseball, which helped keep these institutions afloat during the Great Depression. Mize got used to playing night ball immediately. Batting third and playing right field, he had two hits and two runs batted in, as Greensboro took a 9–8 decision. From that point on and for the rest of his professional career—under the lights or in broad daylight—he never really stopped hitting.

But night ball wasn't for everyone.

At thirty-one and in his eleventh year of pro ball, Greensboro manager Johnny Kane was already an old timer. And he planned to hang 'em up after the season and return to his native Chicago to work as a salesman in the stockyards, an off-season gig he'd had for twelve years—because Kane hated night baseball.[19] All over the country, necessity begetting invention, Minor League teams were installing lights and turning to night baseball to bolster dwindling gate receipts. In 1931 the entire Cigarette Circuit lit up as all eight teams embraced night baseball.

Before heading off to his career in the Windy City's meat-packing market, Kane played second base and managed the Patriots to an 81-56 record—third place again. Charlotte won one hundred games, easily outpacing an improved Raleigh club in second place at 86-50. Charlotte was declared league champion after beating Raleigh in a best-of-seven series, 4–2.

- - -

Mize had hits in his first five games, and Greensboro won seven games in a row. He hit the first home run of his professional career, a two-run blast, in an 8–5 win over Henderson on June 12. A few days later, he hit his second homer in a win over the Charlotte Hornets.

Johnny broke out of a short slump with two hits and an RBI against Henderson and threw out a runner from right field. In his next start, a win against Raleigh on July 23, he stroked two more hits from the seventh spot in the batting order. The next day, Kane dropped him down to eighth. But even buried near the bottom of the order, Mize produced maximum results. His two-run double highlighted a six-run sixth inning win over Henderson on July 29. He hit a two-run homer in Greensboro's 16–6 rout of Henderson the next day. (Ostermueller drove in six runs and earned the win on the mound.) In his next game, still inexplicably batting eighth, Mize had two hits, including a double, and scored a run in a win over last-place High Point, then homered in the next game against the

Pointers, a 3–2 Greensboro win. In a doubleheader sweep of Asheville, he had four hits, including a double and a home run and five runs batted in.

Kane kept him buried down near the end of the batting order, and Mize kept hitting everything. He had two hits and an RBI in each game of Greensboro's first-ever nighttime doubleheader at home, a sweep of the Winston-Salem Twins on August 5. He finished the season with an exclamation point: two hits—one a double—and five RBIs, and he threw out a runner from right field in a 10–7 win over Henderson.

Mize posted a .337 batting average and hit 27 doubles and 9 homers in ninety-four games, nearly all of them as a right fielder. Based on one report, his bat wasn't the strongest part of his game. "His finest quality is a magnificent throwing arm," the *News Observer* of Raleigh, North Carolina, opined on September 13, when it reported that Mize and teammate Fritz Ostermueller would be reporting to Rochester, the Cardinals' top farm club.[20]

The report was slightly misleading. Mize *would* be moving through the Cardinals labyrinth farm system, and he *would* land in New York—but not in Rochester.

3

Scenic Route in the Bushes

> They called it the farm system.
> They wanted to keep you down
> on the farm all they could.　　—Don Gutteridge[1]

The Western Union telegram found its way to Johnny Mize in the tiny, remote village of Norman Park, halfway between the cities of Omega and Moultrie in deep Southwest Georgia: "Have placed transportation and berth for you through your local passenger agent so that you can report to Elmira Baseball Club at Greensboro North Carolina April fourth stop please register at YMCA and eat the Mayfair Cafeteria."[2]

Dated March 31, 1932, it was from Joe Mathes, business manager for the Elmira baseball team, a Cardinals farm club in the eight-team Class B New York–Pennsylvania League. Though only nineteen, Mize had been expecting to join the Class Double-A Rochester Red Wings, one step below the Major Leagues. That was what the newspapers had reported, anyway.[3]

Barely shaving yet, Johnny had passed his pro-ball audition and become a big man in Greensboro, at bat and in the field. And he felt ready for something more than another season of Class B (even if Elmira had deeper roots in Class B). But this was life in the St. Louis Cardinals farm system, where prospects grew, developed, and often withered on the vine—"flow'r's born to blush unseen," as Annie Savoy of *Bull Durham* fame might say.

Branch Rickey, baseball's innovator supreme, had created the farm system—professional baseball's talent factory—with the Cardinals. It was more advantageous to control and develop talent than to try and outbid other ball clubs for the best players from independent Minor League teams. Rickey and Cardinals majority owner Sam Breadon built the foundation of a winning franchise in St. Louis with homegrown prospects who had to compete their way through a sprawling farm system, also known as the Cardinals "chain gang."

Rickey's assembly line would stretch from coast to coast. Before long, the rest of Major League Baseball would follow suit, but the Cardinals led the way. By 1939 their farm system included twenty-nine teams and almost seven hundred players.[4]

Young Mize was beginning to realize the limited choices he had as a professional ballplayer, this being the age of the reserve clause, when players had virtually no control over their careers once they signed their first contract and became the property of the ball club—until they quit or were traded or were sold or were cut altogether. Ballplayers existed as professionals, or not, completely at the whim of the teams. Johnny was ambitious enough to think he'd make it to the big time—and smart enough to read between the lines of the Western Union telegram: *Quit the college sports crap already and get your ass up here, kid.*

- - -

The Elmira club (still operating as the Colonels at that point but on the verge of being known as the Red Wings, like the Rochester club) had already spent a few weeks in Greensboro getting into shape. Well, *some* of the Elmira players were in Greensboro. Others were training in Houston. The plan was to meet back in Elmira a few days before opening the curtain on the regular season in early May.

But Johnny was way down in South Georgia, getting one final taste of college athletics.

On March 5 he ended his college basketball career with the Lions in a 29–22 loss to South Georgia Teachers College (now Georgia Southern University) in the finals of the Georgia small college basketball tournament. Mize, a wide-shouldered forward, led Piedmont to wins in the first two games of the tourney, scoring 18 and 12 points. But the Teachers held him to just 6 points in the championship game.[5]

Four weeks after his college basketball finale, Johnny was back in South Georgia in a Lions baseball uniform for a series of games against small colleges, losing two to the Norman Park College Bears. Johnny had two hits in the first game and pitched a complete game the next day—as a young man he had a strong arm but was no pitcher.[6] On April 4 he played first base and led Piedmont to a win over the Georgia State College for

Men Rams, in Tifton, with a triple and a mammoth home run over a distant center-field fence.[7] "After the game, an old settler came up to me and said, 'Son, I've been watching baseball down here for 35 years and I never seed anybody even hit one out to the fence let alone over," Mize recalled years later.[8]

He played college sports like it was his job. But now Johnny was a legitimate professional. He was glad to have a regular paying gig, even if Minor League ball didn't pay much—especially during the heart of the Depression and especially when the tight-fisted Branch Rickey was paying. So, Mize spent 1932 in Elmira, where he won the praise of local baseball fans while overcoming illness and injury, establishing himself as a full-time first baseman.

- - -

Unlike the relatively new, horseshoe-shaped War Memorial Stadium (opened in 1926) in Greensboro, Dunn Field in Elmira had no lights. It had an old wooden grandstand and had been the site for professional baseball for decades, while War Memorial was designed for football and adapted for baseball. And Dunn Field was a hitter's desert.[9]

Most of the New York–Pennsylvania League ballparks seemed to be hitters' deserts in 1932. Consequently, home runs did not come easily throughout the league that season. Jake Plummer of the Wilkes-Barre Barons led the NYPL with 19 round-trippers in 1932 (in 523 at bats). Mize finished in a tie for fourth with just 8 clouts—3 in his first two games as a Red Wing. Then, he continued to hit for average and produce runs, and although the homers were few and far between that season, they were the kind that left onlookers whistling in amazement.

"Outfielder Mize Gets Two Homers in First Contest," declared the subhead in the May 4 sports pages of the *Star-Gazette* after Elmira's loss in Binghamton. Both shots, to right field, traveled well over 450 feet. Mize hit another 400-plus-foot homer the next day in another loss to Binghamton, but the game's highlight was a slick triple play that Elmira turned on the Triplets.[10] The series against Binghamton was indicative of how Elmira played in 1932—flashes of brilliance overshadowed by failure. The Red Wings finished in eighth place, last in the NYPL for the second year in a row.

- - -

In mid-July 1932 the Cardinals started moving managers around their farm system chessboard. Rochester sent Billy Southworth to Columbus, Ohio, to become skipper of the Red Birds in the Class Double-A American Association. (He'd guide St. Louis to a couple of World Series titles in the 1940s, punching his ticket for the Hall of Fame.) Rochester second baseman George "Specs" Toporcer was promoted to player-manager. And Elmira's skipper, Jack Bentley, was sent to Rochester as Toporcer's assistant.

That brought Clay Hopper back into Mize's life. He joined Elmira as player-manager on July 12 for the Red Wings' win over visiting Hazleton.[11] A few days later in a comeback win against Williamsport, Hopper put himself in right field and sent Mize to left, making both men look brilliant. With the game tied, "Johnny Mize contributed a stellar fielding feat in the ninth inning when he caught Tangema's fly in short left field and threw to Bucher to retire Rabbit on the double play."[12]

Twice in Hopper's first week as manager the team came within a game of .500, but each time the Wings returned to form, dropping close games.

Mize kept hitting, but not with the same power he showed in the first week of the season. In fact, it was right after that first week that the jinx started for Johnny.

First, he developed a case of the measles and couldn't leave his room for sixteen days. Then, he'd barely settled back into the lineup when he injured his leg while sliding into third base against Wilkes-Barre. He aggravated the leg after singling in the fourth. That sidelined him for ten more days.[13] When he returned to the lineup on June 26 against Harrisburg, he did so in style, with two hits, including a double.

In early August, Hopper started playing Mize at first, and he was wearing the first baseman's mitt every day for the final few weeks of the season and playing dependable defense. He also rediscovered his power stroke. At Scranton's Brooks Field on August 30 in a 7–4 win, he had three hits and three runs batted in with two doubles and a homer.

In 106 games that season, Mize batted .326 with 20 doubles, 11 triples, and 8 homers and proved himself at three positions—right field, left field, and first base. Sports writers covering the New York–Pennsylvania

League made Johnny one of two Red Wings on the postseason honorary All-Star squad (pitcher Lefty Heise, a twenty-game winner, was the other).

So, it's easy to imagine Mize's dismay when an Associated Press dispatch made its appearance under this headline on Christmas Day 1932: "Johnny Mize Is Returned to Greensboro."[14]

- - -

Back on familiar ground in 1933, Johnny started bullying Piedmont League pitchers right away, with four hits, including two doubles and five RBIS, in Greensboro's season-opening win over the Bulls in Durham.[15] Playing first base and batting third, he also created fireworks in Greensboro's home-opening win over Charlotte at War Memorial Stadium, with a triple and a grand slam that flew over the right-field fence with room to spare.[16] Like most games in the league, it was played at night, and poor lighting was blamed for numerous dropped fly balls. But the lousy lighting didn't bother the batters. In the next game, Greensboro beat Charlotte 11–10, as the two teams combined for twenty-two hits, including a two-run homer from Mize.

Greensboro would be a powerhouse in 1933, finishing the regular season with a 90-48 record and the league championship. But Mize didn't stick around long enough for the title run, finally earning promotion to Rochester in August. When he left Greensboro, he was the Piedmont League leader in home runs (22) and RBIS (99). He was third in the league with a .360 batting average and had a slugging percentage of .664.

He played his last game as a Patriot on Thursday, August 3, 1933, and as a parting shot, Charlotte lefty Chester Martin belted him with a pitch.[17] Following the 4–3 loss to Charlotte, Mize caught a train to Jersey City, where his new team, the Rochester Red Wings, had doubleheaders scheduled for the weekend. He joined a road-weary Rochester club on Saturday and had an instant impact.

Toporcer installed the twenty-year-old into the lineup immediately, playing Johnny at first and batting him fourth, and according to Rochester's *Democrat and Chronicle*, "Mize broke in right. He slammed a vicious home run drive over the right field wall in the fourth inning of the first game after having walked the first time."[18]

His clout broke a scoreless tie en route to a 7–2 Red Wings victory. He gave Rochester a 1–0 lead in the second game, too, driving in a first inning run with an infield groundout. In the bottom half of the inning, he got his glove on a liner but couldn't hold the ball, which was scored a hit and knocked in a couple of runs for Jersey City, which won the game, 3–1.

Mize went hitless on Sunday but made a couple of fine plays at first as Rochester split the doubleheader with the hometown Skeeters. In taking two of the four games at Jersey City that weekend, the Red Wings looked like a different, sharper ball club. "They had no mental lapses," reported the *Democrat and Chronicle*. "Perhaps it was the injection of Johnny Mize into the game at first base that bolstered the confidence of the boys."[19]

The four-game weekend ended a grueling twenty-four-game road trip for the Red Wings, who headed north for Rochester and a long homestand that would begin with a historic game for the bustling city on the banks of Lake Ontario. Monday, August 7, marked the first night game ever played in Rochester's Red Wing Stadium, where fifteen thousand fans showed up to watch a clash between the second-place Wings and the first-place Newark Bears, the New York Yankees mighty farm club. Part of the Rochester park's left-field fence was moved in to accommodate one of the one-hundred-foot-tall towers for the massive lights (a $23,000 renovation).

"It was a spectacle," wrote the *Democrat and Chronicle's* Henry Clune. The lights, he added, "make the ballpark look like fairy lands. The players tanned to the tint of an old and well stained Meerschaum bowl, looked pasty white under the giant lights. Their uniforms were spotless. The green grass of the infield, clipped like a convict's head, was a delicate emerald under the flood of white light. The infield was almost a pastel. The ladies loved it. It appealed to their aestheticism."[20]

But it didn't appeal to the Red Wings. Newark pitcher Johnny Broaca struck out ten batters in a 4–0 whitewashing of Rochester. The Wings were "as nervous as a string of green chorus girls exposed for the first time to the blinding rays of the Broadway lights."[21] Mize had a single in four at-bats.

It was the beginning a new era in the four-year-old ballpark. "Night baseball is a novelty here this week. Next week it will be an established institution," Clune wrote. "[Warren] Giles, who is president of the Rochester club, thinks it is the coming thing. He has the best night plant in the country."[22]

And his ball club was pretty good too. In addition to Mize, the team had future big league stars like George Selkirk, Ival Goodman, Fritz Oster-mueller. Player-manager Toporcer, who'd been a dependable infielder for the Cardinals in the big leagues, was a Rochester favorite. He helped the Red Wings win four pennants from 1929 through 1932, winning the International League MVP Award in '29. He was named manager only in '32 and guided the team to the league title. In 1933 he directed it to an 88-77 record and a berth in the championship playoff series.

- - -

The International League celebrated its golden jubilee (fiftieth) season with a wild championship series that saw the lowest-ranked playoff participant, the Buffalo Bisons, sneak off with the pennant. Overall, Newark breezed to first place in the regular season with 102 wins. Mize, who led Rochester in hitting (.352) and slugging (.610), kept the Red Wings in second place, four games ahead of the Baltimore Orioles. Buffalo was fourth with a losing record of 83-85, clinching the last playoff spot with a 5–2 win over Rochester in the regular-season finale.

The playoff system was an experiment designed, like night baseball, to bring more fans out to the games.[23] The bracket was broken up into North and South divisions. Rochester and Buffalo were ranked one-two in the North, respectively, with Newark and Baltimore one-two in the South. In an odd playoff alignment, the two division winners, Rochester and Newark, played each other in the best-of-five semifinals, while the division runners-up, Buffalo and Baltimore, met in the other series. Regardless of the baffling bracket, Newark was favored to repeat as league champion. In 1932 the Bears had also won the Junior World Series (the annual postseason clash between International League and American Association champs).[24]

Unfortunately for Mize, a defensive lapse in the first game against Newark, a loss, prompted Toporcer to bench him for most of the series. Rochester rallied to win the next three games, advancing to play its upstate New York rival, the Buffalo Bisons, which swept Baltimore in the other semifinal series. Then Buffalo beat the Red Wings in six games.

Mize, who may have ended the season on the bench, left Red Wings management and fans something to think about: a .352 batting average in forty-two games, with 11 doubles, 3 triples, and 8 home runs. Though he dominated IL pitching, Mize's defense could best be described as mediocre. Nonetheless, Frank Rickey, the man who'd signed him to a professional contract, predicted he'd be a big leaguer in two seasons.[25]

Following their loss to Buffalo in the 1933 championship series, the Wings took off on a postseason barnstorming tour of upstate New York. But Johnny had other plans, and they involved a lovely climate, sandy beaches, and a tropical atmosphere. He also got something he probably didn't expect—some of the best baseball he would experience in his life.

4

Beisból with El Maestro

First there is the swing. Compact, powerful, controlled violence with a slight uppercut. A second later, at sonic speed, comes the explosive crack—Buck O'Neil said it sounded like a dynamite blast when Josh Gibson hit the ball just right.[1]

The crowd gasps as the white streak blasts off through swirling Caribbean trade winds, far and high into the Puerto Rican sky, stopping at an impossible apex before gravity grabs the ball, which hurtles back to Earth at a long angle, crashing down through the palm trees beyond the spacious confines of Estadio del Escambrón and into the rolling tide. Gibson trots around the bases as the crowd finds its collective voice, exhaling a thunderous wave.

The ball flies so high when it leaves San Juan's old ballpark that "[Gibson] was at second base before the ball cleared the fence," Johnny Mize will recall many years later.[2]

- - -

While the Rochester Red Wings wrapped up their fall barnstorming tour with a game against a squad of semipro champions in Naples, New York, Mize was on a ship to sunny Puerto Rico. He'd joined a group of players, mostly Minor Leaguers, traveling as the Richmond Colts, a Piedmont League team during the regular season.[3] This barnstorming version of the Colts was led by Ralph Minatree, a well-traveled Minor League player-manager. He assembled a squad that included several of the actual Colts in addition to players from other teams, such as Mize, Jimmy Jordan (Johnny's former Greensboro teammate, now an infielder with the Brooklyn Dodgers), and outfielder Ted Norbert, recently of Binghamton in the New York–Penn League.[4]

Though they called themselves the Colts, the players apparently wore uniforms borrowed from the Philadelphia Athletics (or possibly the Richmond Athletic Club), as depicted in what might be the only surviving team photo. Piedmont University has the photo in its archives, with

"Richmond B.B.T." scrawled across the bottom of the print. And there is twenty-year-old Johnny Mize of Demorest, tall and still thin, in the middle of the back row, and like the rest of the team, wearing the Athletics' Old English "A" on the left breast of his jersey.

The rag-tag Colts arrived in San Juan on October 12, and over the next few months they played about forty-five games, winning most of them, usually in front of boisterous crowds. "The Islanders take their baseball seriously and even the amateur teams attract thousands to their games," wrote J. Francis Edwards, sports editor of the San Juan newspaper *El Imparcial*, in a December 1933 letter to the *Pittsburgh Courier*.[5]

Puerto Rico and other Caribbean islands had become an alluring hotbed of baseball in the winter months, especially for black players, who received the respect and admiration there that eluded them in the continental United States, where Jim Crow laws and widespread racist attitudes still ruled the day. In Latin America, these men would be "treated as human beings," wrote Raul Ramos on the website Conbasesllenas.com, "and in some instances treated like royalty throughout these enchanted islands and welcoming countries."[6]

Even Josh Gibson, who hit home runs and won acclaim everywhere he played, said the greatest thrill of his baseball career was winning the MVP Award in Puerto Rico.[7]

"We played three or four games a week, sometimes against the native teams, but more often against other visiting clubs from the United States," Minatree reported in the *Richmond Times* after most of his team returned home from the tour. "We sometimes played before crowds reaching 5,000." He said local teams were strong in the field but weak at the plate; "otherwise the competition was keen, especially when we met such clubs as the Caracas, Venezuela club, which is the strongest on the South American continent."[8]

He was referring to the Concordia Eagles, a superteam based in the city of La Victoria, about sixty road miles from Caracas, owned by the son of a Venezuelan dictator and led by a brilliant Cuban athlete whose nickname was "The Immortal."

- - -

From October 1933 through February 1934, when he was twenty and becoming twenty-one, Mize had a grand adventure playing ball in Puerto

Rico and the Dominican Republic with and against some of the best ballplayers who ever lived. In his big league career, Mize's teammates included Joe DiMaggio, Mickey Mantle, Dizzy Dean, and Stan Musial. And he played against Ted Williams, Jackie Robinson, Bob Feller, and Willie Mays. But the best ballplayer he ever saw never wore an American League or National League uniform—because he wasn't allowed to.

"The greatest player I ever saw was a black man," Mize said decades after he'd retired. "His name is Martin Dihigo."[9] Dihigo was a legend in his twenty-nine-year playing career (1922–50), a pitching and batting phenom.

"Martin Magdaleno Dihigo Llanos was considered by infinite masses as the most absolute Cuban ball player of all time," wrote Dihigo's granddaughter, Sundae Yvette Cora, in the prologue of *My Father Martin Dihigo, "The Immortal,"* written by Martin's son, Gilberto Dihigo.[10] Hall of Famer Buck Leonard, one of the best sluggers in Negro Leagues history, said of Dihigo, "I'd say he was the best ballplayer of all time, black or white. If he's not the greatest I don't know who is. You take your Ruths, Cobbs, and DiMaggios. Give me Dihigo. I bet I would beat you almost every time."[11]

Known as "En Inmortal" and "El Maestro" and "El Hombre Team" throughout the Americas, Dihigo was elected to the National Baseball Hall of Fame in 1977, four years ahead of Mize. He's also in the Cuban and Mexican Baseball Halls of Fame.

Dihigo already was a veteran star when he crossed paths with young Mize, described in the Dominican press as "the formidable first baseman of the blonde Americans, who has been the greatest attraction of the visiting team, due to his aggressiveness as a long-distance hitter and the perfection and cleanliness of his movements."[12]

A natural leader, Dihigo had been hired as player-manager for the Concordia Eagles, a team owned by Gonzalo Gómez, son of Venezuelan dictator Juan Vicente Gómez. With Concordia, Gonzalo had built the first Venezuelan team to travel abroad and win tournaments throughout the Caribbean. According to Dihigo, who played in Venezuela from 1931 through 1935, "Gonzalo Gómez had the best athletes that the Caribbean area had in those years."[13]

For a few weeks in 1934, Mize was one of those athletes. Dihigo, a shrewd judge of talent, recruited Big John for his bat and Jimmy Jordan for his glove. Together, the two Americans would help Concordia win that season's Trujillo Cup in the Dominican Republic.

- - -

The 1933–34 Concordia team was Venezuela's version of the 1927 Yankees, and Mize believed Dihigo was the most dangerous member of this Latin American edition of Murderers' Row.

"I played with [Dihigo] in Santo Domingo in winter ball," Mize said. "He was the manager. He was the only guy I ever saw who could play all nine positions, [could] run, and was a switch hitter. I thought I was having a pretty good year myself down there and they were walking him to get to me."[14]

Mize was well into his seventies when he shared his Dihigo comments, which landed in the fiftieth anniversary edition (1989) of the *National Baseball Hall of Fame and Museum Yearbook*. And his memory of that winter was a bit fuzzy. For example, based on a study of available box scores, Mize typically batted fourth and Dihigo batted fifth, so they weren't walking Dihigo to pitch to Mize. Then again, it's completely feasible that Dihigo switched the batting order from time to time.

The taciturn Northeast Georgian was the unsentimental sort who didn't elaborate much on his time playing winter ball in the Caribbean, even though that barnstorming trip proved to be an advanced class in how to play professional baseball, held in an unfamiliar, combustible political environment, in ballparks packed with zealous, often armed fans. Still, "it hardly ever came up," said his son, Jim Mize. "He only mentioned it a few times, in passing."[15]

- - -

According to Minatree, the Colts left two players behind to play for Dihigo's powerful Concordia Eagles: Mize and Norbert. Jordan wasn't mentioned. But when it was game time, it was Jordan and Mize who suited up in Concordia's colors.

Jordan and Mize, who met when they both played for Greensboro in 1930, were from the same part of the world. Jordan had just completed his rookie season of Major League ball in 1933, getting into seventy games at second base and shortstop for the Brooklyn Dodgers.

Like Norbert, Jordan put in some long miles on baseball's backroads, playing with thirteen different Minor League teams across thirteen seasons, plus four seasons in the big leagues (1933–36, all with Brooklyn).

When the young players weren't enjoying the colorful nightlife or the fishing or the beaches, they played ball, mostly on the weekends, often against other professional outfits, including barnstorming teams of Negro Leaguers, like the Brooklyn Giants.[16] Another Minor League team from the U.S. mainland, the Mountaineers of Hazelton, Pennsylvania, led by pitcher George Hockette, was based in San Juan for the winter, while the Richmond Colts settled down in Ponce, a large city on the southern coast of Puerto Rico close to Santo Domingo in the Dominican Republic.[17]

These were the early days of the Trujillo Era in the Dominican Republic, the diverse nation that shares the island of Hispaniola with Haiti. Dictator Rafael Leónidas Trujillo Molina presided over a bloody political regime that lasted from 1930 until the CIA had him assassinated in 1961.

Trujillo seized power in 1930 and would eventually change the name of Santo Domingo, the capital city, to Ciudad Trujillo. An ardent promoter of baseball, he recognized its massive popularity among the people and typically used the game for self-promotion. He may have been a cruel tyrant, but Trujillo was still a politician.

Most famously, baseball-wise, he created a championship team to take on all comers during a sham election in 1937, when Trujillo hired Negro League stars Satchel Paige, James "Cool Papa" Bell, and Gibson, among others, to form the Dragones—with the implied threat that they'd better win, or else. The Dragones took the championship.

When Johnny Mize and his fellow ballplayers visited the country in the winter of 1933–34, passions—over baseball and politics—seemed to be at a tipping point in the old city. "In Santo Domingo the natives all wear pistols on their hips," read a story in the *Reading Times* on January 26, 1934. "Times are perilous down there and a gun is needed for protection."

About one thousand armed soldiers were present at the ballpark, the *Times* noted, "mostly for protection, although when the battle waged hot the 'soldatos' forgot their importance and waved sombreros and guns in acclaim to good plays," adding that the multicultural fans "are real rooters and take their baseball seriously."[18]

- - -

Concordia warmed up for its run in the Trujillo tournament with a series of games in Puerto Rico, which gave Dihigo plenty of opportunity to see Mize and Jordan in action with the Richmond club. Then, for a few weeks in November 1933, fans in Santo Domingo got a preview of the "Americanitos," as the Colts played a series of high-profile games at the new Campo Deportivo Municipal, the city's sports stadium, against two powerful Dominican teams, Escogido and Licey.[19]

The Santo Domingo press wasn't above a little tongue in cheek: Several stories in *Listin Diario* carried the byline "Ty Cobb." The faux Georgia Peach praised Mize and Norbert as "the players with brilliant work."

And then Johnny really showed them something.

Called the "Continental Blondes" by local media, Richmond swept a Sunday (November 12) doubleheader, beating Licey in the first game and Escogido in the afternoon. "The granddaddy of all long hits at the Campo Deportivo Municipal was hit by Mize in the seventh," *Listin Diario* reported. "It was a fly ball that almost touched the ruins of old Memphis."

The abandoned American warship, the USS *Memphis*, was a monument to the United States' arrogant gunboat diplomacy. The armored *Memphis* had been rusting in that spot since August 29, 1916, when it had been thrown violently to the rocky shore by a series of gigantic waves, killing forty-three sailors—*only* forty-three, thanks to the efforts of heroic locals who fought the angry sea and rescued survivors.[20] The defeated ship was left to its beachside grave, a haunted hulk outlined on the blue horizon beyond the right-field fence. It made a tantalizing target for ambitious sluggers like Mize until U.S. president Franklin D. Roosevelt had the wreck removed in 1937.[21]

After nearly touching the ruins of the old ship with his shot in the first game, Mize put on a good show in the five-inning second game too. He singled in his first at bat and next hit a long fly ball to deepest center. The ball was kept in the ballpark by a spectacular leaping catch from center fielder Juan Sonora. Mize drove in a run in the second game with another big fly ball, this time tracked down in deep left field.[22]

The Richmond boys played another Sunday doubleheader with Licey and Escogido the following weekend. This time, the nearly seven thousand *fanaticos* who packed the municipal stadium watched Escogido's Lions whip the Colts, 6–3, and Richmond hold off the Licey Tigers for a 4–2 win in the afternoon.[23]

The Lions' pitcher, Felitto Guerra, mastered Richmond's "famed hitters of Yankeedom" and held Mize hitless in four at bats. In the afternoon game, Johnny botched a throw from the shortstop to let a man on base. He made up for it an inning later by snaring a line drive and completing an unassisted double play at first. He also lined a double to right.[24]

Mize had been impressive enough throughout Richmond's Dominican tour to catch the attention of the fans and the press. More importantly, he'd impressed the best all-around player in baseball, Dihigo.

- - -

Mize and Jordan joined an international lineup of top-tier talent. Juan "Tetelo" Vargas, at twenty-seven, was already a star and perhaps the best player from the Dominican Republic; he'd already made an impression in the Negro Leagues with the Cuban Stars. A speedy base runner who was known to score from first on singles, he hit for high average with power and was versatile in the field, playing infield and outfield for Concordia. Vargas grew up in Santo Domingo and had plenty of fans on his side as Concordia took on the best teams in his hometown for the Trujillo Cup: Licey and Escogido (which featured in its lineup Orlando Cepeda's father, Pedro "The Bull" Cepeda).[25]

The powerful Concordia roster also included Latin American All-Stars Manuel "El Pollo" Malpica, a great catcher from Venezuela who handled Dihigo's pitching with ease and hit for high average, and Venezuelan shortstop Luis Aparicio Ortega, father of Baseball Hall of Famer Luis Aparicio.[26]

- - -

Mize and Jordan jumped into the Concordia lineup for a doubleheader on Sunday, February 4. Dihigo, "throwing invisible balls," struck out fourteen batters in the first game, a 4–0 win over Licey. In the second game, a win against Escogido, Jordan played dazzling defense at second, robbing several batters of hits. But Mize was Concordia's hitting star for the day, with a single and a double in the first game, another double and a "beastly" home run to straightaway center in the second.[27]

The following weekend, Mize didn't have a hit but struck the ball hard in each at bat. Jordan drove in a run with a single, and Dihigo hit a three-run homer in the eighth to lift Concordia over Escogido, 6–0.[28] The same two teams played again the following Sunday, the 18th, and Concordia won, as Mize and Jordan each had two hits and an RBI and Vargas homered.[29]

Then, just like that, the winter adventure was over for Mize and Jordan. Spring training was about to begin, and Dihigo had a couple of new ringers for his club: Josh Gibson and Herbert "Rap" Dixon.

As Mize and Jordan went home on the steamship *Coamo*, *Listín Diario* published a small story, saying, "Mize was the sensation of the last series between our teams and Richmond, and lately, Concordia."[30]

A week later, with Dixon and Gibson in the lineup, Concordia breezed to the Trujillo tournament championship. Gibson homered.[31]

Meanwhile, Mize was back in a Rochester Red Wings uniform; he joined the club in Florida for spring training. Johnny still had to prove himself at first base.

Dihigo and Mize never played together again. The Cuban star would continue his glorious career, building a legend in the shadows of segregation. His Negro Leagues records (which are incomplete) include a .312 lifetime batting average and more than 100 pitching wins. His son Gilberto offers these mind-boggling numbers from his father's first season with Concordia (1932), playing against top competition: 6 wins and 0 losses, with 101 strikeouts in 60 innings.[32]

For Mize, the large young man from a small mountain town in Northeast Georgia, that Caribbean winter was an eye-popping, world-expanding experience. He'd been exposed to different cultures and a different brand of baseball, and it left a lifelong impression, even if he rarely mentioned it.

Johnny Mize would play twenty more years after that winter of 1933–34. He would see and do remarkable things on a ball field and play with and against some of the best athletes in the history of the game. And he would watch succeeding generations of superstars and many, many ball games. (The last thing Mize did consciously in his life was watch a ball game on TV.) But for the rest of his days, the Big Cat never saw anyone play baseball better than *El Maestro*.

5

Can Mize Field This Year?

It is March 1934, and the Rochester Red Wings' brass and the baseball press eagerly anticipate the arrival in training camp of young Johnny Mize. They are not disappointed. The big Georgian seems even bigger. He looks stronger. Maybe it's the dark glow of health he's acquired from spending the winter playing ball in Puerto Rico and the Dominican Republic. He's exuding the confidence earned from having played ball with grown men, hardened veterans from island empires. His shoulders look broader than ever on his six-foot-two frame. Is it possible he's grown to six feet three? He is sharp and energetic in the team's first spring workouts, like he's going to own first base and anyone else who wants his job is in for a battle.

- - -

In Rochester's first exhibition game of 1934, a 13–6 loss to the Brooklyn Dodgers, "Mize was particularly bad on ground balls, letting three go through him, two for hits and one for a miscue," wrote Joe Adams of the *Democrat and Chronicle*.[1]

As Opening Day loomed, one of the top questions in the minds of Rochester baseball fans, according to Adams, was: "Can Mize field this year?"

Adams and the fans needn't have worried.

In a 9–6 Opening Day win over the Orioles in Baltimore on April 18, Mize made an excellent pickup on a hurried throw from infielder Tom Carey to complete a crucial double play and added four hits, including a pair of hustling infield singles.[2] He helped the Wings complete a three-game sweep of Baltimore a few days later in a come-from-behind 6–4 win, with a home run that sailed clear over the bleachers and out of the park. He also made a heads-up, clutch defensive play, taking a throw from right fielder Estel Crabtree and making a strong relay to catcher Bill Lewis, nabbing the sliding Baltimore baserunner at the plate.[3]

At Syracuse's brand-new Municipal Stadium on April 28, Mize hit the first-ever home run out of the ballpark, way over the right-field wall. He had three hits in the 8–7 Wings win and scored the decisive run in the tenth inning.[4]

The Red Wings were in first with an 8-3 record as they arrived in Rochester for their home opener, May 2. The Flower City on the shore of Lake Ontario was buzzing with a festival atmosphere on a Wednesday afternoon. There was a parade down Main Street, with a marching band leading a long procession of motor vehicles carrying local celebrities, including ageless baseball legend Walter "Rabbit" Maranville, shortstop for the Miracle Braves of 1914. Maranville had been a Rochester favorite since 1927, when he led the team (then known as the Tribe) in triples on his way back to the Major Leagues, where he'd help the Cardinals win a pennant in 1928. In May 1934 Rabbit, back with the Boston Braves, was rehabilitating in Rochester from a broken leg he'd suffered in an exhibition game. He waved from the back seat of the parade vehicle.[5]

In these days before television, before twenty-four-hour news could be accessed on a wristwatch or telephone, Opening Day was a holiday that brought entire cities together. Men ducked out of work early, kids skipped school, and more than fourteen thousand fans packed into Red Wing Stadium to watch Rochester whip visiting Baltimore, 9–4, on the power of Mize's bat. He had a double and a homer that landed in the parking lot beyond right field. A front-page photo showed him crossing the plate after the homer.[6]

Rochester completed a four-game sweep of the Orioles with a win that featured another homer by Mize (his sixth of the year), who also played sensational defense. Johnny started one double play and registered the last out of the game on a smart pickoff play. He positioned himself far enough off the bag to let Baltimore baserunner Wally Gilbert take a big lead. Then Mize broke for first, grabbed a quick throw from pitcher Virgil Brown, and tagged the sliding Gilbert out.[7]

The next day, May 6, Rochester thrashed visiting Syracuse. Every Red Wing had at least one hit. The team smacked twenty-one in all—Mize had two, including a double and an RBI. But he didn't finish the game. "It also may be a costly win for the Wings as they suffered their first major injury to a regular when Johnny Mize pulled a muscle in his left groin as he tagged first base in the third inning," the *Democrat and Chronicle* reported. He hustled to first after belting a line drive to right that had seemed destined for extra bases and tagged the base awkwardly. He shambled to second for his double, then left the game for a pinch runner. It was initially diagnosed as a pulled muscle. It was much worse.[8]

- - -

When Johnny returned to action as a pinch hitter on May 30, after striking the ball he limped to first in agony, making it clear that he still was in rotten condition.[9] He tried to get into shape for a series in Albany the following week but felt sharp pain in his thigh with every exertion. So, when the Red Wings reached Montreal for a series against the Royals, Mize was taken for a thorough examination by two of Montreal General Hospital's leading specialists, radiologist William Ritchie and surgeon Frederick Tees. They did not have great news.[10]

"The hopes of a speedy return to the Rochester lineup of Johnny Mize, injured first sacker, were shattered today when an examination revealed a condition that will keep him out for another month or more" was the lede of a special dispatch to the *Democrat and Chronicle* on June 9. The physicians discovered a growth of bone on Mize's pelvis, where his muscle was torn. "Until today it was not known there was a bone condition," the story continued. "Mize's ailment is very rare among ball players, but is common among jockeys, according to the doctors. There was considerable of it among the members of the Cavalry during the late war."[11]

He was sent to St. Louis to be treated by Dr. Robert F. Hyland, the Cardinals team physician, dubbed the "surgeon general of baseball" by Commissioner Landis—a suitable sobriquet for the modest MD because he treated players from all the other clubs too. Hyland, whose salary was paid by the St. Louis Public Service Company (which operated the city's transit system), had an unassuming office on the second floor of the city's streetcar barn.[12] And he didn't charge ballplayers for his services, though he extended or saved the careers of many, including Johnny Mize.

Under the good doctor's watchful eye, Johnny had a chance to try on a Cardinals uniform for the first time. A picture of him wearing the team's regalia while working out in Sportsman's Park in St. Louis appeared in the *Democrat and Chronicle* on June 23, and the following week the newspaper was reporting on Mize's impending return to the Rochester roster. But that would ultimately be up to Hyland, who figured that Mize's pelvis, "was damaged from years of riding mules and horses bareback in his Georgia boyhood," according to William B. Mead in a profile of Hyland in the Society for American Baseball Research's journal, the *National Pastime*, in December 2002.[13]

In 1934 the medical community didn't really know much about femoroacetabular impingement, or FAI, which could be what Hyland and the experts in Montreal observed in the young first baseman. FAI, which typically occurs in young adults and is often related to sports activity—like baseball—is a condition in which extra bone grows along the bones that form the hip joint. That includes the pelvic bone.[14]

But Mize gradually felt well enough to play—at least, he could withstand the pain and hit a baseball with authority. He convinced Hyland and left St. Louis, heading back to Rochester in time for a Fourth of July doubleheader. Mize would need Hyland's extraordinary skills eventually.

"Johnny, stiff and sore in his attempt to come back into the lineup, did not show to best advantage," Adams wrote in his game story in the July 5 edition of the *Democrat and Chronicle*, which featured a photo of Mize swinging a bat under the header "Big Slam of Wing Hitters Returns to Regular Post." Adams continued, "He'll have to improve in condition before he becomes the defensive threat that he was before his injury. Johnny hit the ball well but is unable to run the bases with effect. But regular play will aid him now, he's more rusty than hurt."[15]

- - -

Mize had been leading the league in homers when he was injured. Now he was just trying to get loose again. Meanwhile, the Red Wings, which dominated the league those first few weeks with Johnny in the lineup, had slipped to second place, trailing Newark. In his July 4 return to action, Mize had a hit in each game, as Rochester swept the visiting Toronto Maple Leafs, who were battling the Wings for second.

A few days later, a Sunday, the Red Wings swept a doubleheader from visiting Baltimore. Mize was hitless at the plate but made contact in the field when he and Orioles baserunner Keith Molesworth "engaged in a short but spirited fist fight," according to the *Democrat and Chronicle*'s game report. The fight broke out in the second game, after Rochester third baseman Jimmy Brown made a fine backhanded stop of Molesworth's smash down the line with a baserunner on first. Brown threw to Toporcer to force the runner at second, and Specs, seeing Molesworth rounding first too far, threw to Mize in time to nab the retreating Molesworth. But Johnny dropped the ball. Then, for no apparent reason, Molesworth attacked Mize with his fists. Mize fought back. Police separated the combatants, who were both tossed from the game.

- - -

In mid-September the Cardinals purchased the contracts of Red Wing pitchers Nub Kleinke and Ray Harrell, outfielders Ival Goodman and Tom Winsett, and Mize. They'd stay with the Wings through the playoffs and report to the Cards in the spring.

Not all of them would. Mize would finally get his chance to spend spring training in a Major League camp, but it would not be with the Cardinals. Before any of that could happen, there was work to do in Rochester. The same young man who was letting ground balls slip through his legs back in March put on a first-base clinic in the International League playoff series.

The Wings, who finished the season in second place with an 88-63 record, played fourth-place Albany in the first round, while third-place Toronto played the regular-season champion Newark Bears. Mize was hitless in the first game, a Rochester win. In the second game, another Rochester win, he drove in three runs with two doubles and made a clutch play in the ninth inning, leaning over the dugout railing to grab a foul fly.

In the third game, a 3–2 Senators win in Albany, Mize poled a home run over the center field fence and continued his defensive heroics, preventing a run with a one-handed stab of a looping fly headed for the outfield. He played solid defense and added two hits in a 7–4 win, giving the Wings a 3–1 lead in the series. Mize's spectacular defense in Game Five helped Rochester clinch the series with a 3–1 win in Albany's Hawkins Stadium. "Mize scooped up [Del] Bissonette's savage smash with his gloved hand in the second and he made it look, oh, so easy," the *Democrat and Chronicle* reported.[16]

Toronto upset Newark in the other series, which went the full seven games, setting up a championship playoff between the Red Wings and Maple Leafs. Against the Leafs, Mize continued to play smart at first, but Toronto had the momentum and dominated the Wings, winning the series in five games.

The Leafs' thirty-five-year-old right-hander Sheriff Blake pitched a two-hitter in stopping the Wings in Toronto, 3–0, in the opener. Toronto came from behind to win the second game, 5–4, though Mize had a double and hustled on the bases. He added two more doubles in the third game and made a great play on Carey's wild throw up the line, tagging the baserunner out in the third inning. But Toronto won, 3–2, in thirteen innings to take a 3–0 lead in the series.[17]

The Wings performed one last act of defiance in Game Four, winning 9–2 behind Pete Appleton's pitching and a hitting attack that included a double and two RBIs from Mize.[18] In Toronto's 2–1 Game Five clincher, Mize played well again, making a clutch defensive play in the sixth—Toronto was leading 1–0 when Johnny picked Carey's short-hop throw out of the dirt, recording the out. Then in the eighth, he singled to right center. Toporcer replaced him with pinch runner Jimmy Brown. So, for the second year in a row, Mize ended the season watching from the bench as his team lost the championship series.[19]

Even though he had missed nearly two months with a painful injury, Mize seemed to have recovered well enough to play like an All-Star. In ninety games, he hit 17 home runs and batted .339. The next stop for him as a ballplayer seemed clear enough—he was going to the big leagues.

- - -

Word from St. Louis arrived shortly after the IL championship series ended. As the first pitch was being thrown in the Junior World Series (American Association champ Columbus would defeat Toronto in that year's little fall classic), Mize was slated to suit up with the Cardinals.

"Mize is being brought here to aid the Red Birds in the last two games and the playoff with the Giants, if necessary," Branch Rickey said. "He was one of the leading sluggers of the International and he may come in handy as a pinch hitter."[20]

They didn't use him. But the surging Gas House Gang from St. Louis ended the season with four straight wins over the visiting Cincinnati Reds, winning the National League pennant by two games over the Giants.

Even if he didn't get to play, Johnny had an opportunity to get a good look at big league ball before packing his bags for Georgia. And in a few months, he'd get a much closer look.

6

The Temporary Red

The truth is, the big kid can really sock
almost anything that's pitched.   —Rabbit Maranville[1]

The Johnny Mize era with the Cincinnati Reds began on Christmas 1934.
It was finished before Easter 1935.

The rumors of his leaving—escaping?—the Cardinals' expansive,
black-hole farm system began before Rochester even finished the 1934
International League playoffs.

"Eastern baseball men predict that Johnny Mize, Rochester first baseman, will bring the St. Louis Cardinals, who own him, $100,000," wrote
Chicago Tribune sports editor Arch Ward in his September 17 column.[2]
Two days later in the *St. Louis Globe-Democrat*, W. H. James echoed Ward's
contention, writing that Mize "will bring $100,000 when he is placed on
the block. This is interesting because Johnny is a Cardinal farm product
and if we market him at the quoted price we'll get enough money for him
to pay the salaries of the Dean brothers next year."[3]

By early December the Cincinnati Reds had emerged as the team most
interested in Mize, and a basement price was established: Rickey would
not consider anything less than $55,000.

"A deal to land Johnny Mize, supposedly the best of the minor league
first basemen of 1934, in Red togs for 1935 still is cooking and may come
to a boil in New York," wrote Tom Swope of the *Cincinnati Post*.[4]

Cincinnati's interest was not a big surprise. Having finished last in
the National League every season since 1931, the Reds were now on a
whirlwind spending spree for young talent. Owner Powel Crosley Jr. had
brought in Larry MacPhail as general manager to turn things around,
through trades, player development—whatever would work. Even though

they finished in the cellar again in 1934, MacPhail's first season with the club, the Reds were way ahead of everyone else in at least one respect. MacPhail, one of baseball's true front office geniuses, made Cincinnati the first team to fly in an airplane for road games. And in 1935, after having lights installed at Crosley Field, he made the Reds the first Major League Baseball team to host a night game (May 24, 1935).[5]

Eventually, MacPhail put the pieces together for pennant winning teams, in 1939 and 1940. By then, the combustible redheaded GM had gone to the Dodgers, before moving on to the Yankees. But in the off-season between the 1934 and 1935 seasons, MacPhail was interested in bolstering the Reds by dipping into the St. Louis Cardinals' deep pool of Minor League talent.

Before Thanksgiving the Cincinnati club spent $40,000 to acquire two of the Cards' top farm prospects, third baseman Lew Riggs of Columbus and Mize's Rochester teammate, slugging outfielder Ival Goodman.[6] Then, on December 13 at the Winter Meetings in New York, in addition to plucking shortstop Billy Myers from the New York Giants' farm system, the Reds made a $55,000 offer to the Cardinals for Mize.[7]

It took almost two weeks, but the Mize deal was finally completed on Christmas Eve and announced in the following morning's sports pages. The Reds planned to field an entirely new, young infield in 1935: twenty-two-year-old second baseman Alex Kampouris; Riggs, twenty-five, at third; Myers, twenty-four, at shortstop; and Mize, twenty-two, at first base.[8]

Maybe.

The six-foot-two, power-hitting Christmas gift to Reds fans came with a money-back guarantee—if Mize turned up lame, he could be returned to the Cardinals. The Reds got Mize on a trial basis—manager Charlie Dressen had until May 15 to make up his mind on the young first baseman's condition.[9]

But baseball commissioner Kenesaw Mountain Landis stepped in and vetoed the arrangement. He thought it was unfair for an athlete (Mize) to play for one team (the Reds) while another team (the Cardinals) still had a claim on him.[10]

So, the Cardinals agreed to sell Mize to the Reds with the caveat that, if Dressen found him physically unfit by the end of spring training, he'd be returned to the Cardinals with no obligation to the Reds. It was an agreement that Landis and both ball clubs could live with. If Mize was in good shape, he'd replace Jim Bottomley at first base.[11]

Sunny Jim was thirty-five and nearing the end of a Hall of Fame career. He'd starred at first base for the Cardinals from 1922 through 1932, helping them win four National League pennants and two World Series, winning a Most Valuable Player Award for himself along the way (1928). But he'd been dealt to the Reds before the 1933 season and hadn't hit over .300 since 1931; his run production had fallen off sharply. With Mize in the fold, Bottomley was now expendable.

- - -

Mize spent the winter playing basketball to stay in shape and arrived in Tampa to train with the Reds on February 21 full of confidence, claiming to be in perfect condition. He quickly fell under the tutelage of Reds coach George "High Pockets" Kelly, who'd been a solid defensive first baseman for John McGraw's New York Giants team that won four straight National League pennants (1921–24). Kelly liked the natural way Mize handled himself around the bag, but he worked with the kid throughout the spring.[12]

On February 26, when the Reds finally started batting practice, Mize thrilled team bosses by losing baseballs over the fence at Plant Field.[13] And when the team scheduled its first intrasquad practice game for March 4, Mize suited up with the regulars against the rookies, or "yannigans."[14]

Coincidentally, playing first that day for the yannigans was Frank McCormick, who would edge out Mize for National League Most Valuable Player honors in a few years while helping to lead the Reds into the World Series as National League champs.[15]

In that first practice game, Mize hit a home run to the opposite field, slicing the ball just inside the left field foul pole for two runs in what ended as a 3–3 tie. He added three doubles in intrasquad games over the next few days, preparing for his first game as a Major Leaguer against other Major Leaguers, on Saturday, March 9, against the Boston Braves and Johnny's cousin-in-law, Babe Ruth.

This was the Babe's first game in a Boston uniform after fifteen years with the New York Yankees, lured to the lowly Braves by a vague promise (or unrealistic expectation) to become the team's manager eventually. Johnny didn't waste the opportunity to show off in front of Cousin George (also playing first base that day), singling in a run and playing solid defense. Babe also had a hit and an RBI as the Braves won. The next day, Mize had three hits and three RBIs as the Reds beat Boston.

Daily newspapers covering the Reds—the *Cincinnati Enquirer*, the *Cincinnati Post*, and the *Dayton Herald*—regularly featured photos of Mize and his young infield comrades as the team worked through spring training. The giant apple-faced kid from the Georgia hills was big news in Porkopolis.

One of the more interesting photo series featured Mize and his first baseman's mitt, which he'd customized with a large webbing between the thumb and palm, giving it the look of a fisherman's net. "Once a ball lands in his glove it seldom escapes," noted the caption in the March 13 edition of the *Post*.[16]

And once he hit a ball, it stayed hit, observers were finding out. It didn't seem to matter who was pitching.

He homered off Detroit Tigers right-handed ace Schoolboy Rowe. He went 2 for 3 with a triple and two RBIs against Brooklyn's Van Lingle Mungo. In a game against the Toronto Maple Leafs, he hit the longest home run that had ever been seen at Plant Field, a blast that sailed over a racetrack beyond right-center field, which "furnished a big argument for keeping him with the team, for his injured leg does not seem to be bothering him to any noticeable extent," the *Enquirer* reported.

But it *was* bothering him.

- - -

The *Sporting News* reported on March 14, "Mize appears to be living up to his $55,000 price tag in practically all respects." The *Enquirer* tabbed Mize as "all but a certainty" in its March 24 baseball column. But the next day's edition featured a complete about-face. "Mize's Leg Is Ailing Again; Manager Dressen Worried; Bottomley Is at First Base," the headline screamed.[17]

The plot thickened when Mize started feeling better and Bottomley left the team.[18] And Mize kept on hitting as the Reds toured the South in the final days of spring training. And whenever he did, other players tended to stop what they were doing to watch. "Many of them profess to see in this strapping youngster a future king of clout," the *Post* reported.

But Mize was hurting. Every time he stepped onto a ballfield to start warming up was an exercise in agony. And Reds leadership was still undecided, because Mize continued to hit the ball really well, which was, "something of a phenomenon," according to *Post* sports editor Joe Aston, "because of the physical handicap under which he has been laboring."[19]

Tigers rookie Dixie Howell, a former All-American halfback at the University of Alabama, discovered how phenomenal Mize's power could be, the hard way. Before an exhibition game on April 11 in Lynchburg, Virginia, Howell was warming up with some teammates along the right field foul line during Reds batting practice when Mize lined a baseball that fractured his skull.[20] Howell made a comeback and played several more years in the Minor Leagues, in addition to some pro football.

As Mize continued to impress on the field, MacPhail and Dressen publicly expressed optimism that he'd be a Red on Opening Day, April 16, against the Cardinals. Dressen was calling him the best hitter he'd seen in years and "the greatest rookie first baseman I ever saw."[21]

Grantland Rice, perhaps the most respected and best-known sportswriter in the country, published his forecast for the upcoming season in his widely syndicated column on April 15. Offering his picks for the top hitters in the National League, he predicted that "Johnny Mize, of the Reds," would be among the circuit's top sluggers in 1935.[22]

Rice's column hit newsstands the same day Mize's career as a Red came to a sudden end.

Johnny was playing, and he was willing to keep on playing. But a difficult operation loomed, and the Reds knew it, and they got scared at the eleventh hour.

They re-signed Sunny Jim Bottomley on April 14, and on April 15 (Opening Day Eve), MacPhail returned Mize to the Cardinals and asked for his money back.[23] "MacPhail felt he couldn't afford to gamble on me," Mize told author Donald Honig years later. "So they turned me back, and the Cardinals sent me to Rochester."[24]

And so, Johnny Mize's career as a Cincinnati Red ended before it officially started.

7

All the Way Back

Add to the great moments of
baseball history—the return of
First Baseman Johnny Mize to
the Rochester Red Wings.   —*Democrat and Chronicle*[1]

Buddy Lewis had the kind of line drive power that kept infielders back
on their heels. But this time, the right-handed-hitting Montreal Royals catcher was jammed by one of Rochester righty John Michaels's
heavy, inside pitches. So, he managed just a weak pop-up to the right-
field side. And that was the beginning of the end of Johnny Mize's 1935
baseball season.

The big first baseman broke quickly for the ball, wielding the new,
catch-everything mitt he had designed himself. "I was running down
the line after a foul ball, looking up in the air, and stepped in a hole,"
Mize recalled years later.[2] The pain in his upper leg was jolting. The ball
fell, untouched.

It was the bottom of the sixth of a 4–1 Royals victory in Montreal's
Delorimier Stadium, the second game of a Sunday doubleheader. The
Wings had taken the first game, 3–0, on Mize's towering two-run triple
and Al Fisher's pitching. Johnny's injury was like the one that cost him
two months in 1934. But this time, the muscle tore from the right side of
his pelvis. "That finished me for the season, and I went home," he said.[3]

It was June 30, less than halfway through the 1935 campaign. But after
sixty-five games, during which he led the Rochester regulars in batting
(.317), Johnny Mize's baseball season was indeed over. And for a while it
looked as though his career might be too.

A year earlier, in June 1934, physicians in Montreal had discovered bone growths on Mize's pelvis. Baseball's own "surgeon general," Cardinals team physician Robert Hyland, was aware of the problem. But just days after the Cincinnati Reds returned Johnny to the Cardinals as damaged goods in April 1935, Hyland declared the young first baseman fit and healthy, and ready to play ball, saying an operation was not advisable, at least not yet. So, the Cardinals sent Johnny back to Rochester, where Red Wings president Warren Giles claimed Mize was in perfect physical condition and ready for the rigors of a pennant race.[4]

Of course, this was long before advanced medical diagnostics or free agency or multiyear contracts or a players' union. Teams with large, well-stocked farm systems like the Cardinals routinely gambled on the long-term health and future of their human property. And the players, with little choice in the matter, typically played hurt, until they couldn't. Mize agreed with the owners, saying he was strong enough and eager to play regularly, despite the pain he was still feeling when he tried to bend down or exert himself.[5]

And the local press was giddy, to the point of the absurd. "The flags might well have been flying when Johnny came marching home," read an editorial in the *Democrat and Chronicle*. "Rochester fans now know what the appearance of Blucher meant at the Battle of Waterloo and what Pickett was to Gettysburg."[6]

The editorial writer must have forgotten that Pickett's division was slaughtered at Gettysburg. Speaking of which, like Pickett's ill-considered ideology, the 1935 Red Wings also were a lost cause. They suffered through their worst season yet in '35, finishing seventh at 61-91, and attendance tumbled to under 95,000, having fallen steadily through the years from a high of 328,424 in 1930.[7]

Also, this wasn't Spec Toporcer's team anymore—he was now playing second base for Syracuse. Instead, Johnny was reunited with his former Greensboro manager, Eddie Dyer. It wouldn't last. As the Red Wings foundered in or near the cellar, someone had to be sacrificed, and it was Dyer, on June 1. The kiss of death came a month earlier when team president Giles, speaking to a group of two hundred at an American Legion baseball supper, claimed full responsibility if the Red Wings continued along their humdrum path. It would not be the manager's fault.[8]

"Just as the officials are willing to take the credit for the success we have enjoyed in the past, so are we willing to take the blame if the club does not go well," said Giles, who had a change of heart a month later, when he fired Dyer and hired Burt Shotton.[9] The Red Wings are very likely the only team in baseball history to employ two future, back-to-back National League pennant-winning managers in the same season (and in the same order that they won those pennants). Dyer managed the Cardinals to the pennant in 1946 and Shotton guided the Dodgers to the flag in 1947 (and again in 1949).

Mize played well for both men in '35, until he couldn't.

- - -

Johnny got glove envy in 1934 when he watched Montreal Royals player-manager Oscar Roettger snaring errant throws to first base with one hand and picking up short hops with fluid ease. "I noticed Roettger was getting the ones most first sackers get errors for," Mize said. The newspaper also ran a photo of Mize wearing his new "butterfly net glove."[10]

The veteran Roettger, an ancient thirty-four at the time, was a former pitcher in the big leagues who had switched to first base. His glove was like a large oven mitt with the thumb and flap connected by a leather strip and crisscrossed lacing.[11]

For Mize, seeing the contraption on Roettger's hand was an epiphany. Then, when he saw Hank Greenberg using it during spring training of 1935, he had to have one. Since Mize had first seen him in the Piedmont League back in 1930, Greenberg had become a superstar for the Detroit Tigers, leading the team to American League pennant in 1934 (and he would in 1935 too). After seeing Hank's glove, Mize acknowledged, "If it's good enough for Hank Greenberg then its good enough for me."[12]

So, Mize visited a glove maker and designed his own butterfly net mitt and used it for the first time in a 5–0 win over Newark on May 2. Johnny played well most of the game, handling an unassisted double play. But he also was given an error when he mishandled a bad throw on a pickoff attempt from catcher Tommie West (the Red Wings thought West deserved the error).[13]

But mostly, Mize was playing competently (occasionally brilliantly) at first base and hitting at a .320 clip with the usual power. He hit twelve home runs before the injury put him out of action, the last two blasts as different as they were awe-inspiring.

On June 18, with Shotton now managing, Johnny put on a good show for the 3,500 or so fans at Baltimore's Oriole Park, with a third-inning home run that left the ballpark, sailing over the right-field bleachers. He added a single and made a great defensive play in the eighth, using that new, broken-in glove to dig out a low throw from third baseman Jake Flowers, as the Red Wings won easily, 12–5.[14]

Mize hit his last home run of the season, a murderous drive over the left-center field fence on June 24 in a win over the Bisons in Buffalo in the first game of a doubleheader. He added two hits and an RBI in the second game, another Red Wings win.[15]

A week later, following the mishap in Montreal, Johnny stayed in bed to nurse his leg injury. He was expected to be out of action a week to ten days. In fact, he had played his last game for Rochester. On July 22 Mize returned to St. Louis, asking to be placed on the voluntarily retired list.[16] But Mize told author Donald Honig that it wasn't his idea to quit. "The club doctor recommended that I retire from baseball," he said. "That didn't sound too good to me, so I got another opinion."[17]

- - -

Johnny found his second opinion back in Georgia.

"Mize was written out of the game by one of the greatest medical and surgical clinics in the profession," wrote future Pulitzer Prize winning journalist Ralph McGill in his Break o' Day column for the *Atlanta Constitution* on May 17, 1936, after Johnny had already established himself as the top rookie in the National League.[18]

It was an Atlanta doctor who disagreed, McGill reported, after an examination in a local hospital revealed the presence of calcium plates in the groin. The Cardinals sent Hyland to Atlanta, and he agreed with the diagnosis, according to McGill, who earned lasting fame and respect as an antisegregation editorial writer for the Atlanta newspaper.[19]

Doctors in Montreal had already reported bone growth on Mize's pelvis in June 1934. If McGill's story is accurate, then it took the word of an anonymous Atlanta doctor (McGill doesn't name the Atlanta hospital either) in late 1935 to convince the Cardinals to finally do the right thing for their ailing young prospect. Hyland performed the surgery on November 15.[20]

"It was my most difficult operation," Hyland said later, adding that Mize had "growths in both crotches. These were shaped like icicles and extended into the musculature of both thighs. Cavalrymen are subjected to this trouble. It was a tough job to remove these growths from such a difficult spot."[21]

But the surgery was a stunning success. After a few weeks of rehabilitation under Hyland's supervision, Johnny returned to Demorest. Hyland had admonished him to start a conditioning program back at home, and the Cardinals had determined to invite Mize to training camp in 1936 to see the results for themselves.[22]

"If Mize turns out to be all right," the *Post-Dispatch* reported, "it will be a great Christmas present for the Cardinals."[23]

But they'd have to wait until spring to unwrap it.

8

Cardinals Rookie

A boy we like is Johnny Mize,
Not for the color of his eyes.
Or just because he's over-size,
And has an appetite for pies.
The reason we like Johnny Mize
Is no occasion for surprise.
He's out to trim the other guys
And gets there and tries and tries.   —W. H. James[1]

Before he appeared in his first official big league game, Johnny Mize was cast in poetry. But when he made his big league debut on April 16, 1936, it wasn't the kind of stuff that would inspire flights of lyrical fancy: With two outs in the bottom of the ninth and the visiting Cubs leading the Cardinals 5–3 before 2,500 committed fans in Sportsman's Park, Johnny was sent in by manager Frankie Frisch to pinch hit for pitcher Paul Dean. Chicago's Larry French struck him out, an ironic start for the powerful young Georgian, who would develop a reputation as one of the game's best contact power hitters.[2]

By season's end, Mize probably deserved to be praised in verse. He'd recovered from the surgery and arrived for training camp in excellent shape. He played flawlessly while subbing for Jimmy "Ripper" Collins at first base. Johnny made eighty-two putouts and no errors during the spring training period.[3] And, just as he'd done a year earlier with the Reds, he showed that he could hit big league pitching with authority.

Nonetheless, rumors persisted that Mize would be dealt by the Cardinals to another club. These stories, and the Cardinals' failed attempt to sell him to the Reds a year earlier, only nurtured Mize's suspicious nature.

Year after year there were reports that he was headed to the Giants or the Dodgers or the Cubs or somewhere that wasn't St. Louis. And Rickey's actions over the negotiating table in years to come fed whatever mistrust Johnny felt regarding the Cardinals and baseball as a business enterprise.

"Mize was a cynical man, and like many of his teammates, he disliked Rickey intensely because of Rickey's constant pressure to keep salaries low," wrote Peter Golenbock.[4]

Johnny knew he was valuable, so it probably got under his skin that he had to dicker over pennies every season, when he was usually ranked among the top first basemen in the league. He certainly was a hot commodity in the spring of 1936. Casey Stengel, manager of the Brooklyn Dodgers, was willing to trade two players and cash for the twenty-three-year-old.[5] Or, if Jack Troy of the *Atlanta Constitution* is to be believed, "Casey Stengel would take him and throw in a dozen players for the Cardinals' extensive farm system. Taking him is the only way Casey could get away with it, according to Memphis Bill Terry, who stands ready to outbid anything Brooklyn offers."[6]

But Johnny remained a Cardinal, and the team was intent on finding a spot for him on the roster; it even considered reclassifying him as an outfielder.[7] Mize raised the team's hopes when he reported to spring training in Bradenton, Florida, a trim, muscular 205 pounds on his six-foot-two frame. He handled Frisch's strenuous workouts at full speed and was pain free.

And Frisch, a graduate of the hard-bitten John McGraw school of managing, seemed pleased. Mize proved he belonged. His eighth-inning single tied the score in a come-from-behind win over the Phillies on March 12. Then he singled and tripled in a win over the Dodgers. Against the Yankees in St. Petersburg, he had a base hit and played spectacular defense—including a leaping, one-handed snag of a Red Rolfe line drive.

This was Mize's first chance to see the game's premier first baseman, Lou Gehrig, up close and in his prime (Gehrig would win the American League Most Valuable Player Award in 1936). It also was a preseason meeting of the top two rookies of 1936, Mize and his future teammate Joe DiMaggio, participating in his first training camp with the Yankees.

But the big story Cardinals fans followed closely that preseason was the annual contract drama involving Dizzy and Paul Dean. They settled with the team on March 23 when Dizzy signed for $24,000 and Paul promised to sign for $10,000.[8] Dizzy was a bargain that season, winning twenty-four games and leading the league in a category that hadn't been invented yet with eleven saves. It was Dizzy's last great season. Paul injured his arm in 1936 and won just five games and never won that many again.

- - -

On April 25, 1936, Johnny got the first hit of his big league career, a two-run pinch-hit double to the left-field corner off the Pittsburgh Pirates' Jim Weaver. The hit was wasted, as Pittsburgh rolled, 12–5.[9] It was his fourth plate appearance of the early season, all of them as a pinch hitter. The next day, Mize got his first start as a first baseman, and his triple drove in the Cardinals' first run in their 3–2 win.[10]

After six seasons in the Cardinals' farm system, Johnny Mize had arrived as an impact player in the National League. He'd also arrived in one of the zaniest clubhouses that ever existed in baseball. When they had too much time on their hands, these Cardinals were capable of lapsing into some Three Stooges–type shenanigans. One of Johnny's favorite stories was about the time Pepper Martin, Dizzy Dean, "and a young infielder whose name escapes me, dressed up as a painter, carpenter, and air-conditioning, respectively," and wreaked havoc in a Philadelphia hotel after a rain out.[11]

"The terrible trio," as Mize called them, amused themselves by teasing the hotel barber and his bald customers, then "marched into the dining room, where they explained to the very pompous head waiter that they were going to build a bar and create an entirely new atmosphere."[12]

As if that wasn't horrifying enough to the waiter, the would-be Moe, Larry, and Curly explained that the painting scheme would be determined by the color of the food that was served. Mize continued, "Whereby they requested he bring out a plate of each kind of soup they served. Baffled by the fast-talking threesome, the poor man complied. They then took a spoonful from each of the plates, consommé, tomato, split pea, and so on, and put it all in a glass. They assured the head waiter that by mixing it all up, it would show them the exact color to paint the room."[13]

The only thing missing from the tableau was a pie fight.

Mize had a wry sense of humor. So, when he writes, "A young infielder whose name escapes me," the reader is left to wonder, *Is Johnny winking at me? Is he being coy? Is he the young infielder?* Perhaps. Johnny was one of the boys. And he had great affection for Diz—even named one of his bird dogs back in Demorest after the pitcher. "He is sure named right, too. That's the screwiest dog that ever hit these parts," Johnny told Thad Holt of the *Atlanta Constitution*.[14]

Shenanigans and stunts aside, after the umpire called, "Play ball," the Cardinals were all business. And Mize demonstrated that he fit right in.

In that debut game at first base, for example, against Pittsburgh, he received his first of a league-leading twenty-one intentional walks. Mize tied Gehrig's Major League record of twenty-one, set the year before—which has been since broken many times (first by Johnny Mize, in 1940, when he received twenty-four free passes). But eighty-seven years later, in 2023, Mize still held the National League rookie record for intentional walks in a season.

And that RBI triple he rocketed against the Pirates not only was the second base hit of his fledgling career but also kept alive a rare kind of hitting streak. Johnny set a record when his first seven big league hits went for extra bases (a feat that stood alone until Oakland Athletics rookie center fielder Carlos Gonzalez matched it in 2008). Following that Pirates game, he continued the extra-base-hit streak against the powerful New York Giants, tagging them for three doubles and the first home run of his big league career in two games. His final hit of the streak was a double against Brooklyn.

That first Major League home run, on the last day of April, made the difference in a 3–2 win over the visiting Giants. With the Cardinals leading 2–1 in the bottom of the seventh, Mize hauled his thirty-six-inch, forty-ounce bat up to the plate to face Giants right-handed reliever Harry "Gunboat" Gumbert and promptly deposited the ball onto the pavilion roof beyond the right-center-field fence.[15] It was one of those moments that Mize would not forget—neither would Gunboat.

That victory over the Giants was the second-straight razor-thin win for the Cardinals over the National League frontrunners. The day before, a Wednesday, New York's great left-handed ace Carl Hubbell and St. Louis's sidewinding right-hander Roy Parmelee hooked up to spin a classic, each of them going the full seventeen innings in a game the Cardinals won, 2–1, on a close play at the plate.

With the Cards trailing in the bottom of the twelfth inning, Joe Medwick singled, and Mize hit his second double of the game. Medwick scored the tying run on Charlie Gelbert's single. Later, with darkness descending, umpire Beans Reardon was almost ready to call it quits. Sportsman's Park wasn't equipped with lights yet. St. Louis catcher Virgil Davis opened the bottom of the seventeenth with a double to right. Hubbell intentionally walked Gelbert. With one out, Parmelee gift-wrapped a hard grounder to shortstop Dick Bartell, who misplayed the ball, and the bases were loaded. Then Terry Moore's slow roller to third forced Giants third baseman Travis Jackson to hurry his throw, pulling catcher Gus Mancuso off the plate as Lynn King, running for Virgil Davis, slid home with the winning run.[16]

In addition to being one of the greatest pitching duels anyone had ever seen, the contest provided rookie Mize an early taste of big-game tension between the league's two best teams, and he'd responded with two doubles off the great Hubbell and played well in the field behind Parmelee.

- - -

Mize had joined a great ball club that wasn't quite a dynasty but always seemed to be in contention. The Cardinals had won pennants in 1930 and 1931 (and the World Series in '31). But they truly became the Gashouse Gang with their 1934 pennant run and victory over the Detroit Tigers in one of the classic seven-game World Series.

Frisch had been named player-manager for the final two months of the 1933 season, replacing Gabby Street. By 1934 the Cards fought for another pennant against a tough Giants team led by player-manager Bill Terry. That was the year Dizzy predicted he'd win thirty, then won thirty. Little brother Paul, a rookie, added nineteen victories, and Durocher's great play at shortstop anchored the league's best infield. Third baseman and outfielder Pepper Martin was the team's sparkplug. He and second baseman Frisch, along with role players like outfielder Jack Rothrock, set the table for sluggers Medwick (.319 batting average, 106 RBIs) and Collins (.333, 128). In 1934 Collins led the league in home runs, total bases, and slugging average. That's why Mize was stuck in the Cardinals chain gang Minor League system.

As one of the younger players on the 1936 team, Mize buddied up with rookie Don Gutteridge, and they developed a long friendship. Like many of the Cardinals who didn't live in St. Louis year-round, Mize and Gutteridge roomed at the Gatesworth Hotel.[17] The diminutive but scrappy Gutteridge, from Pittsburg, Kansas, immediately hit it off with Johnny.

"We were both country boys," said Gutteridge, who broke in with the Cardinals later in the 1936 season. "Come to think of it, there were plenty of country boys on that Cardinals team."[18]

Ball clubs traveled by train, so the players became very familiar with each other, sharing the same travel horror stories. Mize and his St. Louis teammates would play games in 100-degree heat, for ten days at a stretch, then board trains that had been sitting in the sun all day.

"You'd strip down to your shorts in the car and then wait for the train to start," Mize said. "Then you had the choice of sitting there with the windows closed and suffocating or opening the windows and inhaling soot and smoke; when you did that you arrived the next morning with your face as black as night and you'd blow coal dust out of your nose for a day."[19]

It gave teams plenty of time to talk baseball, something Mize was happy to do.

"He loved to talk hitting, even as a young player," Gutteridge said. "And that was quite an experience, that first year—the Gashouse Gang. You'd walk into the clubhouse and there would be Durocher, Medwick, Pepper Martin, Dizzy and Daffy Dean. That was a big deal to a guy like me. Johnny never seemed fazed by any of that stuff, though."[20]

Mize seemed ready to supplant Rip Collins. Batting fifth in the order, behind cleanup hitter Medwick, he was hitting well over .300, and the Cardinals passed the Giants, spending most of May and June in first place as the Giants, Cubs, and Pirates gave chase. But Johnny slumped, and Frisch removed him from the starting lineup following a loss to the Pirates on May 28. He played sloppily at first and his 0-for-4 showing left him hitless in seventeen straight plate appearances. The Cardinals were clinging to first place at 24-13. With Mize playing first, they'd gone 21-8. Johnny was second on the team in runs batted in and first in home runs. But on May 29 against the Pirates, Collins was back on first.

"Frisch has decided that, after all, Ripper Collins, his regular first baseman, can do his club more good in the lineup at this time than the brilliant young recruit, Johnny Mize, who suddenly has gone off into a slump that has hurt the Cardinals almost as much as enemy bats," the *St. Louis Star-Times* reported. "With Mize a rank failure in the No. 5 batting position, the Cardinal attack has dwindled to a mere nothing."[21]

Mize's bat was integral in a comeback win for the Cards, who eliminated a five-run deficit to beat Pittsburgh, 9–7, in the last game of their five-game series. Collins led off the bottom of the fifth with a home run to right, the first hit of the game off Pirates righty Mace Brown. That same inning, with two runners on, Frisch sent Mize in to pinch hit for Parmelee, and he hit the ball against the screen above the pavilion roof in right field, his three-run homer reducing the Pirates' lead to one run. Dizzy Dean earned the mound victory with a game-winning, two-run double in the eighth.[22]

Mize's bat was too valuable to leave on the bench. After a few more pinch-hitting jobs, Frisch put Mize back into the starting lineup—in right field, a position he hadn't played in several years. And the rust showed. But he mostly overcame it with his bat. In his first game as a big-league right fielder, Mize lifted the Cardinals to their biggest lead in the standings (four and a half games ahead of the Giants and Pirates) with a virtuoso performance against the visiting Boston Bees. Batting sixth in the order, he had two hits and drove in five of the Cardinals' runs in a 7–5 win, including a first-inning grand slam. Before the game, he confessed that he was as surprised as anyone by his sudden start in right.[23]

"I had been working out at first base during the infield drill," Mize said. "Frisch came along and asked me if I'd like to play in right field. I told him I would, and he said, 'Okay, you're the right fielder in today's game!' I'll play any position here, first base, right field or anything else, just to get into the ball game!"[24]

And when he wasn't starting, he was one of the National League's top pinch hitters with seven hits in fifteen at bats.

But as summer blazed in St. Louis, Collins crumbled, as did the Cardinals' lead. They kept trading first place with the Cubs. And even though the Cards were not fated to win the pennant (neither were the Cubs), when Mize was given another chance as the team's first baseman, he got hotter than July and shot like a comet through August.

- - -

From July 14 through the end of the month, Johnny went on a rampage. Hitting in fourteen straight games, he batted .551 (27 for 49), with 5 homers, 6 doubles, 11 RBIs, and 15 runs. He belted a dramatic two-run pinch-hit homer in the bottom of the eighth to lift the Cards past the Phillies on July 17.

On July 23, in a 4–2 win over the Giants in the Polo Grounds, Johnny had 3 hits, including a home run and double, and 3 RBIS, all against New York starter Freddie Fitzsimmons, who was becoming a favorite foil for Mize.

The rookie had disrespected the veteran knuckleballer in previous encounters that season as a pinch hitter, belting Fitzsimmons hard. Now Johnny singlehandedly crushed Fat Freddie, a big winner for the Giants since 1925. Mize's abuse of Fitz probably inspired the latter's disdain for the big Georgian.

"For as long as I had known [Fitzsimmons], he had hated Johnny Mize, and I had never been able to get him to tell me why," Leo Durocher claimed. Durocher, Mize's Cardinals teammate and later his manager on the Giants, managed Fitzsimmons on the Brooklyn Dodgers for five seasons. "He just didn't like [Mize], the way some people just don't like other people. 'He's a tomato-face,' he'd growl. 'He's a picklehead.' He had all kinds of names like that for him. 'I just don't like him.'"[25]

And for good reason. Picklehead feasted on Fitzsimmons, batting .410 lifetime (16 for 39) against the roly-poly righty.

Mize feasted on pretty much everyone else in August 1936, too, when he put together the longest hitting streak in the Majors that season and the longest of his career—twenty-two straight games, August 2–24. During the streak, Johnny batted .390 (32 for 82), with 7 doubles, 2 triples, 5 homers, 20 runs, and 23 RBIS. But neither his pace nor the Cardinals' pennant hopes would last.

The Giants posted a 24-3 record in August. They were in third place, seven games behind the league-leading Cubs on August 1. By the end of the month, New York was in first place with a four-game lead over the Cardinals, and the Giants never trailed again. St. Louis and Chicago tied for second.

While the Cardinals muddled through September (13-15) and Mize struggled at the plate (.245 average for the month, no home runs over the last two weeks of the season), there were some notably tense moments for the rookie star.

On September 9 in Boston, a loudmouthed spectator in a front-row box seat "tormented Johnny Mize until the Cardinal first baseman charged toward the stand to challenge him," wrote the *Post-Dispatch*'s J. Roy Stockton. "Umpire Magerkurth persuaded Johnny to put away his gun and in a few minutes the fan left the ballpark. He didn't want any part of a player who fought back."[26]

Later in the month there occurred the strange intersection of Hall of Fame careers that has become the basis of a classic trivia question.

Johnny and the Cards ended the 1936 campaign on Sunday, September 27, against the visiting Cubs. The two teams were battling for second-place money, a difference of hundreds of dollars per player (when that was big money). St. Louis was in second, a game in front of Chicago. But the Cubs earned a share of the second-place money with a 6–3 decision, thanks in part to a couple of defensive mistakes made by a rookie first baseman playing in his first and only big league game, Walter Alston. Young Walter, the future longtime manager of the Dodgers who would guide the team to multiple championships and earn induction into the Hall of Fame, was replacing Mize, who had been tossed from the game by umpire Ziggy Sears.[27]

Both teams harassed Sears the entire game over ball-and-strike calls. He'd already run Cardinals coach Clyde Wares and Cubs manager Charlie Grimm out of the game. In fact, "Jolly Cholly" was tossed in the top of the seventh as his own Cubs were rallying for two runs and a 3–0 lead. After Chicago was finally retired in the seventh, Johnny said something while passing Sears that seemed harmless from a distance, but it must have infuriated the umpire. Mize had a slow and easy way of speaking, "even when he is cussing an umpire," wrote Frank Graham in a magazine profile years later.[28] Whatever it was, Sears accused the rookie of using profanity and gave Mize the hook.

And that made Johnny Mize the answer to the great trivia question, "Who did Walter Alston replace in his only Major League appearance?" In addition to his blunders in the field that led to three Chicago runs, Alston came to the plate with two out in the bottom of the ninth and struck out in the only at bat of his career.

So, Chicago tied St. Louis, which meant Cardinal players lost about $300 each in bonus pay. "Cardinal players will be forced to accept approximately $1,000, instead of $1,300 apiece, as their share of the spoils after second and third-place money is pooled and divided among the St. Louis and Chicago players," wrote Ray Gillespie of the *St. Louis Star*.[29]

Despite his weak finish, Mize's rookie season was a significant success. He was leading the league in hitting in mid-August but fell to eighth overall in the National League with a .329 batting average. He was also third in slugging percentage (.577), and though he only played a partial season (126 games, 20 of those as a pinch hitter), his 93 RBIs were good for ninth in the league.

He'd put together a stunning six-week stretch of hitting from July 14 through August 24, during which he hit safely in thirty-six of thirty-seven games and batted .450. That, not his September swan dive (he still drove in twenty runs during the month), was on Rickey's mind when he traded Ripper Collins (and Roy Parmelee) to the Cubs for pitcher Lon Warneke after the season.

As news of the trade broke, young Mize was busy playing baseball for manager Rogers Hornsby and a squad of Major Leaguers in Iowa as part of a barnstorming tour with Satchel Paige, Cool Papa Bell, and some of the greatest players from the Negro Leagues.[30]

Here was an opportunity, once again, to play baseball against great ballplayers whom Mize rarely got to see and to make a little extra money in the process. Barnstorming tour promotor Ray Doan tapped Mize and several of his Cardinals teammates, and players from other white big league teams, to play a series of games against the Negro League All-Stars.

These games were immensely popular with curious fans in small-town America. In a time before national television coverage or high salaries, teams of barnstormers crisscrossed the country, playing local teams or other squads of professionals. These ballplayers made extra money and provided fans in the hinterlands an opportunity to see the baseball heroes they could only read about in their local newspapers.

Under the field direction of Hornsby, now the manager of the St. Louis Browns, the big league squad included Mize, his Cardinals teammates Mike Ryba, Jim Winford, and Art Garibaldi, as well as Ival Goodman of the Reds, Gus Suhr and Jim Weaver of the Pirates, Harlond Clift of the Browns, some Minor Leaguers, and the headliner, teen sensation Bob Feller.[31]

"Oh, they had a heckuva club," recalled Jimmie Crutchfield, an outfielder with the Negro League All-Stars, whose potent lineup included Bill Perkins (Satchel Paige's favorite catcher), Sammy Hughes (the top second baseman in the Negro National League), and Chester Williams (shortstop for the champion Pittsburgh Crawfords).[32] And like the white team, with Mize, Feller, and Hornsby, this squad also featured three future

Hall of Famers: Paige, Bell, and an aging Oscar Charleston, considered by many who saw him play to be the greatest of all time. For this tour, he was Mize's counterpart at first base.

"This was in 1936 when Charleston was big and fat," Crutchfield remembered in Robert Peterson's *Only the Ball Was White: A History of Legendary Black Players and All-Black Professional Teams.* "Even at his age he was as good as anyone playing baseball."[33]

The big leaguers won the first game of the tour in Davenport, Iowa (despite sixteen strikeouts by Paige and his reliever, Andy "Pullman" Porter). The Negro Leaguers won the remaining four contests in dominant fashion. Hughes led all hitters, batting .500, as his team outscored the big leaguers 22–13. Mize, who never could solve Paige (but didn't strike out), led the big leaguers with seven hits in the five games.[34]

From beginning to end, Johnny's first season as a big leaguer had been a resounding success. And somewhere, St. Louis sportswriter W. H. James must have felt a measure of vindication for a little couplet he'd written back during spring training:

When Ripper Collins fails to bat,
Frisch, right before our eyes,
Digs down into his magic hat
And pulls out Johnny Mize.[35]

9

Johnny and Jene

The average player must run the gauntlet
of feminine fans outside the clubhouse after
a big game. They stand around in groups,
lots of them pretty young things. They want
autographs; maybe a closeup view of their hero.
They usually get both while we wives stand back
in a corner under the grandstand, making
ourselves as inconspicuous as possible.   —Jene Mize[1]

The highlight of spring training in 1937 for Johnny Mize was a weekend
trip to Havana, March 13–14, when the Cardinals split a pair of exhibition games against the defending National League champion New York
Giants. The games drew informed, energetic crowds to La Tropical, the
lovely sunken garden ballpark that was the baseball jewel of Cuba.

But it wasn't the games that stood out for Mize—he had a hit and an
RBI in the first game, two hits and a run in the second. No, what Johnny
always remembered most about that trip to Cuba was pretty, young Betty
Jene Adams.

Traveling with the St. Louis party in Cuba was the family of Ray R.
Adams, an executive with the Kellogg's cereal company and a Breadon
friend who routinely attended Cardinals games in a private box at Sportsman's Park. Along for the ride was Ray's nineteen-year-old daughter, who
answered to Jene, "a lovely blonde, curvy, very attractive," said St. Louis
sportswriter Bob Broeg.[2]

Immediately following the Sunday game in Cuba, the Cardinals and
their entourage left for Daytona Beach—they were scheduled to play the

Yankees in a Monday afternoon exhibition. Before the boat from Havana docked in Florida, Johnny and Jene had fallen hard for each other.

Elizabeth Jene Adams was a society girl, the only child of Ray and Gladys Adams, who were a society couple. Ray had a high-paying job as a sales executive, which meant he could send his daughter to good private schools and go to ball games at Sportsman's Park whenever he wanted. Well off by Great Depression standards, Ray and Gladys enjoyed vacationing in Florida and established part-time residence there in 1937.

Johnny and Jene came from vastly different backgrounds and life experiences. It probably would not be a great leap to say the attraction was mostly physical, especially given the circumstances of their meeting—two young, single, healthy people in a tropical setting in the springtime.

Jene was a baseball fan—she'd been attending games with her father since she was a little girl. But more than his batting average, it was probably Johnny's broad shoulders, grey eyes, and self-assured, soft-spoken manner that she fell for.

Johnny had become a prince in her home city, a baseball star in a baseball town that supported two teams (the Cardinals and the sad-sack Browns of the American League, which owned Sportsman's Park, meaning the Cards were their tenants).

And Mize was no fool—Jene was a prize catch, a cultured beauty who spoke French and sang in her college glee club, the only daughter of prosperous parents. And of course, she had those intoxicating curves and a pretty smile, besides.

On August 8, a Sunday, they were married in the Episcopal Church of the Ascension. After the small ceremony that Sunday afternoon, Johnny went to work at Sportsman's Park—the Cardinals had a doubleheader with the Phillies. Jene watched from a box seat as Johnny went hitless in the first game, a Cardinals victory, then rapped two singles in the nightcap, a 6–6 tie called by darkness in the twelfth inning.[3]

- - -

The framed photo of Babe Ruth surrounded by sixty baseballs (his record home run total from 1927) hung in Johnny Mize's Demorest home. It had arrived with a note from Cousin George: "I hope you try to break this record"—an invitation from the Babe himself to chase one of the most cherished records in the game, a request to keep the home run mark in the family.[4]

"Well, that's just what I'm going to do," Johnny told Associated Press writer Bill Boring for a feature story that ran in January 1937. Ruth had even given Mize one of his bats, which Johnny never used in a game, but would swing from time to time over the winter, for inspiration.

"I want to hit more home runs than anybody in the league this year and I'm keeping in shape with the hope of doing it," said Mize, who would fall short of that goal but made it abundantly clear that his rookie season was no fluke. "I hit about as well in the majors as I did in the minors," he added.[5]

And then he hit even better in 1937.

But before that could happen, the Cardinals needed to sign Johnny to a contract. Young Mize was beginning a new tradition for himself: the holdout. Rickey mailed a contract to Demorest three times, and Johnny sent it back unsigned three times.[6]

Rickey did nothing to endear himself to Mize when he went out of his way to blast the young star: "He's not as good as he thinks he is, and I don't care who knows it," he said.[7]

Finally, they reached an agreement. Mize signed for $7,000.[8] Or it might have been $9,000.[9]

At either figure, he was a bargain.

Though he didn't lead the league in any offensive category, Mize finished second in batting average (a career-high .364), slugging percentage (.595), doubles, extra-base hits, total bases, and on base percentage (.427). He was also fourth in home runs (25), third in RBIS (113), third in overall wins above replacement (WAR) and position-player WAR (6.7), and second in offensive WAR (7.1). And he was selected to the first of ten All-Star teams.

It was a stellar season by any standards except, perhaps, Joe "Ducky" Medwick's. His 1937 season was the personal masterpiece in a Hall of Fame career. Ducky won the Triple Crown as the league leader in batting average (.374), home runs (31), and RBIS (154), and just about everything else, and deservedly won the Most Valuable Player.

But he never won, or seemed to want, Mize's friendship. In fact, the Cardinals' two top sluggers had a simmering, ongoing competition that lasted the entire time they played together.

"They were rivals," recalled Bob Broeg. "Johnny was kind of easygoing, and Medwick was kind of hard-nosed, not easy to get along with."[10]

Gutteridge added, "There was some jealousy there, on both sides. Johnny wanted to drive in runs, and so did Medwick. So, there were times when Johnny was on base and Medwick got a hit and complained when Johnny didn't score—and vice versa."[11]

Ducky didn't typically hang out with most of the guys, but he and Leo Durocher were tight.

"They were buddies," Gutteridge said. "And they kind of set themselves apart from the rest of us, dressed better, went to the higher-priced places."[12]

Leo had been best man at Joe's wedding in August 1936. Like Mize, Medwick married a St. Louis girl, Isabelle Heutel, "a dark-haired beauty," Broeg said. "Isabelle and Jene sat together in Sportsman's Park, two very attractive ladies. It made for quite a spectacle; they both liked to dress well, and I think there might have been a little competition going on there."[13]

Meanwhile, the Mizes and Gutteridges—Don and his wife, Helen—spent a lot of time together.

"We went out a lot," Gutteridge remembered. "The four of us most of the time—dinner, movies. We'd eat at each other's home, pick up some steaks, and eat in. And we'd drive to the ballpark together a lot. Then Jene would pick up Helen, or Helen would pick up Jene. Those were good days."[14]

- - -

This wasn't the Gashouse Gang anymore. Paul Dean's pitching career was pretty much over. He made one appearance in 1937, lingered a few more seasons with the Cards and Giants, and called it quits at thirty after a few innings with the Browns in 1943. Pepper Martin got off to a hot start, then suffered a knee injury that shortened his season and, ultimately, his career. Durocher was the only member of the 1934 infield still starting. And Dizzy Dean was about to discover his Achilles heel—actually, it was his toe, then his arm.

Dizzy started strong in 1937, winning his first five decisions. Dean was 12-7 when he was selected to start the All-Star Game for the National League, July 7 in Washington DC. It was also Mize's first All-Star Game, and he contributed an RBI on a long fly to center field, but the American League cruised to an 8–3 win.

In the bottom of the third, Cleveland Indians slugger Earl Averill sent a line drive back to the mound that bounced off Dizzy's left foot to second baseman Billy Herman, who easily retired Averill. But Dizzy had a broken big toe. He missed the next two weeks, then insisted he was well enough to pitch against Boston on July 21. Frisch, in one of the most passively idiotic moves, or nonmoves, by any manager in baseball history, let him. And Dean pitched a good game, but the Cardinals lost. But he began ruining his arm in the process. Unable to throw and step with a proper motion, he favored the toe, overstressed his arm, and was never the same pitcher again.

Dizzy won another game and lost three the rest of the year, finishing at 13-10. Then Rickey traded him to Chicago just before the 1938 season, and Diz recaptured a little bit of his old magic. Though his tired arm managed just ten starts, he went 7-1 with a 1.81 earned run average, winning some critical games (including a shutout of the Cardinals), helping the Cubs win the '38 National League pennant.

- - -

The Cardinals bolted out of the gate in 1937 like they were going to rule the world, winning seven of their first eight games. Then gravity did its thing, and the Giants and Cubs did theirs, making it a two-team race for most of the season.

Chicago had a six and a half game lead on August 13 when the Giants made their move. They caught the Cubs on September 1, then took over first place for themselves on September 2, with help from the Cardinals, and held on to it.

The Cardinals visited the Polo Grounds for a three-game set that began on August 31, a Tuesday. St. Louis won the first game, as Johnny, now batting third in the order ahead of Medwick, had 3 hits, including a home run, and 3 RBIs. Mize was having one of his monster months in August, batting .386 and driving in 29 runs in thirty-one games.

The Giants won the next two games to move into first place, but Johnny did not stick around for the end of the second game, thanks to Gunboat Gumbert, who had him seeing stars.

Mize had abused Gumbert since coming into the league in 1936, when he hit the first home run of his career off the big Giants right-hander. And he continued the abuse in this game, hitting a triple and single off Harry the first two times up. In the top of the sixth, Gunboat fired back. Jene, who had traveled to New York to be with her husband of less than four weeks, watched in horror as Mize, no doubt expecting an off-speed pitch, stepped into a Gumbert fastball with his skull, then fell to the ground in a semiconscious heap. He was carried off the field on a stretcher, and Jene accompanied him to the hospital.[15] Even though she'd been watching baseball all her life and understood the risks, this was the thing she hated most.

"I don't approve of the beanball," she wrote in a 1942 guest column for the *Sporting News*. "Who would? And I know most pitchers wouldn't throw such a cowardly pitch."

What bothered her more than a pitcher's cowardice was when a fan would yell, "Hit him in the head." She called such catcalls "the fullest degree of depravity."[16]

Luckily, though, Mize wasn't hurt too seriously. But in the days before protective batting helmets, as every batter knew, any beaning had the potential to be devastating, even fatal. Cleveland Indians infielder Ray Chapman was killed by a fastball from New York Yankees submariner Carl Mays in 1920. And in May 1937 Detroit Tigers player-manager Mickey Cochrane had been nearly killed by a pitch from Yankees hurler Bump Hadley, probably still fuming over the home run Cochrane hit off him earlier.[17]

For Mize, this was the first of two serious beanings in his career. He'd be smacked upside the head again years later by Harry "the Cat" Brecheen. But Johnny didn't take these things personally. "You know, back when I broke in, throwing at hitters was part of the game. It was expected. If you couldn't take it, you were better off going home," he told Donald Honig. So, it never really bothered Mize. "I figured any guy that threw at me knew I could hit him, because the only reason you throw at a guy is to try and scare him. You let a pitcher scare you, you might as well go up there without a bat in your hands. I always bore down harder against any man that threw at me."[18]

Following the beaning, he sat out several games, joking that he was doing fine because Gumbert's fastball felt like a softball pitch.[19] A week after getting hit in the head, he smashed a double and a triple and drove in two runs in a win over the Cubs, which helped the Giants' cause.

New York won the pennant by three games over Chicago, and for a second straight year it was an all–New York Subway Series, and once again the Yankees eased past the Giants for the championship.

The Cardinals finished a disheartening fourth with an 81-73 record, well out of the race but good enough to have expected more. They got a decent season from Lon Warneke, who came to St. Louis from Chicago in the Collins deal. The veteran right-hander won eighteen games. But it wasn't enough to make up for the loss of the Dean brothers, or the team's weakness at catcher, or its miserable performance against the Cubs (5-17 record), or Durocher's more-anemic-than-usual bat (the man Babe Ruth dubbed "the all-American out," lived down to the nickname, batting .203). The team was two, maybe three players away from being great. From Mize's point of view, this became typical.

"We always had good ballclubs in St. Louis, but most of the time we needed just a little bit more help," he said. "They kept plenty of good ballplayers in the minor leagues in those years, but they kept selling them off." Players like Fritz Ostermueller, Bill Lee, and Cy Blanton had been in the Cardinals' system but went on to have good careers elsewhere.[20]

Johnny added, "I heard that Rickey got 25 percent of whatever he sold a player for. That's why every year he was selling those players." In truth, Rickey got 10 percent, but Mize wasn't alone in believing the 25 percent story. A lot of Cardinals told the same general tale, along with the one about Rickey ensuring that his teams would stay in the pennant race long enough to draw crowds but then fall just short so the players couldn't demand raises for winning championships, according to Mize. "I don't know if it's true or not, but that was the talk," he said.[21]

Idle chit-chat—the truth is, Rickey had agreements with Cardinals Minor League clubs to *not* raid their teams in the middle of a season, especially if they were fighting for a league title. So, he wasn't manipulating the scenario for the Cardinals to barely fail. It was business. "Rickey believed that it was important to keep the goodwill of his minor league customers, and so he refused to take an important player from a team during the season, no matter how badly the Cards may have needed him," wrote Peter Golenbock in *The Spirit of St. Louis*.[22]

But Mize came to his suspicion of Rickey's and the club's motives honestly. By way of example, he shared with author Donald Honig that when he married Jene, club owner Breadon—a friend of her family's—celebrated the newlyweds with a wedding gift of $500. "The next year when I was talking contract with Rickey, he said, 'Well, you made seventy-five-hundred last year.' 'No,' I said, 'I only made seven thousand.' He said, 'Really? Where's that five hundred that Breadon gave you?' That was Rickey."[23]

Mize told it slightly differently to syndicated columnist Jimmy Cannon in 1959. In that story, Mize claimed he was making $9,000 in 1937.[24] At any rate, in both versions of the story, Johnny describes his experience dickering with Rickey. And that's what lay ahead for Johnny: more dickering and another holdout in 1938. This was baseball in an age when players represented themselves in contract negotiations, Mize's least favorite part of the job.

But first, he had to attend to one of the best parts of the job. For the second year in a row Mize headed into the American heartland as part of a postseason barnstorming troupe of big leaguers. This time he was joining Bob Feller for a series of games against the Kansas City Monarchs, undisputed champions of the Negro American League.

This time, fans in the flyover zone would have a chance to see five future Hall of Famers in action: Mize, Feller, and Monarch stars Willard Brown, Hilton Smith, and Bullet Joe Rogan. Brown left a lasting impression on the fans and players who saw him on that tour. In one game, he blasted a two-run homer that just kept going over the left-center-field scoreboard in Davenport's Municipal Stadium and drove in another run with a blistering double, lifting the Monarchs to victory. And he helped preserve that win with a jaw-dropping catch that robbed Mize of an extra-base hit in the top of the ninth. Johnny sliced a long shot off Smith, the best curveball artist in Black baseball, and Brown sprinted after it.

"Mize poled a honey that looked like a sure double, if not a triple," wrote Leo Kautz, sports editor of the *Daily Times* of Davenport. "But Brown came up with an almost impossible one-handed catch while running at full speed to his left, for the third out."[25]

Lon Warneke said Brown's catch was the best he'd ever seen.[26]

Following the tour, Mize proceeded with the second part of his simple off-season plans: "Barnstorm for ten days and then home to Demorest, Ga., for some hunting."[27]

That was Johnny's two-cents' worth in one of those end-of-season feature stories that baseball writers used to bang out every year. In the September 29, 1937, edition of the *St. Louis Star-Times*, Mize and his teammates shared their plans for the off-season, and it excellently encapsulates the many differences between now and then:

LEO DUROCHER: "See the World Series and then beat it back here to play golf. Medwick's my dish at the game."

STU MARTIN: "Get that appendix operation over."

MIKE RYBA: "Barnstormin' with Doan first and then I'll go to Punxsutawney, Pa., my home. I'll hunt and maybe dig me a little coal."

MICKEY OWEN: "Go to work in a lumber camp up in Oregon and try to put on about twenty-five pounds."

While his teammates did some huntin' and fishin' and diggin' and cuttin' (and appendix losin'), Johnny met Jene in St. Louis, then the two drove to Demorest, stopping in Atlanta to visit his mother on the way.

Back in Demorest, Johnny spent much of the off-season walking the woody hills with his dogs and enjoying quiet evenings with his new bride. It was a lifestyle that gave him plenty of time to think about what he expected from the Cardinals and himself in 1938, probably while swinging at phantom pitches with the Babe's bat.

10

Rule of Three

I'd like to write a story about
a player on this ballclub.
I'd like to write a story
about Johnny Mize.   —Frankie Frisch

The Fordham Flash shared the story he'd like to write, delivering a flow of effusive praise in a piece written by Sid Keener for the April 1, 1938, edition of the *St. Louis Star-Times*. It came under the headline and subhead "Mize Is Now Best First Baseman in Game, Frisch Says; Believes Cardinal Slugger Will Soon Become One of Baseball's Greats."

Frisch ripped the local press for not giving Mize enough credit and for consciously favoring Medwick over the youngster, then said, "Mize is a manager's ball player. He never grumbles, never complains and is there every day—practice games, bush league games and pennant games. He hits to all fields. He snatches high throws and scoops 'em out of the dirt. By 1939, maybe it'll be 1938, big Jawn should be one of the great stars in this game. There's my story about Johnny Mize."[1]

But before Mize could follow Frisch's happy script, there would be a few plot twists.

- - -

It is an overcast June day in Chicago, and the good-luck charm flutters down from above, twinkling as it crosses the edge of Johnny Mize's gaze and falling gently at his feet in the visiting team dugout at Wrigley Field.[2] The Cardinals are about to do something unusual for 1938—take their second game in a row from the Cubs, who will win the pennant this year.

Mize is taking it easy today on manager's orders. Frankie Frisch has grown impatient with the struggling first baseman. So, Johnny sits here, idly sur-

veying the game from a distance, when the little glimmering thing catches his attention. He watches it land and bounce lightly.

It's a little horseshoe pendant that has somehow become separated from a fan in the grandstands. Perhaps it's been tossed with the intention of finding someone who needs it.

Mize reaches down and grabs the thing, looks it over in his big hand, and thinks, I can use all the help I can get.

- - -

Since June 19, Mize had been collecting splinters in his rear end because of a horrid batting slump. Frisch replaced him with Don Padgett at first base, and Mize waited. But he probably didn't worry. Wasn't in his nature. He took his hits and his slumps in stride. He'd already demonstrated what a streaky hitter he could be in his first two years in the big leagues.

But now it was July, middle of the season already. The All-Star Game had come and gone (National League won, 4–1; Mize didn't make the team), and Johnny was batting .261 at the break.

"Here in 1938, Johnny Mize is the year's biggest bust," Keener wrote in his column of July 2. "They say the pitchers found his weak spot—a slow dropper on the outside of the plate." Forgetting the fact that a slow dropper on the outside of the plate is everyone's weak spot, perhaps Keener was burying the kid a bit too quickly with his parting shot: "They come and go in a hurry out on the baseball diamond."[3]

Mize figured out early on that he didn't really trust these scribes who were always looking for an angle. Now the writers were on him for what they perceived to be his stubborn refusal to accept Frisch's advice.

Perhaps Mize was refusing. Or he might have been working through it the best way he knew how: trying to hit the ball back through the middle of the diamond. He did this in batting practice, concentrating on just meeting the ball squarely. Also, when Mize was struggling, he did not tune out helpful advice. "During a slump, be open to all theories," he preached. "If someone makes a suggestion that sounds reasonable, try it. You lose nothing."[4]

He was making contact, but the baseballs weren't falling in or flying out. At the All-Star break, he had a mere four home runs to go with his sickly batting average. And he was hitting a lot of grounders to first and second.

"It never fails that when a ballplayer is in a slump, he might tag the ball well a couple of times but always, right at someone," Mize claimed. "This is also when the fielders start robbing you of base hits as well. The ballplayers call this the 'At-em' ball. No matter where you hit it, it's always at someone."[5]

While he was relegated to the bench for several weeks, Mize worked hard to lose weight, wearing a rubber suit, pitching batting practice. He was about 15 pounds lighter, down from the bloated 235 he'd been in March.[6]

And according to Frisch, Mize eventually did start taking his advice. "We changed his stance a little," Frisch said. "I've been trying to get him to do it for a long time. Get his right foot around closer to the plate."[7]

Despite his lousy start in 1938, Johnny was a celebrity in St. Louis. Every baseball fan knew who he was. He was in the headlines. His picture was in the newspaper, in the sports pages, and in advertisements. One of the city's Municipal Baseball Leagues had even borrowed his name for the Johnny Mize Junior League (there was also a Medwick Junior League). He was a fan favorite. "Johnny was very popular," Gutteridge said. "The kids, they'd follow us to the car, and I'd have to wait for him to sign every autograph before we could go home."[8]

They may not have been clamoring for his autograph lately, but his fortunes were about to change. Frisch sent him in to pinch hit against the visiting Pirates with two out and Gutteridge on base in the bottom of the ninth. He responded with a line drive double, putting two men in scoring position. But that's where they stayed, and the Cardinals lost.

Frisch was convinced. Padgett hadn't been hitting. He wanted Mize back. So, the next day, July 9, after three weeks of exile, Mize started at first base. He hit a home run, then hit two doubles the day after that. The Cardinals were still losing games, but Johnny had started a hitting spree that lasted the rest of the season.

The pitchers all started looking alike again.

- - -

Johnny Mize hit a full 5 percent of his career home runs in just six games. That is, he hit three home runs in a game on six different occasions, a record he held by himself for decades, which has since been tied (by Sammy Sosa and Mookie Betts as of 2022). That's 18 home runs out of Mize's career total of 359—slightly *more* than 5 percent.

The first of these six games, on July 13, 1938, served notice that Mize was just fine, even if the Cardinals were not. Sportsman's Park drew 7,846 fans to the annual Tuberculosis Day game against the Boston Bees.

Pitching for Boston was right-hander Jim Turner, who won twenty games as a thirty-three-year-old rookie in 1937, when he led the National League in earned run average (2.38) and shutouts (5). While he wasn't as effective in '38, Turner was a dependable starter for manager Casey Stengel (and he would become Casey's pitching coach on the Yankees, 1949–59).

Mize previously had very little luck with "Milkman Jim," who worked at his family's dairy during the offseason. He had four singles in twenty-three at bats against Turner in their entanglements so far. And the Tuberculosis Day ball game started badly for Mize, who grounded into a double play his first time up in the bottom of the second inning. The Bees were ahead 7–0 when Johnny came up in the bottom of the fourth with one out and Medwick on first. He hit the ball on top of the pavilion roof in right.[9]

His next two homers, also against Turner, left the premises altogether. In the sixth with two out and Boston leading 8–2, Mize's solo shot to right landed on Grand Boulevard. He hit the boulevard again in the eighth with Medwick on base, driving in all the Cardinals' runs in the 10–5 loss. Maybe it's fitting that such a breathtaking performance should take place on Tuberculosis Day. The little horseshoe pendant that landed at Johnny's feet in Chicago circled the bases with him every time, taped to the inside of his belt.[10]

Then, about a week later, he did even better. The Giants were breathing down Pittsburgh's neck in the National League race when they came to St. Louis and split a four-game set, July 19–21. New York won the bookend games, and the Cardinals swept the Wednesday doubleheader in front of 12,886 fans. In the second game of the twin bill, Johnny hit the trifecta again, his three homers providing five runs in a 7–1 win. He might've had four blasts but got under a Slick Castleman pitch in the fifth inning, flying out to right field.[11]

He hit the first two off Castleman, with two out and two on in the first inning and leading off the fourth with a smash that landed on Grand Boulevard. He led off the eighth with his third blast, against reliever Bill Lohrman. This one, too, left the premises altogether, bouncing on the boulevard.

Mize had become the first and still only player to hit three homers in a game twice in a span of eight days. He also became the first big league player to hit three home runs in a game twice in the same season. Not even the Babe did that.

Speaking of which, Johnny's Cousin George was back in baseball that year. Two years earlier, 1936, Babe had joined Christy Mathewson, Walter Johnson, Honus Wagner, and Ty Cobb in the inaugural class of the National Baseball Hall of Fame. Ruth had hoped to become a manager since retiring in 1935, but it never happened. Instead, Larry MacPhail signed Ruth for $15,000 to put on a Dodgers uniform. His job was to just be Babe Ruth, to be seen by the fans.[12] He also took part in batting practice and long-distance hitting contests and coached first base.

For Mize, it meant the opportunity to meet his big-shot cousin-in-law on a regular season ballfield. There were probably some visits to the Ruth pad during these Cardinals trips to New York. And there also was the opportunity for some friendly competition with the Babe.

In a pregame slugging contest on August 3 in Brooklyn's Ebbets Field, Johnny won the $50 first prize with a 391-foot clout. Medwick won $25 for second place. The Babe and Brooklyn slugger Dolph Camilli finished out of the money. Mize's buddy on the Cardinals, Don Gutteridge, earned the biggest pregame prize, taking home $250 for winning the finals of what had been an ongoing eighty-yard-dash contest to determine the fastest man in the National League.[13]

A day earlier, as the Dodgers were winning both ends of a doubleheader against the bumbling Cards, Johnny had a chance to show off a little bit for the Babe. In the first game, leading off the seventh against Freddie Fitzsimmons, he hit the ball over the right-field screen for a home run. And this wasn't just any baseball. The two teams had agreed to use an experimental yellow ball in the first game—they were collaborating with color spectrum experts at Columbia University, who claimed that yellow was the most visible of all colors.[14] The golden sphere didn't catch on, but the home run stuck.

- - -

How to explain Mize and the Cardinals of 1938? The team was never very good, and the best expression of its overall frustration may have been the afternoon in Boston near the end of July, when Pepper Martin struck out with men on base and the Bees won, 3–2. Afterward, a furious Martin took it out on Mize's precious bats, smashing them on the ground.[15] No matter. Johnny, who had already become famous for carrying more bats than anyone else, could always get more.

"He always had more bats than anybody," said Don Gutteridge. "When you hit like he hit, they buy you all the bats you want."[16]

After his slow start, Mize was otherworldly for most of the 1938 season. The difference between before the All-Star break and after is stark. Over the last eighty-seven games of the season, he hit 23 of his 27 home runs for the year, drove in 74 of his 102 RBIs, and batted .389, finishing at .337 for the season, second in the National League.

He very nearly won the batting crown. Ernie Lombardi was leading, but Mize batted .446 in September, closing the gap. Lombardi was hitting .339 to Mize's .338 as the two sluggers met in a head-to-head battle, September 27–29. Both men were hitless in the first game, a 3–1 Reds win, which dropped them both to .336. Mize briefly led the league after going 3 for 4 in the second game. His double to left field in the sixth provided the winning run for the Cardinals in their 8–7 triumph. Lombardi had two hits, but Johnny led Ernie, .339 to .337. The next day, Thursday, Mize went hitless in five at bats, while Lombardi added two more hits to retake the lead. He finished with a .342 average to win his first batting title—Lombardi led the National League again in 1942 when he was a Boston Brave.

Johnny's final 1938 report card was noteworthy: league leader in total bases (326), slugging percentage (.614), and, though it wasn't recognized by stat-chasers back then, on-base average plus slugging percentage, or OPS (1.036). But his magic number that season, of course, was three—Johnny led the National League in triples with 16, demonstrating hustle on the base paths, even if he faltered in the field—he also led National League first basemen in errors (15), contributing to the Cards' defensive woes.

St. Louis made 199 errors as a team, second highest in the league—only the miserable Phillies (45-105 that season) had more. And while the Cardinals had the highest team batting average and slugging percentage in the league, their pitching was inconsistent. Ultimately, Frisch paid the price with his job. He was fired September 11 and replaced by his friend, Cardinals coach Miguel "Mike" González, for the final sixteen games of the season (the team went 8-8 for Mike).[17]

"How do I stand around here?" Frisch asked Breadon the Friday before he was fired. "He didn't have an answer to my question, but he told me he'd let me know Sunday. I went in to see him, and I was in the room only a few minutes when he told me he decided to have a new manager in 1939. We parted friends."[18]

While the move made González the first Latin American manager in the big leagues, there was an element of cruelty involved—Mike did not want his pal Frank to go, and he knew his appointment was only temporary. In an unbylined blurb, González is tactlessly quoted using ham-fisted vernacular, in which the word "is" is spelled "eez," and the new manager is quoted saying, "I weel see Meestair Reekey."[19]

The Cardinals' sixth-place finish in 1938 was their worst since 1932, and their 71-80 record the worst since 1924. The team never reached .500, and attendance plummeted to seventh in the league. But still, Rickey had begun strengthening the team with the addition of twenty-two-year-old rookie right fielder Enos Slaughter of Roxboro, North Carolina.

He was another rural southerner on a team filled with them. But Slaughter was special. He was that rare Cardinal who only spent two seasons in the Minors—but he batted .325 and .382 with a bunch of extra base hits and RBIs, so the future Hall of Famer "would prove to be one of the toughest, most durable, and most exciting players ever to wear a Redbird on his sleeve," wrote Peter Golenbock in *The Spirit of St. Louis*.[20]

Slaughter, whom Mize affectionately called "the peanut farmer," batted .276 as a rookie in 1938 (his lowest average in thirteen years with the Cardinals) but showed incredible hustle, cracking the top ten in the league with 10 triples while playing in just 112 games.

Another rookie who debuted that season with St. Louis and saw limited action was twenty-five-year-old right-handed pitcher Mort Cooper, who would join Slaughter and center fielder Terry Moore as part of the nucleus of a Cardinals team destined to win three straight pennants (1942–44). In that stretch, Cooper would squeeze enough juice out of his perpetually sore arm for three 20-win seasons, topped by 1942, when he posted 10 shutouts, led the league in ERA (1.78), and won the Most Valuable Player Award. One of his favorite victims that year was the slugging first baseman for the New York Giants, who looked helpless as he went 1 for 13 against Cooper: a fellow named Johnny Mize.

- - -

On Wednesday morning, March 9, 1938, Pope Mize unlocked the front door to his gas station in Demorest, Georgia, where he had a hefty chunk of the local market in the fill-er-up business. It didn't hurt that Pope's little brother was the best left-handed hitter in the National League. While Skippy was playing for the Gashouse Gang, Pope was really working in a gashouse.

Pope saw the telegram lying on the floor as he opened the door to the station. He almost collapsed from the shock. It was from Jimmy Dykes, White Sox manager, asking him to name his terms for a contract. An Associated Press story also claimed that "26-year-old Pope wired Dykes that he was ready to play ball but would talk terms later." Pope is quoted saying he'd report the following night, "ready to start all over in a game that I thought had closed its door in my face."[21]

Pope had failed in a tryout with the Moultrie Steers of the Class D Georgia-Florida League in 1936. Now he was getting a new chance to have a professional baseball career, though it would be brief. He spent several months playing in the outfield for the Lubbock Hubbers of the Class D West Texas–New Mexico League. Then he returned to Georgia, where he finally caught on in the Georgia-Florida League, with the independent Cordele Reds.

Johnny had always claimed his big brother could hit, and Pope proved it that season, pounding the ball hard and for good average. But his fielding and throwing were suspect, and he was injured much of the time.

Also, Pope was one of the oldest players on the Lubbock team and one of the few married men. His wife, Mary Cathleen, moved with him to Texas for those few months. She made for a pretty picture in the *Lubbock Avalanche-Journal* on June 12, when the paper ran a photo, above the fold, of players' wives. A week later, after her husband already had been cut from the team, the same newspaper reported that Mary Cathleen "has teeth as perfect as the movie stars display."[22]

Pope was nearly twenty-eight by then, not the twenty-six or twenty-three that most papers reported that season. They also referred to him as Johnny Mize's younger brother from time to time.[23] Either way, that 1938 season would be Pope's only turn at organized professional baseball. And while Johnny was setting records in the National League that year, vying for a batting title, Pope could be proud that, at the very least, his .337 batting average in the Minors matched his brother's.

The peanut shells (along with the Chicago Cubs) had barely been swept from the 1938 World Series (the Yankees won their third-straight title) when the rumors began. Chicago manager Gabby Hartnett, vowing to shake up the lineup of his pennant winning club, was showing interest in acquiring Medwick or Mize from the Cardinals. Cubs owner Phillip K. Wrigley was supposedly offering $150,000 and players.

"While Breadon and Rickey did not exactly turn down Wrigley, they intimated that Medwick certainly would be retained, while only a most attractive offer will lure Mize from the Mound City," wrote Joe LeBlanc in Chicago sports journal *Collyer's Eye and the Baseball World*.[24]

The Cardinals kept denying anything was afoot. But the rumors persisted right up until Mize signed his contract with the Cardinals. In a January 26 story by the *Globe-Democrat's* Martin Haley, Cubs executive Clarence Rowland claimed, "We did all we could to get Mize and there's no sense in trying further."[25]

For his part, Mize wanted to handle the negotiations a little differently this year—no more dickering through the mail with Rickey. In early January, while trade rumors were swirling, he told writer Dick Farrington he was through doing business with the Mahatma that way.

"[Rickey] will outpoint you every time in a letter," Mize said. "I'm not the smartest guy in the world, but I'd rather meet him face to face when it comes to terms."[26]

They came to terms on January 27, 1939, a month before spring training. Johnny signed for $12,500. Mize told Farrington he was "well satisfied."[27]

"And being satisfied and in excellent condition," Farrington wrote, "there is no good reason why Johnny should not lead the league in hitting this year."[28]

11

Best Hitter in the National League

> When you can win the cleanup job
> from a hitter like Medwick you must
> have something besides a toothpaste
> smile and a Demorest, Ga., accent.   —Jimmy Powers[1]

It's one of those strange blips that jumps out at anyone who pores over baseball statistics, something that deserves bold type or italics: Don Padgett's .399 batting average in 1939.

Padgett was a fine utility player for the Cardinals from 1937 through 1941. He'd even been cast as a potential replacement for Johnny Mize by Cardinals bosses trying to light a fire under the young Big Cat. But no one ever took those threats very seriously, including the easy-going Mize.

A lifetime .288 hitter, Padgett batted .271 in 1938 and .242 in 1940. But the blip—playing ninety-two games, mostly as a catcher, he turned into Ty Cobb in 1939 and was a major contributor to a good Cardinals ball club. Padgett's $6,000 salary made him one of the year's best bargains.

It was Padgett's career year, and though his average was the highest among all National League players, he didn't have enough plate appearances to qualify for the batting crown. That honor went to his Cardinals teammate, the club's starting first baseman, the guy Padgett was supposed to replace.

"About the only question that still surrounds Johnny Mize's climb toward the batting championship of the National League is how high a ceiling he can reach," the *New York Daily News* pronounced on September 3.[2] Mize had raised his average to .360 by then and would get as high as .366 before leveling off to win the batting championship with a .349 mark.

The combination of Mize, Joe Medwick (.332, 117 RBIs), Enos Slaughter

(.320, 52 doubles), and the team's new pitching ace, Curt Davis (22 wins, 7 saves), helped make St. Louis a pennant contender under rookie manager Ray Blades, a former Cardinal outfielder who managed Rochester to a third-place finish in 1938. He'd been elevated to field boss of the mother club and was familiar to most of the players in St. Louis, having managed in the team's farm system for years.

But Blades had a bit of a despotic tendency that grew tiresome on a ball club with a reputation for shenanigans. "It wasn't long before the martinet manager outwore his welcome," wrote Peter Golenbock.[3]

Don Gutteridge noted, "He was a different kind of guy than Frisch. Ray was intent and serious. Frisch was intent, but he had a humorous side. Ray Blades never did."[4]

Blades could be fierce and a perfectionist. His style had worked well in the Minor Leagues, guiding mostly boys on the cusp of adulthood. That style didn't go over so well with the grown men in the big leagues.

"I don't think Blades was a very good major league manager," Gutter-idge told Golenbock. "He was great in the minor leagues but not in the big leagues, all the difference in the world. In the minor leagues, you take what talent you get, and its more teaching because your job as a minor league manager is to send kids to the big leagues."[5]

Blades and the players didn't get along very well. That was especially true with Joe Medwick, already known for being moody. Ducky was mood-ier than usual in 1939 because, after a contentious battle with Breadon and Rickey, he'd reluctantly agreed to a $2,000 salary cut (to $18,000) for the season, despite batting .322 and leading the league in doubles and RBIS in 1938—yeah, Rickey and Breadon could be brutal negotiators.[6]

On top of that, Medwick's pride had been hurt when he was fined by Blades for not hustling (it was only $25). Then in late July, Blades started pulling Medwick from ball games for a defensive replacement. The Mad Hungarian finally blew his top when it seemed Blades was trying to show him up or teach him a lesson. On August 1, a Tuesday, the Cardinals were leading the visiting Boston Bees, 4–3, in the top of the ninth with two out, a runner on first, and two strikes on the batter. That's when Blades stopped the game to replace Medwick with Lynn King in left field.

"Medwick promptly heaved his glove high into the air across the foul line, stalked after it sullenly and then kicked it around viciously before he picked it up," wrote Martin Haley in the *St. Louis Globe-Democrat*'s

August 2 game account. Blades, who didn't take any official action against Medwick for his public outburst, added, "I don't care how mad he gets just so we win."[7]

Mize didn't enjoy a spectacular relationship with the intense Blades either. "Once in a while they'd spit back and forth," Gutteridge said. "But mostly, Blades left Johnny alone. How do you get on a guy who is hitting .350 and leading your ball club?"[8]

- - -

St. Louis was awash in new managers. Less than twenty-four hours after Blades was introduced as the Cardinals new skipper on November 6, 1938, Browns president Don Barnes named Fred Haney as manager of his club.[9] Poor Fred—the 1939 St. Louis Browns was the worst team in the franchise's history, and that's saying something. Haney, who would later manage the Milwaukee Braves to consecutive pennants (1957–58) and a World Series victory (1957), "guided" the Browns to a 43-111 record in 1939. Meanwhile, Blades presided over a Cardinals club that won ninety-two games and nearly won the National League pennant.

Nonetheless, Haney outlasted Blades in St. Louis. Breadon was more impatient than the Browns' leadership. When the Cardinals got off to an awful start in 1940, Blades was fired in early June. Haney would finally be fired in June 1941.

But in 1939 Blades was being hailed as a "miracle man" in this new era of Cardinals baseball.[10] Medwick was the only starter from the 1934 Gashouse Gang still playing every day. Pepper Martin was still valuable, but as a part-time utility player. And the sparkplug of the 1934 Cardinals infield, shortstop Leo Durocher, was now managing the Brooklyn Dodgers.

This version of the Cardinals featured Enos Slaughter, Terry Moore, Don Padgett, and Johnny Mize. It was a good team, but not good enough to overtake the Cincinnati Reds, which grabbed first place on May 19 and held on to it. The Cardinals matched the mighty Reds in head-to-head competition, as the two teams split their season series, 11–11.

And Mize, seemingly intent on showing the Reds what they had missed by letting him go, feasted with gusto on their pitching, particularly in Cincinnati's Crosley Field, where he logged a .442 batting average with 5 homers and 16 RBIs against the National League's best pitching staff. Johnny was particularly unkind to Paul Derringer, the former Cardinal whose nickname was "The Control King." Derringer, who once lost 27 games in a season, had become an ace in Cincinnati, where he posted four 20-win seasons, including his career high of 25 in 1939. Mize was unimpressed. In fact, he was merciless on the big right-hander, batting .555 (10 for 18) against him in 1939.

Derringer's teammate, Bucky Walters, had more luck with Mize, holding him to a .305 average. The former third baseman turned pitcher, Walters led the National League with 27 victories and a 2.29 earned run average in 1939, winning the National League Most Valuable Player Award, easily outdistancing the runner-up—Johnny Mize, who finished second in MVP voting, just ahead of Derringer.

But in his final start of the regular season, Walters came up short against the Cardinals, giving St. Louis a last gasp of hope for a pennant. Then Derringer strangled it out of them the following day.

- - -

Cincinnati was in the middle of a long drought, but the clouds hanging over Crosley Field held the promise of rain as an overflow crowd of 34,194 played hooky and packed the ballpark for a Tuesday afternoon double-header between the hometown Reds and visiting St. Louis Cardinals on September 26. These were the first two games in a four-game series that could decide the pennant.

The pesky, can't-take-a-hint, won't-go-away Cardinals had been dead on July 30, trailing the Reds by twelve games. That day, St. Louis began a ten-game winning streak, its longest of the season. And that's when Mize began a forty-game stretch of mighty hitting. Through September 10, he batted .432, with 10 doubles, 6 triples, 6 homers, and 37 RBIs. And the Cardinals won thirty of those games, edging closer to the Reds, which struggled through August but played like champs the final month of the season.

The Cards and Reds were the hottest teams in baseball as they prepared to meet. St. Louis had won eighteen of its previous twenty-one games, and the Reds had won sixteen of twenty. Cincinnati, managed by former St. Louis skipper and future Hall of Famer Bill McKechnie, had a record of 93-54 and led in the standings by three and a half games over St. Louis (89-57) as it began its four-game series with that Tuesday doubleheader.

The rain held, and the two teams ended the day in the same place—

three and a half games apart. Cincinnati won the first game, 3–1, as rookie pitcher Gene Thompson scattered nine hits (Mize had two of them). Mort Cooper held the powerful Reds to four hits in the second game, a 6–0 Cardinals victory that ended Cincinnati's eight-game winning streak.

Some skillful maneuvering by McKechnie made it possible for his two aces to pitch the next two games of the series. Walters was initially going to pitch the second game of the Tuesday doubleheader, but after Thompson handled the Cardinals in the first game, McKechnie chose to save Walters for Wednesday, and that would leave Derringer for Thursday's series finale.[11]

Wednesday's rhythm belonged to "Fiddler" Bill McGee. A multitalented musician for Pepper Martin's Mississippi Mudcat Band, McGee played an assortment of instruments—guitar, mandolin, harmonica, piano, trumpet—to go along with an assortment of pitches—overhand fastball and curve, sidearm fastball and curve, changeup, and a wicked sidearm sinker. The Reds could hardly touch any of them, as McGee held them to four hits and beat Walters, 4–0, cutting the Reds' lead in the race. A win by the Cardinals on Thursday would leave them just one and a half behind with three games left on the schedule in Chicago. (The Reds had three games in Pittsburgh.)

Those games would not matter, though. Derringer and the Reds simply outlasted the Cardinals, winning 5–3 to clinch Cincinnati's first pennant since 1919. The Cardinals knocked Derringer around, getting fourteen hits. But they stranded eleven baserunners. Mize contributed to Cincinnati's victory with an error in the second inning. After Bill Werber tripled, Mize fumbled Lonny Frey's bouncer to first, and Werber scored to give Cincinnati a 3–2 lead. Derringer drove in the winning run himself with a sacrifice fly to right in the sixth inning. Slaughter made a perfect throw home to catcher Don Padgett, but Wally Berger slid under the tag. Harry Craft homered in the eighth for the Reds' final run, and Derringer did what he couldn't do before—he had his way with Mize, striking him out to end the game.

The Cards lost two out of three in Chicago, and the Reds beat the Pirates two out of three to win the pennant by four and a half games. Then they got swept by the Yankees, which won their unprecedented fourth-straight World Series.

--- - ---

Once he got hot in July, Johnny never was seriously challenged for the batting title. Trailing him were Medwick and Reds first baseman Frank McCormick, who both hit .332. McCormick was Cincinnati's best hitter, with 128 RBIs and 209 base hits, both tops in the league.

But this was Mize's year as the best all-around hitter in the National League. In addition to winning a batting title, he won the first of his four home run crowns, outlasting the Giants' Mel Ott down the stretch. As Johnny warmed up for the last game of the season against the Cubs, the two were tied with twenty-seven homers each. The Cubs were ahead, 1–0, when Johnny led off the top of the eighth against Claude Passeau and hit the right-hander's sailing fastball over the right-field fence to tie the game and pull one ahead of Ott to win the homer race.

Despite falling a few games shy of first place, the Cardinals also had reason to celebrate. They'd corrected their course and seemed poised for the next big thing. But they were still a few moves away from getting back to the promised land. The key question was, who would be going along for the ride?

Mize was the kind of player the team could build around for many years. He was still only twenty-six years old, and he'd just enjoyed his best season yet. Besides leading the league in home runs and batting average, Johnny had the most total bases (353), highest slugging percentage (.626), and best OPS (a career-high 1.064) in the National League. His on-base average of .444 was second in the league, and he placed third in triples (14), doubles (a career-high 44), and RBIs (108). Latter-day statisticians have figured out that Mize also had the highest offensive WAR (7.6) in Major League Baseball.

Johnny's success paid off beyond the ballfield, as endorsement deals rolled in, plastering his face in newspaper and magazine ads throughout the country, from companies like Granger pipe tobacco, Wheaties, Beech-nut chewing tobacco, Gillette razor blades, and Louisville Slugger, among others. One large newspaper ad that made the rounds a few years later featured a photo of Mize and Cardinals teammate Mort Cooper happily smoking Chesterfield cigarettes while duck hunting.[12]

Despite his growing popularity, or because of it, Mize was once again being mentioned as trade bait. But it was Medwick who seemed expendable this time. Breadon said as much with his pronouncement that Joe would be traded if anyone was to offer enough in return.[13] But Rickey denied any such nonsense by offering two predictions on the 1940 National League season: the Cardinals would win the pennant, and Medwick would not be sold or traded.[14]

"Joe Medwick will be playing left-field for the Cardinals in the 1940 World Series," Rickey asserted.[15]

Branch Rickey may have been the most innovative baseball executive in history, but his predictions were way off.

12

The Temperament of Genius

I could probably have hit .400 any
season I wanted, but what would it
be like if I didn't hit those long ones?
It would be just like playing golf.   —Johnny Mize[1]

Butch Yatkeman had seen plenty since becoming a batboy for the Cardinals as a green sixteen-year-old in 1924.[2] Now he was the team's longtime
equipment manager, making sure that cleats, gloves, bats, and protective
cups were in the players' lockers before each game. He'd hung uniforms
for everyone from Rogers Hornsby and Grover Cleveland Alexander to
Bud Teachout and Flint Rhem. He'd been with the team through five
pennants and World Series. By the time spring training was taking shape
in St. Petersburg, Florida, in 1940, Butch had been around long enough
to have seen or dealt with most of the habits, superstitions, demands,
compulsions, phobias, and other peculiarities that take place within the
walls of a baseball clubhouse.

To say that he knew all the Cardinals' dirty laundry would be more than
just a literal truth. But Butch had never seen anything like this before.
Who needed all these bats?

Johnny Mize had ordered thirty brand new hickory Rogers Hornsby
models, fresh from the factory in Kentucky. And he already had thirteen
nearly new bats from the year before. Forty-three bats for one guy? At
barely five feet tall, Yatkeman was not the stoutest of pack mules, and
someone was going to have to move these things. This time, instead of
keeping his mouth shut like he usually did—that was his Cardinal rule—
Butch decided to say something.

When Johnny got there, the first thing the big man noticed was the harried look on Yatkeman's face. Butch glared at him and said, "Come here." Johnny followed him into the equipment room, where Butch pointed at the bats and began, in Mize's words, "complaining vigorously." His bats would take up an entire moving trunk by themselves, Butch bitched.[3]

"I asked him how he expected me to work without my tools—for which he had no answer," Mize remembered.[4] Given his already foul mood at the time, Butch would have been well within his rights had he sarcastically replied, "Hornsby didn't need a trunk full of bats to hit .400 three times."

It wouldn't have mattered if Butch had said that or started belting out the National Anthem in pig Latin at the top of his lungs, because Mize wasn't listening anyway. Still clad in his Florida toggery, his wide red face lit with Christmas-like wonder at the sight of the bats, Johnny approached his precious tools. He had to inspect the new arrivals.

"They were carefully wrapped in two containers," wrote *Star-Times* sports editor and columnist Sid Keener, who was there to witness the scene. "He had ordered 30 models, divided into two weights—fifteen at 36 ounces and fifteen at 40 ounces."[5]

But they were wrapped haphazardly, neither size packed exclusively together—the thirty-six ouncers intermingling with the forty ouncers. So, Johnny got to work separating the lighter bats from the heavier bats. Butch offered to help weigh them. It was part of his job, after all. But Mize insisted on doing it himself, which probably didn't please the equipment manager, who was still going to have to pack all these war clubs eventually.

For Mize, this was all very natural, this fastidious weighing of bats. He took his job seriously. Keener called it the "temperament or idiosyncrasy of a genius."[6]

Johnny eagerly explained to Keener why all of this mattered: he carefully studied pitchers and the weather and used a heavier bat on cold days or against slow ball pitchers, and the lighter bat against speed ballers and on hot days, and he was well aware that his ticket in the big leagues was the piece of wood in his hands, not his glove.

"I must hit to hold my job with the Cardinals," he said. "I'm not overlooking any points, either. Even to the extent of being a bit temperamental with the bat. It's my job to hit for this club—to drive in runs. If I fail to deliver you know what's going to happen? A new man in my place."[7]

So, Mize began the 1940 season with his forty-three bats, and he hit exactly forty-three home runs that season with his Hornsby bats, breaking Hornsby's team record of forty-two four-baggers in a season.

"That year Mize might have had a chance to break Babe Ruth's season record of 60 home runs," Peter Golenbock wrote in *Dynasty: The New York Yankees, 1949–1964*. "But a temporary wire mesh fence was erected above the low right-field wall, and many of the 31 doubles and 13 triples he banged off the screen instead of going into the stand for home runs."[8]

Johnny also wondered what would have happened if he'd started the season with sixty-one bats, musing, "But I imagine that would be too many bats to ask a club to buy for you."[9]

It didn't matter how many bats he had. Mize knew how to use every one of them like a scalpel. When he was young, he held a forty-ounce bat down near the nob, and when he was older, he'd choke up about an inch with his thirty-six-ounce club.[10]

Gutteridge remembered Mize using a thirty-four-ounce bat from time to time. He recalled a game when the Cardinals were facing a hard-throwing lefty who had been giving Mize fits. "We were at home in St. Louis and John says, 'Next time I get up there, I'm gonna get one of those light bats, and I'll get around on that high fastball, you watch.'"[11]

The next time up against the guy, Johnny swung at his first pitch, and the ball landed on Grand Avenue.[12]

- - -

Johnny Mize became the Big Cat in 1940—maybe. He was twenty-seven, and if his version of his nickname's origin story is accurate, then it had to be 1940, in the summer. As Mize wrote in his book, *How to Hit*, "It was while playing for the Cardinals that I was tagged with the nickname 'The Big Cat.' The man responsible was Joe Orengo, who played second base."

Orengo played every position in the infield during his six-year career with five big league teams. But the only time he ever played second base for the Cardinals was from June 7 through September 1, 1940. So, if Johnny's story is accurate, that's when he became the Big Cat.

"One day the infielders were having a pretty bad time and were making some bad throws to me at first base," Mize recalled. "After digging a few out of the dirt, Joe Orengo called over to me, 'Atta boy, John, you look like a big cat.' Some of the writers overheard the remark and asked Joe about it later. The nickname has stuck with me ever since."[13]

But the writers didn't really start calling him Big Cat in print until later in the 1940s, when Johnny was swinging a big bat for the New York Giants. So, maybe it took a while to catch on with the ink-stained wretches. Besides, the nickname wasn't original with Mize, anyway. By the time Orengo would have bestowed the mantle on Mize, there already was another Big Cat in baseball. Babe Phelps, the six-foot-two, 225-pound, hard-hitting, slow-moving catcher with the Brooklyn Dodgers, was known as the Big Cat to his teammates.[14]

Buddy Blattner, who played with Mize on the New York Giants for three years (1946–48), remembered the story behind the nickname differently.

"We gave it to him on the Giants, and it was a pretty good moniker," said Blattner, who followed his five years in the big leagues with a long, successful career in sports broadcasting in radio and television, including a seven-year stint in the booth with Dizzy Dean on the nationally televised *Game of the Week*.[15]

"It was because he was a big pussycat," Blattner said in a 2001 interview from his home in the Missouri Ozarks. "It was more of a teasing nickname."[16]

Bill Rigney, who was on the Giants, claimed, "I was the guy who called Johnny Mize the Big Cat because he was so slow covering ground at first. It wasn't meant to be a compliment."[17]

However and whenever the nickname came to Mize, in 1940, "Big Cat" fit because he was the best player in baseball.

- - -

The Ray Blades and Joe Medwick eras in St. Louis ended less than a week apart in June 1940, a bit of poetic timing since they couldn't stand each other. A 10–1 loss against the visiting Brooklyn Dodgers convinced Breadon it was time to replace Ray.

On Friday, June 7, with the Cardinals in sixth place at 14-24 and the Giants coming to town for a four-game series, Breadon swung the axe. Blades was out, and Billy Southworth, who'd been the Cards' manager in 1929, was back in.[18]

"After our miserable showing in the night game against the Brooklyn

Dodgers last Tuesday, I thought over the entire matter, and then decided on Southworth as my man," said Breadon, who made the decision alone, without Rickey's knowledge or blessing. "I felt a complete turnover was necessary if we were to get up in the pennant race."[19]

Rickey learned about it in the newspapers, after telling reporters a day earlier that rumors about a managerial change were not true. "When the change was announced, Rickey felt embarrassed," Peter Golenbock wrote in *The Spirit of St. Louis*. "It was the first major public rift between Breadon and Rickey."[20]

Breadon agreed with writers who criticized Blades for changing pitchers too often.[21] They could not foresee the advent of the middle reliever, the setup man, and the closer.

After the agreeable Mike González babysat for about a week and the team had slipped to seventh place with a 15-29 record, Southworth arrived to take the reins, managing the team to a 69-40 record the rest of the way, a great showing, but too little, too late, as the Cardinals finished 84-69, in third place, trailing the second-place Dodgers, and far behind the Reds, which breezed to another pennant with a 100-53 record.

Southworth would do the job without Joe Medwick in his lineup because Ducky was dealt to the Dodgers on June 12, a day after Breadon denied any such thing would happen. The Dodgers also landed Curt Davis, the Cardinals' best pitcher in 1939, in a blockbuster deal that sent $150,000 and four obscure players to St. Louis (outfielder Ernie Koy, pitcher Carl Doyle, and two Minor Leaguers, infielder Bert Haas and pitcher Sam Nahem).[22]

Medwick's departure meant that Mize was now batting clean-up. The Cardinals might miss Medwick's bat, but not the tension that came with it. St. Louis fans had been booing Joe unmercifully for what they perceived as nonchalant play—at least, that was Breadon's excuse for trading him. "Medwick was through with the Cardinals," Breadon said. "The fans had sent me that message."[23]

But a year before Medwick was dealt, the Cardinals brought up a rookie shortstop who would help spark a new Cardinals championship team in the 1940s. A defensive wizard, Marty Marion was tall and rangy at six-feet-two, 170 pounds, and his agility in the field made him one of the team's vital cogs. He was named MVP in the National League in 1944. As a newcomer, he quickly fit right in and picked up on the friction between his two slugging teammates.

"I'll never forget my first year with the Cardinals when Johnny Mize and Joe Medwick were there," Marty Marion said in Golenbock's *The Spirit of St. Louis*. "They were jealous of each other. Every time Mize would get a cheap hit, you'd be sitting next to Medwick, and he'd say, 'They never give me those cheap hits.' And the same thing with Mize."[24]

Gutteridge said they used to call Joe "the 'Mad Hungarian,' and this was years before Al Hrabosky had that nickname. It's because Joe was Hungarian, and he seemed to be mad all of the time."[25]

Marion remembered how Medwick would hit line drives off the shins of the batting practice pitcher, then laugh about it. After being traded to the Dodgers, when his skills were sharply deteriorating, Medwick became a much nicer person. "It's funny what a nice guy you can be, hitting .250," Marion observed. "And a son of a bitch when you're hitting .350! That's baseball."[26]

As for Mize, well, he wasn't a mean son of a bitch whether he was hitting .350 or .270, but he was preoccupied with those tools of his. And he never let Medwick's quick temper, or quick fists, bother him. Donald Honig asked Mize if he'd ever had any trouble with Ducky, who was not shy about decking a teammate when the mood hit. "Mize allowed a thin smile and shook his head," Honig remembered. "'Joe knew who to pick on,' he said."[27]

Whatever aggression Johnny demonstrated occurred on a ballfield with a precious bat in his hands.

"All he wanted to do was rub his bats down," said Marion. "He had forty-two bats in the bat rack, and we had two! Back in those days, you didn't get to order many bats. I'd go up to the secretary of the club and say, 'I need some bats.' Well, they'd issue you two. But they gave Mize all he wanted."[28]

- - -

Mize put those bats to great use in 1940, like when he delivered his next three–home run game early in the season.

On Monday, May 13, the Cardinals met the Reds in Cincinnati for a replay of a game that had been flooded out in April. They didn't finish this time, either, but Johnny turned in an unforgettable performance:

3 home runs, 4 runs, and 4 RBIs, as the teams played fourteen innings and called it a wrap with the game knotted, 8–8.

Mize opened the second inning against Reds lefty Johnny Vander Meer and lined a solo homer over the center field fence. In the third, Mize popped the ball up behind home plate, but Reds catcher Ernie Lombardi couldn't catch it. Given another swing, Johnny homered into the right-field seats, scoring Medwick. The game was tied 7–7 in the top of the thirteenth inning when Johnny hit his third homer of the game, a solo blast off lefty Milt Shoffner over the left-field fence. But the Reds rallied to tie it 8–8 in the bottom half of the inning on Bill Werber's RBI single. Werber matched a Major League record that day with four doubles in the game and set a new one—he became the first player to do it twice, having smacked four two-baggers in a 1935 game when he was with the Boston Red Sox.

The big hits came in clumps for Johnny that year. On July 13, at home in the first game of a doubleheader against the Giants, he hit for the cycle: a homer in the third inning, a double in the fifth, a single in the seventh, and a triple that became an error-assisted home run to win the game in the ninth. His line drive to deepest center field bounced hard off the concrete and was picked up by left fielder Jo-Jo Moore. Giants' shortstop Billy Jurges fumbled Moore's throw, and Southworth signaled Johnny to keep running. Jurges recovered and threw to catcher Harry Danning, who fumbled the ball, and Mize scored the winning run.

Two months later, Mize entered the record books as the first player to hit a trio of home runs in a game four times. His threesome against the visiting Pittsburgh Pirates on September 8 also made him the first player to accomplish the feat twice in a season in two different seasons.

This time, it was a 16–14 loss to Pittsburgh (it must have frustrated Mize that his team *lost* most of the games in which he belted three out of the park). Mize hit his homers to three different spots on the pavilion roof beyond the right-field fence. The Cards were already trailing when Johnny led off the bottom of the third against lefty Dick Lanahan and hit one to the roof. He did it to Lanahan again in the fourth, his two-run blast tying the game, 8–8. With the Cardinals trailing 12–8 in the sixth, he turned on a fastball from right-hander Johnny Lanning and sent that ball to the roof, scoring Terry Moore ahead of him to make it 12–10. That made it three straight homers for Mize, the second time he'd done that, another record. He scored four runs in the game and drove in six, the last one with a sacrifice fly to deep center field in the eighth inning.

When the day's work was done, Mize had forty-one homers, one behind Hornsby's single-season club record, more homers than anyone had hit in the National League since Hack Wilson belted fifty-six in 1930. Newspapers with nothing better to do even printed a chart showing that Mize was "only" four games behind Ruth's 1927 pace.[29] Of course, the Babe went on a ridiculous home run binge in the final weeks of the season, whereas Johnny would do just the opposite. Nonetheless, it wasn't the last time Mize would be compared to the Babe in the newspapers.

Following his eruption against Pittsburgh, Mize went twenty games without hitting a home run, his longest drought of the season. He still hit the ball very well—he had four hits, all singles, and six RBIs in a win over Brooklyn on September 18. He finally tied Hornsby's record on September 25 against the Reds, smacking a Bucky Walters pitch into the center-field bleachers of Sportsman's Park, a 450-foot rocket, in the fourth inning of the Cardinals' 4–3 win.

Two days later, he became the Cardinals' single-season home run champion with number 43 in an 11–1 rout of the visiting Cubs. It came in the bottom of the fifth off Ken Raffensberger with no one on base.

Although Mize didn't hit any more homers in the final two games of the season, against Chicago, he did go 3 for 6 in those contests, raising his batting average to .314, good for fifth in the league. His 43 homers led the big leagues, far ahead of National League runner-up Bill Nicholson of the Cubs, who had 25. (Hank Greenberg had 41 clouts to lead the American League.) Johnny's 137 RBIs were also best in the National League, as was his slugging percentage (.636), total bases (368), and offensive WAR (7.7), all career highs. He also led in OPS (1.039) and runs created (147) and was second in runs scored and base hits and was third in on-base average and triples.

He was the most feared hitter in the National League—pitchers intentionally walked him twenty-four times, a new Major League record. And of course, there were the two three-homer games. At twenty-seven years old and in his prime, Johnny Mize was probably the best player in baseball in 1940.

So naturally, Frank McCormick of the Reds was named Most Valuable Player in the National League.

- - -

The Reds had breezed to the pennant after battling Brooklyn over the first half of the season. Cincinnati finished with a twelve-game lead over the second-place Dodgers, and sixteen games ahead of the disappointing Cardinals, which had been picked to win the pennant by almost everyone with an opinion.

But the hiring of Southworth had rallied the team, and it was a sign of greater days to come for St. Louis. Mize performed wonderfully for his new manager. "Billy Southworth was a completely different fella from Blades," Gutteridge said. "He and Johnny got along well—Southworth recognized his ability and knew he would produce for him every day."[30]

McCormick had a fine year at a time when sports writers usually gave the MVP Award to someone on the pennant-winning team. He led the league in hits with 191 and at bats with 618, batted .309, and drove in 127 runs. He wasn't in Mize's class as a hitter that year and probably wasn't even the most valuable player on the Reds. That would have been Bucky Walters again, whose WAR exceeded Frank's, 6.9 to 5.4. For the second straight year, Walters led the league in wins, ERA, complete games, and innings pitched.

In the final analysis, given the benefit of sabermetrics and common sense, Mize emerges as the best player that year. Bill James, the author who basically invented sabermetrics, tabs Mize as the best player in Major League Baseball for 1940.[31] James also selected him for his 1940s Major League All-Star team (along with guys like Joe DiMaggio, Ted Williams, and Stan Musial).[32] He also named Mize the best player who never won the MVP Award. "Mize was probably the best all-around player in the National League in 1940 and 1947, and the second-best in 1937, 1939, and 1948, third-best in 1942," wrote James, who ranked Johnny as the sixth best first baseman in history (behind Eddie Murray and ahead of Harmon Killebrew).[33]

For the reserved Cardinals first baseman, though, the postseason honors, or lack of them, didn't bother him as much as the preseason contract negotiations, and his next tête-à-tête with Branch Rickey would be one for the books. It was a verbal tug of war that Mize would complain about for years.

After the 1939 season, when he'd been the batting champion, Rickey tried to shortchange his performance, saying, "Well, your home run production stayed pretty much the same." No mention of the batting title or the fact that his twenty-eight home runs still led the league. "So the next year I hit 43 home runs, which is still the Cardinal club record, and led the league in runs batted in," Mize said. "But my batting average went down."[34]

The Mahatma brought this up during contract negotiations for 1941, saying, "Well, your batting average wasn't so good—would you be willing to take a cut?"[35]

Johnny was incredulous, telling Donald Honig, "I led the league in hitting, then I led the league in home runs and runs batted in, and he wanted to know if I'd take a cut!"[36]

They were two men cut from completely different patterns. Mize was the tight-lipped, slow-talking southerner who just wanted to play ball and be left alone to do that, and the voluble, influential Rickey was a thrifty, creative man reshaping the game. But they had one important thing in common as the 1941 season approached: their days in St. Louis were numbered.

13

Goodbye, St. Louis

Who will be the last team standing, the Cardinals or the Dodgers? This pennant race feels more like a heavyweight bout than a baseball season. The two rivals have been going back and forth at the top of the National League since April, neither one of them taking a very big lead, poking and jabbing each other, scoring points, neither one delivering a knockout punch.

Now, with ten days left in the 1941 season, the Cardinals are in excellent position to catch the Dodgers, because while Brooklyn is losing to the Pirates in Pittsburgh, St. Louis is hosting the seventh-place Boston Braves. A win today puts the Cardinals back into a tie for first. That is on Johnny Mize's mind as he gets into his crouch at first base while Boston takes its turn at bat in the top of the third.

St. Louis right-hander Mort Cooper still isn't 100 percent following his arm injury—Frank Demaree's three-run homer in the top of the first has given the Braves a 3–1 lead. But Mort retires Boston in order in the second, and he's looking strong here in the third, striking out Sibby Sisti. After Johnny Cooney's bloop single to left, Mort gets Bama Rowell to pop out to shallow center. That brings up left-handed-hitting center fielder Gene Moore.

Trying to keep Cooney honest, Mize plays close to the bag. And so, he's in perfect position to catch the grounder that Moore sends his way.

Except, Mize does what he sometimes does. He makes the simple play look difficult and fumbles the ball. Moore is racing down the line to first when Johnny picks up the loose ball with his bare right hand, dives back to the bag, his arm fully extended, touching first base with the ball just before Moore's toes, ending the inning.

Johnny's landed on his right shoulder with the full force of his 225-pound body on the infield dirt, and there is a sharp pain. Maybe it's nothing, Mize thinks, as he jogs into the dugout. *If the Cardinals can get something going here in the bottom of the third, he'll bat fourth in the inning, right after Musial, who Johnny has taken a shine to. Everyone likes the kid who made his debut the day before, September 17, with two hits and an RBI, helping the Cards beat the Braves, 3–2.*

Here in the bottom of the third, after Musial lines a two-out single to center, Mize walks to the plate wondering to himself, Why did Rickey take so long to bring Musial up to St. Louis? The Dodgers might be chasing us now. *Then he smashes a vicious line drive off the leg of Boston pitcher Manny Salvo for a double, his league-leading thirty-ninth of the season.*

But Mize and Musial are stranded on second and third, as tough Salvo recovers and retires Estel Crabtree. Then he finishes the game, and the Braves win, 4–1, helping Brooklyn maintain its hold on first place. Mize is in agony because of the shoulder, but he finishes the game, his last as a St. Louis Cardinal.

- - -

The year 1941 was one of epic numbers in the American League: .406 (Ted Williams's batting average) and 56 (Joe DiMaggio's hitting streak). And over in the National League, it was finally next year for the long-suffering Brooklyn Dodgers, who withstood a courageous chase by the wounded Cardinals to win their first pennant since 1920, under the scrappy, mouthy manager, former Gashouse Gang ringleader Leo Durocher.

Only seven years after their World Series triumph over the Detroit Tigers, the Gang was ancient history, its players scattered to other teams or into retirement. Pepper Martin had gone back to the bush leagues. Dizzy Dean would pitch one game in 1941 and post an ERA of 18.00 in his last season with the Cubs. Paul Dean was barely playing for the Giants, his arm essentially dead.

In Brooklyn, though, a bit of the old St. Louis fire was burning in the spunky Dodgers. Besides Durocher, there was Joe Medwick, playing a critical role for Dem Bums, batting .318, scoring 100 runs. There also was Dolph Camilli, having his best season in an honorable career, smashing 34 homers and driving in 120, winning an MVP Award that should have gone to his twenty-two-year-old teammate, Pete Reiser, who chased fly balls into outfield walls with reckless abandon and was the best all-around player in baseball in 1941.

The writers who voted for the Most Valuable Player in those years were not always the most reliable judges of talent. For the second year in a row, they botched it in the National League. All Reiser did was win the batting crown (.343) and lead the league in total bases, runs, triples, and slugging percentage. He tied Mize for the lead in doubles and had the best offensive and overall WAR.

Meanwhile, the Cardinals clubhouse resembled a hospital ward in 1941. Pitcher Mort Cooper missed six weeks with an arm injury. Enos Slaughter broke his collarbone and missed forty games. Walker Cooper, Mort's little brother and the team's slugging rookie catcher slated to start that season, suffered a shoulder injury and was limited to just sixty-eight games. Third baseman Jimmy Brown and star centerfielder Terry Moore also missed weeks of action because of injuries—Moore was drilled in the head by Boston Braves pitcher Art Johnson and missed almost a month.

Then there was Mize. Before his season-ending shoulder injury, he'd battled a painful fractured index finger on his left hand. Mize couldn't remember when it happened (probably during a game against the Pirates in late May), but X-rays showed a chipped bone.[1] But it hurt like hell when gripping a bat, making contact, catching balls at first. It didn't help that Johnny kept playing—he aggravated the injury.[2] The digit was placed in a splint, and Johnny missed most of June.

He didn't get back to first base until June 19 against the Phillies, entering the game as a pinch hitter in the bottom of the sixth inning, when he drove in two runs with a single. He stayed in the lineup as the Cardinals won in eleven innings. Then, starting again at first base, he collected five hits over the next three games and kept right on hitting, like he'd been doing since early May.

In the thirty-five games he played from May 5 through July 1, Mize batted .398 with a .483 on-base average. The only thing he couldn't do—probably due to the aching digit—was hit home runs. In fact, the 1941 season would represent a new low for Mize in the power department. He finished with just sixteen homers for the season, and just two in that thirty-five-game stretch.

The second of those came on July 1. The same day that DiMaggio set a big league record by hitting in his forty-fifth straight game, Mize had his best performance of the year. Playing in Pittsburgh, he cracked four hits, including that home run and a double, scored three runs, and knocked in five. The Cardinals won to retake the top spot in the National League, and Mize raised his average to a league-high .369.

"I hate to look up at the plate when that bird is batting against us," Pirates manager Frank Frisch moaned afterward.[3]

After hitting only four home runs through June, Mize hit four in July and six in August. And though his batting average through those two months was only .288, he drove in forty-eight runs in fifty-seven games, on his way to one hundred RBIs for the season. His average tumbled from its midseason high down to .317 by season's end, good enough for fifth in the league.

None of this impressed Fat Freddie Fitzsimmons, the Brooklyn pitcher who hated Mize, and he let everyone know it during a crucial game against the Cardinals late in the season.[4]

- - -

No one could ever explain the animosity Fat Freddie had toward the Big Cat—not even Mrs. Fitzsimmons.

"For some reason, Fred hated Mize," recalled Helen Fitzsimmons in 1955. "We never knew why, because they have long since become good friends. It may have been because he was a great hitter, and in Fred's book all hitters were his mortal enemies in those days."[5]

That makes sense, considering how Mize had routinely abused the right-handed knuckleball specialist. Fitz had pitched thirteen seasons with the Giants, winning a bunch of games, and was considered all but washed up when the Dodgers traded for him in 1937. He posted a remarkable 16-2 record in 1940 when he was thirty-eight. In '41 Durocher picked special spots for old Fitz, and he picked them well. Fred went 6-1, including one of the Dodgers' biggest wins of the year in Brooklyn's final series with the Cardinals, which featured a confrontation against Mize at a crucial point in the game, celebrated with gusto (and some artistic license) by Leo Durocher in his two autobiographies, *The Dodgers and Me* and *Nice Guys Finish Last*.

The Dodgers had a one-game lead on the Cardinals when they visited St. Louis for the three-game set, September 11–13. Before the series, Durocher had rested Fitzsimmons for nine days, saving him for the Cardinals. And Fred had something to prove. The Cards had split a four-game series in Brooklyn back in late August. Fitz took the loss in the final game, 3–1.

Though Fitz was an affable guy off the field, "once he got out on the mound, you just couldn't talk to him," Durocher insisted. "He'd snap his head at you and stomp around and snarl out his words like a lion chewing meat."[6] So, Leo sicced the lion on the Cardinals in their series opener on Thursday, September 11.

Whereas Durocher's memory of what happened was a little off, the result was inarguable: the Dodgers beat the Cardinals, 6–4, in eleven innings to take a two-game lead. Freddie scattered ten hits in ten innings in a gutsy performance and earned the win. Relief ace Hugh Casey retired the Cards one, two, three in the bottom of the eleventh for the save.

In Leo's version, the Dodgers had been robbed in the eighth when Reiser tripled and the Cardinals' 1941 ace, Ernie White (17-7, 2.40 ERA), supposedly balked, but it wasn't called by umpire Al Barlick. So, the score was tied 4–4 in the bottom of the eighth. That's when Leo said the epic Mize-Fitz battle took place, with two out and the bases loaded.[7]

In fact, it was the bottom of the third inning with nobody out and runners on first and second—not as dramatic as Durocher's version but still a critical juncture in an important late-season ball game. Fitzsimmons got in trouble when Jimmy Brown, Johnny Hopp, and Dan Padgett all singled to start the inning, scoring Brown with the game's first run. So, the irritable Fitzsimmons, trailing 1–0, was already fuming when Mize came to bat next with two runners on base.

When Durocher visited the mound, Fitz snarled, "You're not going to take me out of this fucken ball game, Durocher. Get back to the bench. That picklehead, he ain't going to hit me. I'm going to knock his cap off."[8]

In Durocher's story, Fitz's first pitch was a fastball behind Mize's head that nearly got away from the catcher, Mickey Owen. Then he threw a perfect knuckleball for a called strike, and waddled toward the plate shouting, "Get ready, picklehead, you're going down again." Another fastball aimed at Mize's head, followed by another knuckleball for a strike for a 2-2 count. And Fitz stalked closer to home plate, growling, "Right at that thick picklehead skull of yours!"[9]

Then came the inevitable fastball aimed at Johnny's head, which supposedly sent him on his ass, his cap and bat flying in the air, making it a full count.[10]

Whether the story is embellished or not, this kind of thing was typical of the Cardinals-Dodgers in those days. "We had fights all the time," said lefty Max Lanier, who joined the Cardinals in 1938 and became one of their aces, leading the league in earned run average in 1943. Durocher was particularly adept at instigating trouble. "He was the best bench jockey," Lanier said.[11]

Meanwhile, Lanier said, Mize was basically the opposite. "I liked John. He was a laid-back guy, didn't have a lot to say," Lanier recalled. "He could hit, and he wasn't a bad fielder."[12] And, as Leo himself pointed out, Mize was a nice guy. But Fitz didn't care, because he was a picklehead with a bat.

"It's gonna be right where you like it, tomato-face," Fitz yelled at Mize. "And you're never going to get your bat off your shoulder."

Then he threw a perfect curveball that dropped over for called strike three.[13]

Newspapers covering the game didn't mention any melodrama or histrionics by Fitz, who didn't have a great fastball. So, it's unlikely Mize hit the dirt to avoid his pitches. As Musial and others observed, Big John would just lean back on his left foot and bend his body away from the pitch—graceful as a big cat.

Whatever the details, Fitzsimmons got Mize for the first out in the inning. The Cards scored another run to take a 2–0 lead, and the Dodgers rallied for four runs in the fourth, capped by a Dolph Camilli home run. They won it in on Dixie Walker's two-run single in the top of the eleventh.

The teams split the next two games, and the Dodgers left town in the same position they were in when they arrived, two games up on the Cardinals with fourteen games left to play (the next twelve on the road). Brooklyn won ten down the stretch, finishing at 100-54, two and a half up on St. Louis (97-56). Then the Yankees beat Brooklyn in five games in the World Series.

- - -

Though the season ended in disappointment for the Cardinals, they had seen the future, and he wore number 6. In twelve games, Stan Musial had twenty hits and batted .426, which was tremendous but still too little, too late for St. Louis that year. And that really bothered Mize, a clubhouse lawyer who blamed Rickey for not bringing the kid up sooner. "We might have gone ahead and won the pennant," Mize fumed.[14]

It had been a whirlwind year for the kid from Donora, Pennsylvania. Musial had been a southpaw pitching sensation in the Class D minors in

1940, then injured his arm while playing the outfield late in the season. He figured it'd be better by spring training in 1941. It wasn't. Pitching for Albany, Georgia, in an outing against the Major League Cardinals, Mize and Terry Moore hit long homers off him. By the end of spring training, it was evident that Musial was finished as a pitcher. So, he became an outfielder with help from Ollie Vanek, manager of the Springfield, Missouri, farm club.

Stan was hitting everything in sight, batting .379 with power in late July when he was promoted to Rochester, where he helped the Red Wings reach the playoffs. Then the Cardinals brought him to the big club for the final two weeks of the season. Musial was batting .546 after five games as a big leaguer, and the team was on the train from St. Louis to Pittsburgh when the fellas realized who he was.

"He was sitting with Terry Moore in a Pullman car," according to Golenbock. "Musial mentioned the home runs that Moore and Mize had hit off him in spring training. Moore called over to Mize, 'Hey, John, you won't believe this. Musial is the left-hander who threw us those long home run balls this spring.'"[15]

With the 1941 season and its thrills and records fading into past tense, the trade gossip started again. Larry MacPhail wanted to send Camilli to the Yankees and bring Mize to the Dodgers.[16] Johnny found out about it while he was hunting in the Ozarks. It was December 7.

"A guy told me I was wanted on the telephone. As I was walking to the phone he said to me, 'By the way, the Japanese have bombed Pearl Harbor.' I thought he was nuts. Didn't pay him any attention," Mize said, going inside the country store to grab the phone. It was his father-in-law, Ray Adams, with an urgent message: get in touch with Leo Durocher right away.[17]

Still puzzled over the strange news he'd heard about Japanese attack, Mize called Durocher, who asked him if he wanted to play with the Dodgers.

"I told him it didn't mean a damn to me where I played," Mize said. "Then I got into the car and turned on the radio and found out that fellow was right about Pearl Harbor. That was a hell of a piece of news, and I didn't know what to think about it. When something like that happens, you don't know what's coming next until it comes."[18]

There was the sense in St. Louis that Mize had worn out his welcome. Partly, it was because he seemed to be outgrowing his uniform.

"Branch Rickey, sharp-eyed mastermind for the Cards, noted too much excess poundage on that Mize frame months ago," wrote Sid Keener of the *Star-Times* in his December 11 column. "Mize's name is on the Cardinals' roster at this moment, but you can write your own ticket that he will be among the missing when the 1942 squad makes its debut at Sportsman's Park next April."[19]

It wouldn't take that long for Johnny to go missing.

1. Teenaged Johnny Mize was a multisport athlete for Piedmont College in Demorest while still a high school student. Courtesy of the Johnny Mize Collection, Piedmont University Archives, Demorest, Georgia.

2. Nineteen-year-old Johnny Mize hit three home runs in his first two games with the Elmira Red Wings. Years later, he was elected to the Elmira Baseball Hall of Fame. Courtesy of National Baseball Hall of Fame.

3. The brooding young slugger. Johnny spent parts of three seasons in Rochester with the Red Wings in the St. Louis Cardinals' expansive "chain gang" farm system. From Society for American Baseball Research, Rucker Archive.

4. Johnny quickly established a reputation as one of the best hitters in the International League as a member of the Rochester Redwings. He batted .334 in three seasons with Rochester. Courtesy of the Johnny Mize Collection, Piedmont University Archives, Demorest, Georgia.

5. Even as a rookie slugger with the Cardinals, the Big Cat was inspiring poetry: "When Ripper Collins fails to bat / Frisch, right before our eyes / Digs down into his magic hat / And pulls out Johnny Mize." Courtesy of National Baseball Hall of Fame.

6. One of the guys: Johnny was always easier going with his teammates than he was with the press. Here he is teasing Cardinals teammate Terry Moore in 1940. Courtesy of National Baseball Hall of Fame.

7. The Big Cat and his new bride on their wedding day. Johnny met pretty society girl Jene Adams during a spring training trip to Cuba. They fell in love and were married five months later, on August 8, 1937. Courtesy of the Johnny Mize Collection, Piedmont University Archives, Demorest, Georgia.

8. "Nobody had a better, smoother, easier swing than John," said Mize's Cardinals teammate Don Gutteridge. "It was picture perfect." From Society for American Baseball Research, Rucker Archive.

9. "He was very nice with fans, especially kids," said Johnny Mize's old friend and teammate Don Gutteridge. "If we drove to the park together, I'd have to wait on him to sign all those autographs." Courtesy of National Baseball Hall of Fame.

10. The Big Cat (*far left*) brought his big bat to the New York Giants and the Polo Grounds in 1942. He quickly fit in with his new ball club, which included teammates (*left to right*) Joe Orengo, Dick Bartell, player-manager Mel Ott, and Bill Werber. From Society for American Baseball Research, Rucker Archive.

11. The Big Cat's first spring training as a Giant, in 1942. Johnny happily shows sports journalist and cartoonist Jeane Hoffmann how his ailing arm feels, as an amused Giants manager Mel Ott looks on. Courtesy of the Johnny Mize Collection, Piedmont University Archives, Demorest, Georgia.

12. (*opposite top*) Johnny Mize is inducted into the U.S. Navy by Lieutenant Commander Charles K. Saltsman in St. Louis. Next stop for the Big Cat was the Great Lakes Naval Training Station. Courtesy of M. Shawn Hennessy, Chevrons and Diamonds Collection.

13. (*opposite bottom*) Two Hall of Fame sailors. Former Philadelphia Athletics catcher and Detroit Tigers player-manager Lieutenant Mickey Cochrane was Mize's manager for the Great Lakes Naval Training Station Bluejackets. Courtesy of M. Shawn Hennessy, Chevrons and Diamonds Collection.

14. (*above*) Anchors aweigh for big league first basemen. In 1945 Elbie Fletcher of the Third Fleet squad and Johnny Mize of the Fifth Fleet squad were part of a junket of ballplayers that toured Pacific islands in the final months of World War II. Courtesy of M. Shawn Hennessy, Chevrons and Diamonds Collection.

15. The Big Cat as a Giant. After the war, Johnny Mize emerged as the best home run hitter in the National League. Courtesy of National Baseball Hall of Fame.

16. The Big Cat was a menacing sight as a Yankees pinch hitter as he approached the batter's box in the late innings with a ball game on the line. Courtesy of National Baseball Hall of Fame.

17. The Big Cat and his bats. Johnny was fastidious about his tools but also happy to lend them out to teammates in need. As a Yankee, Mize suggested Phil Rizzuto use one of his bats. Rizzuto started hitting and won the Most Valuable Player Award. From Society for American Baseball Research, Rucker Archive.

18. (*above*) The Mizes of Florida. Johnny and Jene Mize spent as much time as they could in Florida, first in DeLeon Springs and then DeLand. He stayed busy managing orange groves, his liquor store, and other business interests. Courtesy of the Johnny Mize Collection, Piedmont University Archives, Demorest, Georgia.

19. (*opposite top*) The Demorest home of Johnny Mize, which he called Diamond Acre, got a historical marker in the front yard in 2000. Photo by the author.

20. (*opposite bottom*) John and Marjorie Mize were a popular couple in Demorest, Georgia, where local leadership had a granite monument erected in the Big Cat's honor. Marjorie was Johnny's alter ego: loquacious and lively. Courtesy of Patricia Pye-Kudrik Manchester.

21. (*opposite top*) The Johnny Mize Athletic Center, as seen when it opened in 2000. Photo by the author.

22. (*opposite bottom*) The Johnny Mize Museum in the lobby of the Johnny Mize Athletic Center on the campus of Piedmont University features photos, trophies, uniforms, and artifacts from the Big Cat's Hall of Fame career. Photo by the author.

23. (*above*) Piedmont College named an award in Mize's honor, given annually to the school's top student-athlete. Courtesy of the Johnny Mize Collection, Piedmont University Archives, Demorest, Georgia.

24. Judi Mize, who used a baseball bat as a cane and was devoted to her parents' legacy, was the last member of the Mize family to live in Diamond Acre in Demorest. Photo by the author.

25. Jim Mize (Johnny's stepson) and Jim's infant son, Alex, inspect some of the Big Cat's artifacts during the museum grand opening in 2000. Photo by the author.

14

Land of the Giants

> When you hold out a couple of times
> against the Cardinals you know you're
> finished with the organization.　　—Johnny Mize[1]

St. Louis newspaper readers were confronted by the latest grim news in triple-digit bold type. "War with Axis" screamed the top front-page headline in the *St. Louis Star-Times* on Thursday, December 11. Beneath that were the stories: A few days after the Japanese bombed Hawaii, Germany and Italy had declared war on the United States. Congress acted unanimously on President Franklin D. Roosevelt's call to respond in kind. U.S. planes had sunk a Japanese destroyer off North Luzon and two other Japanese warships off the coast of Wake Island.[2]

The war was everything.

For temporary respite from that horrible news, readers could flip inside to the sports section, where they learned that the St. Louis Browns were refused permission to increase their number of night games at home from seven to fourteen. Then they moved over to Sid Keener's column to read about the ongoing Johnny Mize trade rumors. And as they chuckled over Keener's snarky feints and jabs, rumor already was about to become fact.

The press had Mize going to the Dodgers in a swap for 1941 Most Valuable Player Dolph Camilli, reserve catcher Herman Franks, and an undisclosed amount of cash.[3] The press was wrong.

Branch Rickey delivered the news in Chicago at the annual Winter Meetings, on Thursday evening, December 11: Johnny was going to the New York Giants. Rickey had hammered out the details in his room at the Palmer House with Giants farm system director Bill Terry and Mel Ott, the veteran superstar who had just become New York's manager.

One of Ott's first goals after being named field skipper of the Giants was to get Mize, and he convinced team owner Horace Stoneham to ante up whatever it would take to land the Big Cat. It took backup catcher Ken O'Dea, pitcher Bill Lohrman, and $50,000 in cash.[4]

Mize was still on his hunting trip in the Ozarks when reporters reached him with the news and asked him for his thoughts. "I was pretty certain I wouldn't be with the [Cardinals] in '42," Mize told the Star-Times, which reported that he had earned $16,000 in 1941. "You've got to play somewhere, and wherever I go I'll do my best. And the Giants look like they're coming back. I've always liked Mel Ott and I think we'll get along fine."[5]

Johnny and Ott did get along fine. But the Big Cat wasn't sure about his new home.

"I wasn't too crazy about playing in the Polo Grounds, because I wasn't that much of a pull hitter," he said years later. "Maybe if I'd have gotten there earlier in my career, I might have become a pull hitter, to take advantage of that short right field, but after hitting straightaway for so many years, I didn't want to start changing around."[6]

Meanwhile, Ott had made the first big deal of his managerial career and was sure that Mize was exactly what his ball club needed. "I know what kind of baseball New Yorkers want and I promise to give it to them," he said after the Mize deal was completed.[7]

And in New York, the trade was applauded. It was seen "as a signal that Horace Stoneham would not take kindly to being the one New York team out of three to be excluded from the World Series," Noel Hynd wrote in The Giants of the Polo Grounds: The Glorious Times of Baseball's New York Giants. Hynd added, "Giants fans were elated to have acquired the Big Cat right under the nose of Dodger president Larry MacPhail."[8]

- - -

There was some apprehension in Giants training camp when Johnny's shoulder started giving him trouble.

At first, Ott was delighted because Mize, who often began the spring with extra winter baggage, was in better shape than he'd been the year before. And Johnny looked good in a pair of exhibition games with the Dodgers in Havana on February 28 and March 1. He had a hit and an RBI in each game, and ever since reporting to Miami in late February, he'd looked good in daily drills, except when he tried to throw. Some days it was so stiff, he couldn't comb his hair.

So, Ott sent him to a specialist in Miami, Dr. Cecil Ferguson, who'd been a Giants pitcher thirty years earlier. A student of pioneering athletic trainer John "Bonesetter" Reese, Ferguson diagnosed Mize's problem as a "misplacement of a large tendon, which seems to have slipped its moorings a couple of inches," wrote John Drebinger in the *New York Times*.[9]

Ferguson treated Mize's "dilly-dallying deltoid tendon" (as the *New York Daily News* called it), putting it back in place and taping the shoulder. Mize rested the arm, not throwing with any force for a few weeks. Soon, he was playing regularly but not hitting particularly well, which kept the Giants brass and fans wondering if he was going to be a bust. Mize wasn't vexed.

"I don't see why anyone is worrying," he said in a *Daily News* story on April 7, a week before Opening Day. "I never hit in the Spring. I can recall hitting but two homers in all the Spring games in which I've ever played."[10]

As soon as the season started, Mize showed Giants fans why there was no need to worry about his bat. In the season opener against the Brooklyn Dodgers, facing his former Cardinals teammate Curt Davis, Johnny strode into the right-hander's sidearm offering and blasted a shot off the Polo Grounds right-field roof. The three-run homer was too little, too late, because the Dodgers had built a 7–0 lead by then and won the game, 7–5, in front of 32,653 fans who witnessed the beginning of the Johnny Mize era in New York.

- - -

Everybody got along with Mel Ott.

"It's because Mel didn't have much to say," said Giants third baseman Bill Werber, who retired after the 1942 season because he was making more money in the insurance business. "Ott was a very nice guy, like Leo Durocher said—quiet and friendly. But, too nice to be a manager, I think."[11]

Ott was the first outfielder to be a player-manager since the days of Ty Cobb with the Tigers and Tris Speaker with the Indians in the 1920s. In 1942 the multiple roles would extract a mental and physical toll on Master Melvin. Managers were not limited to two trips to the mound per pitcher in those days, so Ott often made many trips—calling timeout, then jogging from deep right field on his old, stubby legs several times an inning.[12]

"The pressures on Ott manifested themselves in other ways, too," Hynd wrote. For years, Ott had a nervous habit of tapping his foot on the ground. "Now he wore a bare spot in the outfield grass."[13]

Other, larger pressures were preying on the nerves of everyone: the war, for example. It impacted baseball in various ways. President Roosevelt had encouraged the lords of the game to keep it going as a necessary recreational balm for a tired nation supporting the global conflict. The most dramatic impact, of course, was on the rosters throughout pro baseball. Before the season ended, a few of Mize's new Giants teammates were called into the armed forces—Willard Marshall to the marine corps, Babe Young to the coast guard.

But in 1942 most of the top stars were still wearing baseball uniforms. Ted Williams was winning the Triple Crown in the American League (and being snubbed by an obstinate press in Most Valuable Player voting). Joe DiMaggio was leading the Yankees to another pennant, Stan Musial was coming into his own as the Cardinals won a pennant, and Johnny Mize was a popular addition to the New York Giants, with fans and teammates, although at least one Giant took exception to Mize's laid-back style. Nicknamed "Rowdy Richard," veteran infielder Dick Bartell was the scrappy type of ballplayer described by teammate Bill Werber as a "banty rooster."

"If there were ever two unalikes, it was Bartell and Mize," Werber recalled. "Both were great assets to a ballclub, Bartell for his aggressive spirit and Mize for his powerful bat."

While Bartell was rambunctious, "John's disposition was on the phlegmatic side and unless he had a bat in his hands facing the pitcher, he was mostly asleep," Werber claimed. "With that bat in his hands and the game on the line, he was a fearsome sight."[14]

Werber remembered a comical encounter between Bartell and Mize during a doubleheader against the Philadelphia Phillies on August 15. The Giants won the first game, helped by Mize's two hits, including a triple, after which he hustled home to score on a wild pitch. He had a hit and a run in the second game, another Giants victory.

It was Johnny's defense in the second game that got under Bartell's prickly skin. In the first inning, Mize's wild throw to the plate allowed the Phillies to take a 2–0 lead. Then, with the score tied 2–2 in the third, Phillies shortstop Danny Murtaugh (who later managed the Pittsburgh Pirates to two World Series titles) hit a routine grounder to Giants shortstop Billy Jurges, whose throw to first got past Mize. Murtaugh hustled toward second, but according to Werber, Mize nonchalantly went after the ball and the runner took third, later scoring the go-ahead run.[15]

When the inning ended, Johnny plodded into the Giants' dugout. "He grabbed a towel to wipe the sweat from his face, and Bartell got all over him, told him to get the hell out of the game if he didn't want to play," Werber wrote in *Memories of a Ballplayer*.[16]

Mize, indifferent, calmly waved Bartell away and continued wiping himself down. Now Bartell was about to blow his top, and with balled-up fists he pushed himself into Mize to make his point. The Big Cat responded by slowly looking up with a weary expression and, as Werber recalled, "pushing his forefinger against his thumb, said in a very tired voice, 'Go sit down, Dick, or I'll pinch your head off.'" That corner of the dugout erupted in laughter and, Werber added, "Mize and Bartell remained friends."[17]

- - -

It was the Dodgers' pennant to lose, but they didn't lose it as much as they had it ripped away from them by the Cardinals, who were unstoppable in the second half of the season. A very strong Brooklyn club with Leo Durocher calling the shots set a new franchise record that season with 104 wins and had a ten-game lead on St. Louis on August 6. Then the Cardinals went 43-9 the rest of the way, finishing with 106 wins and the pennant.

It's almost as if St. Louis didn't miss Johnny Mize at all. Almost. For the rest of his days, Stan Musial would wonder, what if they'd kept the Big Cat? Wasn't it enough that St. Louis ruled baseball for much of the '40s, winning pennants in 1942, 1943, 1944, and 1946 and the World Series in '42, '44, and '46? Not for Stan. He believed the Cardinals could have been the Yankees.

"We dealt away Johnny Mize and Walker Cooper to the Giants," Musial told columnist Jimmy Cannon. "With our pitching staff and with Mize and Cooper along with Whitey Kurowski and Enos Slaughter, I think we might have won, maybe, five more pennants."[18]

So, yeah, Stan Musial hated the deal that sent Johnny Mize to New York.

"That one really got to him," Musial's former son-in-law, Tom Ashley recalled. "He thought they were shortsighted. He would talk about all the games they would have won if they had Mize in the lineup."[19]

The Big Cat's replacements at first base for the Cardinals, Johnny Hopp and Ray Sanders, both hit .250-something in 1942. But they weren't expected to replace Johnny's bat—they were supposed to have been better, more agile fielders. More agile, perhaps. But in 1942, Johnny had a higher fielding percentage than any other first baseman in the National League (.995). He also led the league in range factor—a statistic that didn't exist in Mize's day but was introduced by author Bill James in the 1970s as a measurement of how many successful defensive chances a player makes, as opposed to fielding percentage, which is basically an assessment of how well a player manages to avoid errors. Well, Mize not only demonstrated better range than the Hopp-Sanders tandem but also made fewer errors, committing only eight to their twenty combined miscues.

Regardless, the Cardinals had turned in one of the great team performances in baseball history. They didn't have a single batter with one hundred runs batted in but led the league in runs, just ahead of Brooklyn. The two teams were almost identical in every offensive category that season. But the Cardinals had a slight edge in pitching, led by the right-handed duo of Mort Cooper and Johnny Beazley. Mize's old Chesterfield and duck-hunting chum Cooper won twenty-two games, including ten shutouts, and posted a league-leading 1.78 earned run average. Beazley, in his first full season after breaking in the year before with one appearance, went 21-6 while splitting his time as a starter and reliever. He finished second in the National League to Cooper with a 2.13 ERA, Beazley's one great season. He missed the next three years in the military and won only nine more games in four seasons after the war.

But in 1942 Beazley and Cooper combined for a 6-0 record against New York (each going 3-0). Cooper was particularly difficult on Mize and his teammates, holding Johnny to one hit in twelve at bats and posting a 0.26 ERA against the Giants.

For their part, the Giants helped keep the Cardinals alive in the pennant race by taking two out of three games from the Dodgers in a critical early September series in the Polo Grounds, with Mize playing a lead role, thanks in part to a Leo Durocher idea that backfired.

Most of Leo's hunches and mind games seemed to work that year for Brooklyn. For example, he criticized one of his best starting pitchers, right-hander Kirby Higbe, in the August 19 edition of the *Brooklyn Eagle*.

"Trouble with Kirby's been that he's not been able to get his curve ball over," he told writer Harold Parrott. "When he does get it over, it's right over the middle, an invitation to swing."[20]

This was the kind of thing Durocher did to send a message or fire up guys who responded to such things—guys like Higbe, who went on to win his next three decisions, including a ten-inning whipping of the Giants on August 23 in Brooklyn.

Maybe Leo was a little overconfident for the three-game weekend tilt, September 5–6, in the Polo Grounds. By then, St. Louis had closed to within three games of the Dodgers. The Giants won the first game on Saturday. Then Brooklyn's lanky lefty Max Macon mesmerized the Giants in the first game of Sunday's doubleheader, winning a 6–2 five-hitter.

Through five innings of Sunday's second game, Higbe was in control, holding the Giants to two hits and leading 2–0. In the bottom of the sixth, New York loaded the bases on three bloop singles, and Ott made it 2–1 with an RBI groundout. Now Mize was at the plate with two men on base. From the bench, Durocher directed Higbe to throw a curve. Kirby shook him off, but Leo was insistent and flew out of the dugout to set his pitcher straight.

"I told you to throw the big sonofabitch a curve, and I mean throw him a curve," Durocher demanded.

Leo had earlier criticized Higbe's curveball to the media, and Kirby wanted to make sure he'd heard his manager correctly: "Leo, he's the best goddamn lowball hitter in baseball, and you want me to throw him the curve. Right?"[21]

Damn straight, Leo indicated. Higbe shrugged, did what he was told, and then "Mize gave it a terrific ride," wrote Jack Smith of the *Daily News*. "It hit high against the roof of the upper right field stands and caromed back onto the field where [Dixie] Walker gave it a gloomy and disgusted kick."[22]

The three-run blast lifted the Giants to a 4–2 win and left the Dodgers just two and a half games in front of the charging Cardinals. A story in the *Brooklyn Eagle* asserted, "Johnny Mize is still a Cardinal at heart" after his homer trimmed Brooklyn's lead.

Meanwhile, Big Mort Cooper (nearly Mize size, at six feet two, 210 pounds) got stronger as the pennant race got hotter. He put a stranglehold on the MVP Award in September, going 5-0 and tossing shutouts in his last three wins of the season, including a three-hitter against the Dodgers on September 11 in Brooklyn—a win that moved the Cardinals to within a game of the league lead. Max Lanier beat the Dodgers the next day, 2–1, leaving both teams with 94-46 records. The Cardinals went on to win twelve of their last thirteen games to take the flag, then dominated the Yankees in the World Series, 4–1. Beazley was the pitching hero with two complete-game victories.

The Giants, who finished a respectable but distant third in the National League (85-67), were never in the pennant hunt. But once again, Ott and Mize battled for the league's home run crown, trading places this time. Master Melvin's thirty blasts were tops, and Mize's twenty-six tied Brooklyn's Dolph Camilli for second. It was a tight race for both home run and RBI honors, as the three sluggers battled down to the last day.

Entering September, the home run race looked like this: Ott, 25; Mize, 23; Camilli, 21. Ott bashed three out in the final week of the season to distance himself from the other guys, including a grand slam in Boston. Camilli passed Mize with his twenty-sixth home run on September 25 at Ebbets Field against the Braves. Dolph also went on an RBI binge the last week of the season, driving in 11 to give him 109 for the season.

On September 26 the Braves visited the Polo Grounds for a season-ending doubleheader. The day ended in bedlam as a mob of kids swarmed over the ballfield in the eighth inning of the nightcap. That game featured a Braves rookie southpaw named Warren Spahn, getting a final sip of coffee before shipping out to serve in the army for the duration of the war. The Giants, who were beating Spahn and the Braves when the kids mobbed the field, had to forfeit the game to Boston when umpires and cops couldn't restore order.

More than eleven thousand fans were in attendance, including thousands of "sturdy young war scrap contributors," according to the *New York Times*. They saw the Giants bury the Braves in the first game, 6–4.

Johnny had 4 hits, including a double and his 26th home run, plus 2 RBIs to give him 109, bringing him even with Camilli in both categories. Ott hit his 30th homer and drove in 2 runs to also finish with 109 RBIs. That left Ott, Mize, and Camilli tied for the league lead in runs batted in. Johnny had a single and an RBI in the truncated second game to give him the RBI championship with 110. In addition to that, he also had the best slugging percentage in the league (.521) and batted .305, good for fifth in the league.

This was a temporary new and strange era for the game. In addition to players leaving their teams to enter military service, the signs of the times included sales of war bonds at home plate; air raid wardens roaming the grandstand, looking skyward; foul balls being collected from the fans, for servicemen; and of course, scrap drives like the one that put a premature end to the Giants' season.

With two out in the top of the eighth of that forfeited game, the Braves' Max West hit a grounder to Giants second baseman Mickey Witek, who tossed the ball over to Mize at first for the final out of the inning and, as it happened, the season. Johnny squeezed the ball and trotted off the field as an unstoppable surge of children invaded the green diamond.

The Big Cat's greatest baseball thrills still lay ahead, but it would be three and a half years before he played in another Major League game.

15

War Clubs

There's a saying around Great Lakes
that you can throw a baseball anywhere
on the station and at least two big
leaguers will try to catch it.　　—Dan Polier[1]

The reality of global war and the escapism of sport merged on May 8, 1942, at Brooklyn's Ebbets Field, where the Dodgers hosted the Giants in Major League Baseball's first official wartime fundraiser. A record high 42,822 tickets were sold—a number that far exceeded the ballpark's capacity of 33,000.[2] Patriotism put the people in a giving mood—a goodly number of generous folks bought tickets with no intention of showing up. Before the game, Brooklyn club president and general manager Larry MacPhail claimed he had five thousand paid-for tickets in his pocket, the ducats returned to the Dodgers by big-hearted fans who suggested they be resold.[3] One guy, a contractor, bought about a thousand tickets then sent them to his employees in Trinidad as keepsake souvenirs.[4]

Before the game, while fans were still buying (and rebuying) tickets, hundreds of midshipmen and sailors put on a pregame show for the fans, marching in formation while a band played. In the end, approximately $60,000 was raised.

"The money you have paid to see this game goes to the support of dependents of Navy men killed in this war," Commander Gene Tunney, former heavyweight boxing champion, told the fans before the first twilight game in Major League history. "Everyone here had to have a ticket to get in—groundskeepers, ushers and peanut vendors included. Even the ball players and umpires had to pay their way in—for a change."[5]

That brought big laughs from the crowd, which included about three thousand servicemen, their tickets purchased by team sponsors and radio listeners. And they all were treated to an exciting ball game, a 7–6 Dodgers decision.

Of the twenty-four men who played in the that first war-benefit game, thirteen served in the armed forces during the war. And by this time in 1943, Johnny Mize would be hitting home runs for Uncle Sam.

- - -

Long before the Japanese attack on Pearl Harbor, the United States, including some baseball players, prepared for war. While Imperial Japan extended its grasp in the Pacific and fascist forces fired the first shots of the war in Europe, the United States bolstered its ill-equipped, under-sized army. President Roosevelt signed the Selective Training and Service Act in September 1940, requiring every male between twenty-one and thirty-six to register for twelve months of military service. "The draft put nearly two million men in uniform by the end of 1941," wrote author and historian Gary Bedingfield. "It was the greatest defense program in the history of the nation."[6]

Some players took the initiative and volunteered. Among the first was Minor League outfielder Billy Southworth Jr., son of the Cardinals' manager. "My baseball career can wait," said the young Southworth, who enlisted in December 1940, a year before the attack on Pearl Harbor.[7] He died in a training flight in February 1945, after completing twenty-five bombing missions over Europe.[8]

One of the first Major League players to be drafted was Mize's American League counterpart and former Piedmont League foe, Hank Greenberg, who got the call on May 7, 1941—a few months after he'd been named Most Valuable Player. Bob Feller, the Cleveland Indians' superstar pitcher, enlisted in the Navy shortly after the Pearl Harbor attack.

Mize had been deferred from military duty with a draft status of 3-A because he was the sole provider for his aunt and grandmother in Demorest. But in March 1943, with fathers now being taken into the service, Johnny was reclassified as 1-A.[9]

The Sporting News, after interviewing Giants manager Mel Ott, reported that the thirty-year-old first baseman suffered from hemophilia.[10] He was also heavier than ever, weighing in at 244 pounds when he passed his physical in St. Louis on March 25.[11]

Shortly before the physical, Johnny visited with Si Johnson, his former Cardinals teammate who had a farm in rural Sheridan, Illinois (about sixty-five miles west of Chicago). Mize, who used to travel to Sheridan to hunt and fish, confided in his pal that he planned to enlist in the navy.[12]

"I was ready to join up whenever I was called and had made up my mind that I was going into the Navy," Mize said. "I guess I like this branch of the service."[13]

So, he was sworn in by Lieutenant Commander Charles K. Slatsman, the St. Louis–area officer in charge of naval recruiting. Johnny had a week to spend with Jene, then he was off for the Great Lakes Naval Training Station north of Chicago. His "training" was not your typical bootcamp. See, he was almost immediately sent into action—Lieutenant Gordon "Mickey" Cochrane needed Johnny to play first base and bat fourth.

- - -

Cochrane was the great catcher from Connie Mack's championship Philadelphia Athletics of the late '20s and early '30s, who later became the player-manager of the Detroit Tigers, guiding them to two pennants. A nearly fatal beanball ruined his playing career, but now he was in great shape at forty and wore a confident smile as the 1943 season opener against the Louisville Colonels of the American Association approached—his Bluejackets won, and his new star, Johnny Mize, drove in two runs with a triple and a single.

Very soon, the competition got tougher for the Great Lakes team, but Johnny and his fellow sailors were up to the challenge. Just two years and twenty pounds earlier, Mize had starred for the Cardinals in a wild pennant race. Now his old chums from St. Louis—the defending *world champion* Cardinals—were doing their part in the war effort by stopping off at Great Lakes to take on the Bluejackets.

The Cardinals were on their way to another pennant. This time it would be no contest—they won 105 games, 18 ahead of the second-place Reds in '43 (meanwhile, the Mize-less Giants finished last). The Bluejackets didn't seem impressed.

Cochrane had a roster of sailor ballplayers that was probably as good as most Major League teams. In addition to Mize, there was second baseman Johnny Lucadello, pitcher Frank Biscan, and outfielders Joe Grace and Glenn McQuillen from the St. Louis Browns; pitchers Johnny

Schmitz and Vern Olsen of the Cubs; Tom Ferrick of the Cleveland Indians; Bob Harris of the Philadelphia Athletics; and George Dickey of the Chicago White Sox, the younger brother of Yankees star catcher Bill Dickey. About halfway through the season, Detroit Tigers' star outfielder Barney McCosky joined the team.

With that kind of lineup, the Bluejackets' 5–2 win over the Cardinals can't really be considered an upset. Great Lakes' pitchers struck out eleven batters and gave up three hits—two of them solo homers, one by catcher Walker Cooper, the other from Stan Musial, an inside-the-park job in a pinch-hitting role. Mize led Great Lakes with three hits, driving in one run and scoring another.

The Cardinals were just the first of twelve teams from the National or American leagues to visit Great Lakes' Constitution Field in 1943—the Bluejackets beat the Cubs twice.

They reeled off eighteen wins in their first twenty-one games through June 22 following a 2–1 win over the Cleveland Indians.[14] Mize had two hits as the Bluejackets triumphed in the bottom of the ninth on Joe Grace's RBI single.

"The Great Lakes Naval Training Station is staking a claim for the baseball championship for the U.S. armed services—and there isn't a challenge in sight to dispute the claim," *Stars and Stripes* reported on June 24, a few days after the Cleveland game. "It's just that Lt. Gordon 'Mickey' Cochrane's sailor boys are in a class by themselves."[15]

The Great Lakes boys were basically a seventeenth Major League team. They lost a thriller to the Yankees, 8–6, on July 9. Mize had a hit and two RBIs and scored a run. That game gave the Jackets a 1-1 record against the two teams that had a stranglehold on the World Series in 1942 and 1943, the Cardinals and Yankees.

The Bluejackets came back to beat the Dodgers, 9–8, with a ninth-inning rally, then took down a squad comprised of Boston Braves and Cincinnati Reds players and lost to the Philadelphia Phillies and their eighteen-year-old pitcher, George Eyrich. That gave Cochrane's team a 7-6 record against Major League competition.

"The last time we played the Cubs, [manager] Jimmie Wilson told me that we could win the National League pennant," said Cochrane. Then the longtime American League star felt compelled to add a wry jab at the senior circuit: "I wouldn't want to end up in a minor league now."[16]

- - -

The Bluejackets would ultimately break even against bona fide big league competition in 1943. They met their match in a historical contest against the Chicago American Giants of the Negro American League.

Great Lakes was 41-8 on August 7, 1943, when the Giants became the first Negro League team to play at the training station.[17] The Great Lakes facility was behind some other U.S. military outposts when it came to integrated baseball.

Other bases already were fielding integrated teams—the Fort Lewis Warriors (near Tacoma, Washington) and Salt Lake City Army Base Wings, for example. The integrated Fort Lewis team played against not only other service teams but also Minor League teams from segregated circuits, like the Pacific Coast League.[18]

The following year, Mize would play in an integrated league of military ball clubs in Hawaii. Also in 1944, Great Lakes would field a team of Black players in addition to a white team, though the teams would not be integrated.

But in August 1943, in northern Illinois, here was something new: the nation's top military baseball team hosting a traditional Negro Leagues powerhouse.

The *Chicago Defender*, an African American newspaper covering the game, reported that the Giants "startled the 10,000 Bluejackets who were out to enjoy an afternoon of baseball and (so they thought) to see their team win."[19] That should serve as an adequate hint of what transpired.

The American Giants were a charter member of the Negro National League, previously owned and operated by Andrew "Rube" Foster, the father of organized Black ball. The Giants, which joined the Negro American League (NAL) in 1937, were now managed by Ted "Double Duty" Radcliffe—so nicknamed for his habit of pitching the first game of a doubleheader and catching the second. For this game, Radcliffe was the catcher and manager, and he played like the NAL's Most Valuable Player—an award he would win that season, at the age of forty-one.[20]

With a lineup of frontline players, the Chicago club gave the Great Lakes boys a Major League whipping, 7–3, smashing nineteen hits, as popular former WGN broadcaster Bob Elson, now a navy lieutenant, announced it all over the public address. It wasn't lost on the American Giants that the Bluejackets had already beaten some other good big league clubs.[21]

Mize led all players with four hits, including an RBI double, but the Jackets could not overcome resilient Giants starting pitcher Gentry "Jeep" Jessup, who had recently gone fourteen innings to beat the Cleveland Buckeyes in an NAL game. Now he went the distance against Great Lakes. Overcoming twelve hits and seven walks, he stranded nine Bluejacket baserunners, assisted by a sharp infield that turned three double plays—Ed "Pep" Young at first, Art Pennington at second, Ralph Wyatt at shortstop, and Double Duty's younger brother, Alex Radcliffe, at third.

Johnny had ridiculous numbers that summer, batting .418 with 17 home runs and 103 RBIs, as the Bluejackets won fifty-two of their sixty-three games. For Johnny, it was the kind of performance that would have kept him locked down with any other ball club. But this was the military in war time, which meant that Mize would be moving on—not traded or sold, but transferred and reassigned.

- - -

For the second year in a row, the Great Lakes baseball team was the best in the armed services, and not everyone was happy.

"There has been a lot of talk lately about the way the Navy is supposed to be keeping its athletes, especially the major league baseball players, in cold storage at the Great Lakes Naval Training Station, while the not-so-talented guys are knocking their brains out on destroyers in the South Pacific," wrote Sgt. Dan Polier in the lede of his feature article in the February 6, 1944, edition of *Yank*.

The article was a response to critics of service baseball who claimed there was increasing discontent among families of servicemen in combat zones, who didn't think it was fair that "so many major leaguers are fighting this war in cleated shows."

Polier added, "If this is true—if, for example, the Navy is following a well-organized plan to keep Johnny Mize safely anchored in drydock until he can return to the New York Giants—then neither the Navy, Mize, nor the Giants know anything about it."[22]

By the time the article was published, Mize and most of his fellow Bluejacket teammates had been hustled out of Great Lakes—in September, right after the baseball season. They were sent to the Naval Training Station at Bainbridge, Maryland, for more training—some of which did not involve bat, ball, or cleats.

"The greatest scene to come out of the war on the home front is that wherein we see Johnny Mize in a Mae West life-jacket poised, trembling, on a ten-foot springboard preparatory to the propulsion of his 230 pounds into the chilly deep far below," wrote syndicated columnist Caswell Adams of the International News Service in an October dispatch.[23]

Even though Mize must have made quite the splash, he was not long for Bainbridge.

Johnny got sick—perhaps the training in cold autumn waters did not suit his southern constitution—and developed a case of pneumonia.[24] He was reportedly eligible for medical discharge, but doctors at the naval training station thought otherwise, and by mid-January, Johnny was bound for Hawaii.

Military baseball exploded across the Hawaiian Islands during each year of the war, as professional players were yanked into the armed forces. By 1944 about 340 big leaguers were in the military, scattered around the world, in addition to more than 3,000 Minor Leaguers.[25]

Eleven U.S. military bases were in Hawaii, with thousands of troops, an avid civilian baseball community, and lots of fan interest. There were the Hawaii League, Honolulu League, and competitive military leagues, including the 14th Naval District League, Seabee League, Army Post & Command League, Central Pacific Area (CPA) League, and Schofield Barracks League.[26]

And leading the baseball parade was the Big Cat.

"Watch out for Johnny," wrote the *Honolulu Star-Bulletin*'s Blues Romeo, whose name seems conjured from Damon Runyon's universe. "Oahu parks already are moving their fences. When it's all over, he hopes to stay in baseball, and he's almost sure to keep on bothering the guys who mend the fences."[27]

A few weeks after Romeo's warning, Mize put on a hitting clinic. Leading a team of Major Leaguers against the Pearl Harbor Submarine Base team, he had a homer, double, and two singles, as the big leaguers won easily.

It was fine preparation for one of the biggest sporting events Hawaii had seen—a war-bond game between Major Leaguers and Honolulu League All-Stars, April 29, at Honolulu Stadium. The price of admission was purchase of a $25 war bond. Much of the pregame hype was devoted to whether Mize would hit a ball out of the stadium, something that had never been done.

"Talking with Earle K. Vida, president of the Honolulu baseball league, Mize, who will play in the war bond game Saturday, sized up the stadium and said he believed he could knock one over the right-field bleachers," the *Star-Bulletin* reported on April 27. "Even the mighty Babe Ruth was unable to do this when he played here."[28]

The game lived up to the hype. The Major Leaguers won in twelve innings, 4–2. Mize didn't hit a ball out of the stadium, but he hit the longest ball of the game, a 425-foot double that bounced over the centerfield wall. He also scorched a single to right field in the first inning and scored what proved to be the winning run in the top of the twelfth.

Mize and his mates were a formidable bunch and would have been competitive with any team: Pee Wee Reese at shortstop, Barney McCosky in center field, Hugh Casey on the mound—the Brooklyn relief ace played the role of starting pitcher in this game. But Honolulu wasn't intimidated. Among the All-Stars were several Minor League players, including future Washington Senator outfielder Sam Mele.

"The greatest ball game of the season," wrote the *Star-Bulletin*'s Carl Macado. "That's what 17,000 spectators saw."[29]

Between the war bonds and the auction of autographed bats and balls, the event raised more than $1 million.

- - -

A decade earlier, as a young man of twenty-one, Johnny Mize spent some time in an island paradise, where he got involved with a bunch of ballplayers who were among the best in their profession. And here he was again, living on an island, mixing with a bunch of first-class ballplayers, among the best in the business. This group of luminaries included Bill Dickey, Dom DiMaggio, Pee Wee Reese, Phil Rizzuto, Virgil Trucks, Schoolboy Rowe, and Johnny Vander Meer, among others. These were Johnny's teammates on a well-stocked navy All-Star team, assembled to beat a team of army All-Stars in an upcoming armed forces "World Series."

It was planned as a seven-game series but would eventually be extended to ten games, rotating to different ballparks in Hawaii, giving as many people as possible a chance to see big leaguers in action. "With a buildup of Major League talent in Hawaii, a soldier-sailor clash on the ballfield was inevitable," wrote Gary Bedingfield in *Wartime Baseball in Hawaii 1944: Here Come the Big Leaguers*.[30]

The army roster was impressive, too, with a pair of future Hall of Famers: Yankees teammates Joe DiMaggio and Joe Gordon, though DiMaggio would not play. He was in the hospital and had missed most of the baseball season. But he'd already left an impression, batting around .400 with eight home runs, including a 435-foot clout in his first game in Hawaii on June 5, then a 450-foot monster that left Honolulu Stadium a few days later.[31]

The ballplayers also were spread out among military-base teams that played in the various Hawaii leagues. Mize was now an athletics specialist at the Kaneohe Naval Air Station. That team played in the CPA League, also known as the All-Service League—the best collection of baseball talent on Oahu, the most populous of Hawaii's eight islands.

The CPA League featured plenty of professional baseball talent, including some Black players. The Schofield Barracks Redlanders had scrappy future Negro Leaguer Frank "Wizard" Williams, a line-drive-hitting outfielder. Hal Hairston, later with the powerful Homestead Grays, pitched for the Wheeler Wingmen. The South Sector Commandos had former Homestead Grays and future New York Black Yankees hurler Nathaniel "Sonny Boy" Jeffries on their roster. For the Army-Navy Servicemen's World Series, Hairston, playing for the army, would be the only Black player on either team.[32]

Thousands of miles away in St. Louis, the Cardinals and Browns were battling in the Streetcar World Series. But the best collection of talent in the world at that time was probably in Hawaii playing for the navy. The powers that be had agreed that every game would be played, even if the series had been decided—the much-needed entertainment would be good mojo for servicemen and servicewomen. The series accomplished that, even if it wasn't very competitive. The navy trounced the army.

The first game in the series was September 22 at Furlong Field at Pearl Harbor, where twenty thousand fans watched Virgil Trucks pitch a four-hit shutout, while Dom DiMaggio provided the game's biggest highlight, a leaping catch in deep center field to rob army slugger (and future American League batting champ) Ferris Fain of extra bases. The navy kept dominating from there, winning the first six games, and seven of the ten.

The combatants ended the series October 6 with a fourteen-inning, 6–6 tie in the only contest that was played on the island of Hawaii (the Big Island). Mize, who batted over .400 in the series, leading all hitters, belted a two-run homer in the first inning, giving the navy an early lead.

It was one of five home runs hit in the game, which was called on account of darkness.

The 7,500 people in attendance at Hilo's Honolulu Park was a record sports crowd for the Big Island.

"Without a shadow of a doubt, it was the greatest exhibition of baseball ever played in our fair city and it paled to insignificance the battle royal of St. Louis in the current World Series," wrote Bert Nakaji of the *Hawaii Tribune-Herald*, tweaking the Cardinals-Browns clash, won by the Cards in six games.[33] The game in Hilo finished the army-navy series for the year, but it did not finish the army or navy teams on the Big Island. They each had a date with a locally based service team, the Red Wings, which beat the army stars and almost beat the vaunted navy squad, which held on to win 5–4, thanks to Mize's double in the tenth inning.

- - -

The word came in early February 1945: a bunch of Major Leaguers were leaving Hawaii on a tour of forward areas in the Pacific. Mize would be joining McCosky, Reese, Trucks, Vander Meer, Rowe, and a horde of big leaguers, assembled by Lt. Bill Dickey, divided into two squads, Third Fleet and Fifth Fleet (Mize's team).

Following a send-off game against a team of army air force stars (the army guys won in an upset), the two navy squads spent the following months playing baseball at Majuro, Roi-Namu, and Kwajalein in the Marshall Islands; Ulithi and Peleliu in the Carolines; and Saipan, Tinian, and Guam in the Marianas in front of crowds of eager servicemen.

Following the junket, instead of returning to Hawaii, the players were assigned to the Mariana Islands, where they helped design ballfields, organize athletic activities, and play ball. Johnny was stationed on Tinian, which had been held by the Japanese until a force of U.S. Marines, after a weeklong battle, secured the strategic island, just 1,200 miles from Japan. Within months of taking Tinian, U.S. B-29s were bombing the Japanese mainland. All told, B-29s would fly about twenty-nine thousand missions out of the Marianas, the most famous coming on August 6, 1945, when the *Enola Gay* departed on its horrific date with destiny, dropping an atomic bomb on Hiroshima. Two days later, another B-29 Superfortress took off from Tinian with a second nuclear weapon, which was dropped on Nagasaki, ending the war.[34]

This wasn't Great Lakes or Hawaii by a long shot. This was the closest to the war that Mize got. Hundreds of Japanese soldiers were still hiding out in the many caves on Tinian. (The last one wouldn't surrender until 1953, eight years after the war ended.)[35]

Before the atom bombs were dropped, not long after he arrived on the island, Johnny started making his postwar plans. That is, he started getting back into baseball shape. He had gained a lot of his weight back.

"When I got up to 245 pounds, I decided something had to be done about it if I was going to play ball again when the war was over," Johnny told Frank Graham, for a profile in the January 1953 edition of *Sport* magazine.[36]

There was a tent on the island with some gym equipment; each midday he'd close the tent flaps for a few hours. Wearing a sweat suit, he'd go through a round of calisthenics, push-ups, bends, and jerks, losing forty pounds before the war ended.

But he was still large enough to be noticed by a soldier, Private First Class Howard Norman Bornak, who wrote to sports columnist John Flynn of his hometown paper, the *Berkshire Eagle*. His letter, printed in the July 6, 1945, edition, mentioned the progress being made on sports facilities on Tinian—a baseball field was completed, and a basketball court was in progress. He also wrote, "There are quite a number of big-league ball players here but the only one I have seen so far is Johnny Mize. When I was in China I had Hank Greenberg for my commanding officer."[37]

By the time the young MP's letter had been published, Greenberg was out of the army and back with the Detroit Tigers after missing almost four full seasons wearing olive drab.

Hank helped lead the Tigers to the American League pennant, then played like a superstar in the World Series, hitting two home runs, driving in seven, and scoring seven. And when the Tigers finished off the Cubs in Game Seven at Wrigley Field on October 10, Johnny Mize was there too.

"Johnny Mize, discharged at Great Lakes Tuesday, turned up in the Cub dugout yesterday," United Press International reported in its Series coverage. "The former Cardinal-Giant first baseman is eager to get back into uniform."[38]

16

Agony of Defeat

We sing now of the verdant springtime.
Of trailing arbutus and the jolly crocus, of
the robin and bock beer signs, of the circus
coming out of hibernation—and BASEBALL!   —Dan Daniel[1]

Four years of war felt more like an eternity, and after so much death and tragedy and disruption, Americans were eager—no, *desperate*—to get back to normalcy, or something like it. Baseball was the ticket. It had been a welcome morale booster, per President Roosevelt's suggestion, for a tired nation working overtime to support the war effort—a small sample of "normal" to sustain a baseball-hungry public in trying times.

Baseball during the war had been plenty of fun for the loyalists who imbibed. But it was, inevitably, a compromised product. How else to explain the ascension of Pete Gray, the one-armed outfielder who played for the Browns in 1945? As remarkable and gifted as Pete was (he batted .333 and was MVP of the Southern Association in 1944 while playing for the Memphis Chicks), could he have reached the American League before the war? He sure didn't stick around afterward.

But now the stars had returned from their distant outposts around the globe, and the fans showed up in record numbers to watch them again. Attendance in 1946 was nearly twice what it had been a year earlier (New York's three ball clubs alone brought in a combined 5.3 million fans, the Yankees becoming the first team to surpass 2 million).[2]

From 1943 through 1945, with fuel rationing in place, spring training was held close to the ball clubs' home cities. But in 1946 they were all going to Florida, or the coast—or in the case of the Yankees, who had been training the past few years in Asbury Park, New Jersey, to Panama.[3]

And with a wave of players returning to action, or trying to, the ball clubs had more men than ever in camp.

"Nearly 1,000 players—all listed on the rosters of their clubs—will crowd major league training camps this spring in the greatest assemblage of talent ever witnessed," the Sporting News reported. "Returning veterans will swell the number."[4]

But before the former servicemen went to spring training, their teams requested they take part in some preliminary training, presuming they had some catching up to do. Mize showed up ready to play as one of the first arrivals at the Giants' training camp in Miami. He told AP writer Joe Reichler he was in the best shape of his life at age thirty-three, a trim 205 pounds. "The former Cardinal gave an indication Monday of what he may mean to the Giants this season by larruping for 400 feet the first ball served him," Reichler wrote.[5]

Giants manager Mel Ott managed the team through two miserable seasons (dead last in 1943 and fifth with just sixty-seven wins in 1944) and one mediocre campaign (fifth again in 1944 but improved to 78-74). He was pleased with the energy of his players in spring training 1946, especially returning war veterans like Mize, Sid Gordon, Hal Schumacher, Babe Young, and Dick Bartell, back for his nineteenth season in the majors. Ott faced a logistical challenge with seventy players in camp. "Our major problem just now is hustling the pitchers into shape so that the regular batting drills can get started," he told John Drebinger of the New York Times. "Until then it's going to be difficult keeping such a big squad of infielders and outfielders busy."[6]

Not that he was worried about first base—well, not anymore.

From 1943 to 1945, Ott's mantra was: "Who's on first?" The Abbott and Costello bit perfectly captured the uncertainty of the war years, when the Giants' rotating first sackers were Joe Orengo, Nap Reyes, and Phil Weintraub (among others).

"First base no longer presents a problem of any sort," Drebinger wrote. "For that post is definitely clinched by Johnny Mize, the mighty mauler from Georgia. Big Jawn's general appearance and early form already have removed the last lingering doubt as to his ability to pick up where he left off three years ago."[7]

Expectations were high for the mighty mauler, and Johnny lived up to them, as long as he was physically capable.

Even though the war was over, "it could be argued that the New York Giants played one more year of wartime-style baseball, even if the rest of the league didn't," Noel Hynd wrote in *The Giants of the Polo Grounds*. They were that bad in 1946.

But club brass had reason to be optimistic as spring training began. Proven stars were returning: Mize, Gordon, Bartell, Schumacher, Young, Willard Marshall, and Dave Koslo. In January, Stoneham paid the St. Louis Cardinals $175,000 for Walker Cooper, perhaps the best catcher in the league. And there were promising young players, like infielders Bill Rigney and Buddy Blattner and pitchers Monty Kennedy, Marv Grissom, Mike Budnick, and Sal Maglie, who wasn't exactly young at almost twenty-nine. But he was newish, with just one season of Major League ball behind him, 1945, when he went 5-4 with a 2.35 earned run average and 3 shutouts.

The Giants were champs on paper. Then, disaster struck.

It came from south of the border, in the form of wealthy Mexican brothers Jorge and Bernardo Pascuel, who were buying up big league ballplayers to upgrade the Mexican League. They lured some top players, like Vern Stephens of the Browns (American League home run leader in 1945), Cardinals ace Max Lanier, and Dodgers catcher Mickey Owen, among others. But the Giants provided the Pascuels with a buffet of talent, as New York players began jumping ship: Maglie, Danny Gardella, Roy Zimmerman, George Hausmann, Nap Reyes, Adrián Zabala, Harry Feldman, and the team's only relief specialist, Ace Adams.[8]

Maglie made the leap on March 31, just before camp broke. Sal was cast as a villain, according to *Daily News* columnist Jimmy Powers, who wrote that Maglie "acted as unofficial agent for the millionaire Mexicans." Maglie said offers also had been made to other Giants, including Ernie Lombardi, Bartell, Gordon, Young, and Mize.[9]

The season opened on a high note for the Giants. Ott hit home run number 511—the last of his career—as New York beat the visiting Phillies. The Giants were in third place with an 11-10 record in May. Then they lost six straight and never reached breakeven again, withering away in the second division for the rest of the long season.

Cooper, the expensive slugging catcher, struggled through multiple injuries, limiting him to just eighty-seven games in 1946.

Then there was the Big Cat. Hynd wasn't exaggerating when he wrote, "Mize's case was particularly perverse."[10] It was a twisted sort of cruelty that plagued the Giants in '46, particularly Mize. Even the games that didn't count were big trouble.

The Giants were already in last place on July 1, when they hosted the Yankees in the first game of a best-of-three exhibition series for the Mayor (William) O'Dwyer Cup. The Yankees won, 3–0, the big blow coming from Joe DiMaggio, who crushed a 447-foot triple in the second inning. The next game in the series, a fundraiser for sandlot leagues, was scheduled for August 5 in Yankee Stadium.

In the meantime, Mize went on one of his typical July hitting binges, batting .377 for the month with 23 runs batted in and 7 home runs, the last two in a doubleheader against the Reds at the Polo Grounds on July 28. The second one, against his old nemesis, Gunboat Gumbert, gave him a league-leading 22 homers, 6 ahead of his nearest competitor, Pittsburgh Pirates rookie outfielder Ralph Kiner.

A week later, the Giants were in Yankee Stadium for the second Mayor's Trophy game. Once again, the Yankees triumphed, this time, 3–2. But the Giants had already lost something more than the meaningless (except for the sandlot urchins) ball game. In the top of the first inning, Yankees relief ace Joe Page threw an inside pitch that hit Johnny on the right hand, making a loud-enough crack that umpire Art Passarella mistook it for a foul ball. Bartell, now a coach, and Ott argued the call, presenting Johnny's mangled hand as evidence, and the ump changed his mind.[11]

Mize trotted to first, then left the game for a pinch runner and went to St. Elizabeth's Hospital for X-rays, which showed a broken bone below the wrist. He was expected to miss two or three weeks. He'd miss five. Then he'd make a comeback—kind of.

- - -

You can't, or shouldn't, make this up: Johnny returned to action on Friday the thirteenth.

The sad-sack Giants had just ended a six-game losing streak on Thursday, September 12, against the sixth-place Reds, as Monty Kennedy tossed a two-hitter in front of the smallest crowd of the season in the Polo Grounds to that point (1,960).

On Friday, Johnny was back in a ball game for the first time since

Joe Page's wild spitter broke his hand. This time it was an even smaller crowd (1,835 people, who may also have enjoyed seeing flies tortured). Cincinnati quickly tested Mize's right hand. In the top of the first inning, with a runner on first, the Reds' second batter, Benny Zientara, bunted toward first base. Mize fielded the ball cleanly and made a good throw to second baseman Mickey Witek, covering first on the play.

While he didn't have to make any more throws, John completed several double plays. He also grounded into a double play, flew out to left, and walked. But the hand was fine.

In the top of the eighth, with a runner on second, two out, and a 4–1 Cincinnati lead, Reds All-Star second baseman Lonny Frey, a left-handed hitter, got under a Woody Abernathy pitch, pulling it high and foul, to Johnny's left. Mize drifted over and crashed into the wall separating the ballfield from the stands, making the clutch catch, but breaking the big toe on his right foot in the process.

Another freak accident in a year of hoodoo, and Johnny Mize was done for 1946.

The Giants, too, were done. The Friday the thirteenth loss to Cincinnati began another six-game losing streak. New York's 61-93 record was the team's second worst in its history. (The 1943 team was 55-98.) The Giants had powerful bats, hitting more home runs than any other team in the National League. But their pitching staff also gave up the most home runs.

In some ways, the National League race was a repeat of 1942. The Dodgers led most of the way, building a seven-and-a-half-game lead on St. Louis in July. And once again, the Cardinals, now managed by Mize's old Minor League skipper, Eddie Dyer, stormed back to catch Brooklyn. The teams both finished at 96-58, forcing the first tie-breaker pennant series in history.

St. Louis won the best-of-three affair in two games, then beat the Boston Red Sox in the World Series, a seven-game classic highlighted by Enos Slaughter's famous mad dash home from first on Harry Walker's base hit. After years of war and substandard baseball, fans were rewarded with a memorable season from start to finish.

It was a pity for Mize that he couldn't finish it because his injuries cost him a certain home run title. Kiner caught and passed the Big Cat, finishing with twenty-three homers, the lowest number to lead the National League since Hack Wilson's twenty-one in 1926. Kiner felt that he had won the home run race in a "cheap" way, according to the *Pittsburgh Post-Gazette*, which reported, "If Johnny Mize hadn't been out a large part of the season—first with a broken hand and now, permanently, with a broken toe—Ralph knows he wouldn't be on top."[12]

Still, the rookie outfielder had tied the Pirates team record for homers in a season. The next year, he would crush it.

But this was Stan Musial's year. The Man, who had won the Most Valuable Player Award in 1943 as a twenty-two-year-old, won the award again with a National League best .365 batting average, plus league-leading numbers in runs, hits, doubles, triples, slugging average, and total bases.

Mize's .337 batting average would have been second in the league, but he didn't have enough at bats to qualify. He had the second highest slugging average and the best on-base percentage in the league, but it was the same deal—377 at bats in 101 games was not enough to place him among the leaders.

Despite the painful way the season had ended for him, Johnny was upbeat when he spoke with Atlanta sportswriter Jack Troy upon returning to Georgia in late September.[13] He was visiting his mother and grandmother before departing for De Leon Springs, Florida, where he and Jene would spend the offseason. He was getting used to Florida.

He joked with Troy about his unlucky day against the Reds and said, "Cooper and Lombardi were in the hospital when I left to come home for a visit. Manager Mel Ott is holding up very well under the setbacks. He figures it's just one of those years." Johnny also said he had a very good chance to lead the league in homers in 1947, "provided, of course, some new hitting sensation doesn't appear on the scene."[14]

17

Chasing the Babe

It is morning in Boston, and the Big Cat rolls out of his bed in the Hotel Kenmore, fumbles for his cigars, lights one, and starts puffing. Even before the first sip of coffee, particularly when on the road, he starts the day with a cigar. The pungent smoke surrounds his moon head, fills the room. Behind him in the other bed, Bill Rigney stirs, blinks, grimaces, waves at the smoke, and says, "Oh, swell, John."[1] Grumbling, he turns away from his Giants teammate, pulling the covers over his head.

Johnny Mize ignores his teammate, walks to the window overlooking Commonwealth Avenue, lifts the shade. "Gotta check the wind," he says under his breath, opening the window, letting the cool April morning air and the sound of traffic below rush in to fill the room with his cigar smoke.

From up here on the sixth floor, Mize can see Fenway Park three blocks away. More important, he can see its center-field flagpole rising above the green monster, Old Glory with her thirteen stripes and forty-eight stars, flapping in the wind. Johnny stares a minute, studying. He grins.

"The wind will be blowing out today," he says out loud. Rigney grunts.

The Giants are playing the Braves later, and Braves Field is a mile or so down Commonwealth. But Johnny believes he can read the wind, and he's feeling confident.

He stretches, just like a big cat, the cigar clenched in his jaw, shuts the window, turns to Rigney and says, "Roomie, I'm gonna hit one or two today."[2] Then Johnny grabs the morning paper from out in the hall to read the box scores and find out what Musial did yesterday.

- - -

The 1946 baseball season was good for the country. The 1947 season was much, much better.

Attendance soared higher than ever, and for good reason. A lot of people wanted to witness the most significant baseball event of the twentieth century: 1947 was the year of Jackie Robinson—the year that baseball finally lived up to its claim as the National Pastime, removing the invisible but defiantly stubborn barrier that kept Black players out of Major League Baseball since the 1880s.

Branch Rickey, flouting baseball's unwritten Jim Crow edict, signed Robinson following the 1945 season, pilfering him from the Kansas City Monarchs, for whom Jackie played following his stint in the Army. A former multisport star at UCLA, Robinson spent 1946 with the Montreal Royals, the Dodgers' farm club in the International League, where he won the batting title (.349), led the league in runs (113), and led his team to the pennant, winning the heart of the city and earning a chance to stick with the Dodgers in '47.

Rickey's plan worked, in part, because baseball's original commissioner, the xenophobic Kenesaw Mountain Landis, was dead. In his place was former U.S. senator and Kentucky governor Albert "Happy" Chandler, whose public thoughts on integrating baseball could be summarized like this: if Black men could fight for their country at war, they could play ball in America.

At twenty-eight years old, Robinson had the maturity, courage, strength, pride, and sensibility to withstand the scrutiny and abuse that came his way in the National League. Jackie responded like a superhero, leading the Dodgers to the 1947 pennant, winning the Rookie of the Year Award, lifting baseball and America to new heights. So, 1947 surely was the year of Jackie Robinson, whose story transcended the sports pages.

But it also was the year of the greatest home run race in National League history (before the steroids era), the year Johnny Mize and the Pirates' Ralph Kiner battled neck and neck as they tried to catch Babe Ruth (Johnny's cousin George). Not since the Babe and Lou Gehrig put on a home run derby in 1927 in the American League (with Ruth hitting his magic 60 and Gehrig finishing with 47) had there been anything quite like this.

Mize got the early head start when he belted 7 homers in his first ten games. Over the long season, both Mize and Kiner would set records that were still standing seventy-five years later. Mize became the only player in history to hit more than 50 home runs and strike out fewer than 50 times in a season (51 homers, 42 strikeouts). And Kiner hit 8 homers in a four-game stretch in September to break a record that he himself had set earlier in the season—he hit 7 in four games in August, tying a mark established by former Yankee second baseman Tony Lazzeri.

Mize, the first left-handed batter in National League history to surpass 50 bombs in a season, led the Giants in crushing the record for home runs by a ball club, which had been 182, set by the 1936 Yankees (Gehrig, DiMaggio, and their brutish pals). The Giants hit 221.

The season-long home run derby, said Mize, "was one of the most phenomenal and most interesting developments I have run into in my career," adding that much of the credit belonged to manager Ott for the incentives that he put in place.[3]

"Starting with the training season, he paid $2 for every homer, you got $1 for a triple, $1 for a run batted in," Mize explained, adding that there were penalties too. "If you failed to bunt a man to second, it cost you two bucks. If you left a runner on third with one or two out, it cost you $2. If you missed a sign, another deuce. If you failed to touch a base, the assessment was $1."[4]

Ancient Giants coach Hank Gowdy was the bookkeeper, and he made sure to collect or pay off every day of the season.

"Certainly, the money was not important," Mize said. "The system of fines and rewards made a very interesting competition, and you would be surprised to know how many runners went for extra bases just for the dollar that they were able to claim from Gowdy for a triple."[5]

Despite putting on the greatest power display anyone had ever seen with their bats, the slow and slugging Giants only managed to reach fourth place at 83-71. It was a marked improvement, and they did draw more than 1.6 million people, a new franchise high. The Giants had plenty of bang for their bucks—the press called them "The Window Breakers" that year.[6] But they didn't have enough pitching or speed.

The ace of the staff was twenty-six-year-old right-handed rookie Larry Jansen, who was 21-5 with a 3.16 earned run average. Only the novel brilliance of Jackie Robinson, whose league-leading 29 steals matched the Giants' entire team total, kept Jansen from winning top rookie honors.

"One came away from the 1947 season with the impression that if the Giants had only had a bona fide pitching staff, they could have been in the pennant race," wrote Noel Hynd. "Maybe even the World Series."[7]

- - -

Growing up near Los Angeles, Ralph Kiner developed his hitting prowess by playing baseball or fast-pitch softball all year in the sunny climate of Southern California. He signed a contract with the Pirates right out of high school, spent two seasons in the Minor Leagues, then entered the navy air corps in 1943. Coincidentally, he was stationed in the same place as Mize in Hawaii—Kaneohe Naval Air Station. But he hardly touched a bat because he was busy flying Martin PBM Mariners, scanning the Pacific in search of enemy submarines.[8]

Kiner tried to kill the ball every time he swung a bat. His rookie season with the Pirates in 1946, he edged out Mize for the home run championship, but he also struck out a league leading 109 times. That season would be the last time Ralph led the league in strikeouts, and the first of a record seven straight years that he led the National League in homers.

In 1947 he was a different man, thanks largely to Hank Greenberg, whose contract had been sold to the Pirates after a salary dispute with the Tigers. The great first baseman was a four-time American League home run champion (including 1946). Greenberg helped lead Detroit to four pennants, and now he'd spend his last season in the National League with a miserable seventh-place team, playing for a manager he didn't respect, future Hall of Famer Billy Herman, who he thought was too lenient.[9]

The Pirates were glad to have Greenberg. The ball club even built a bullpen in front of the leftfield fence in Forbes Field, shortening the distance for home runs, and named the area Greenberg Gardens. By the end of the 1947 season, it would be better known as Kiner's Korner.

"What saved me was Hank Greenberg," said Kiner, who lived in a hotel near Pittsburgh's Forbes Field but roomed with Greenberg on the road. "That was quite a thrill because as a kid in the 1930s I was a big Detroit fan and he was one of my idols. Nobody helped me in any respect until Hank."[10]

Inspired by Greenberg, who had nearly matched Ruth with his 58 home runs in 1938, Kiner started putting in extra hours before and after games, working on his hitting and everything else, including sliding, which he hated.

"Hank improved my hitting by telling me to move on top of the plate," Kiner said. "He gave me a lot of inside information about pitchers so I'd know what to look for. I'd say he gave me an accelerated course on how to play baseball."[11]

Greenberg helped in other ways too. When Kiner started the season in a slump, notching just 3 homers by the end of May, the Pirates considered sending him to the Minors. Hank went directly to team owner Frank McKinney to plead Kiner's case, saving the kid's job.[12]

The Pirates still stunk, of course, finishing 62-92, but it wasn't because of Kiner (or Greenberg, who belted 25 home runs in just 400 at bats). Ralph, in addition to his 51 homers, batted a career-high .313, scored 118 runs, drove in 127 more, and led the league in total bases (361), slugging average (.639), and OPS (1.055).

The home run race between Kiner and Mize captured a lot of attention, and at the time, Kiner was put off by Mize, perceiving the Big Cat as a bit of a grump. They became good friends years later, their wives getting to know each other and the two couples hanging out together during Hall of Fame weekends in Cooperstown. But in 1947 it was all serious business, and to Kiner, Johnny did not seem like an easy man to get along with.

National League pitchers would have agreed with Ralph on that last point, particularly Johnny Sain on April 24 in Boston, when Johnny broke one of his own records by blasting 3 home runs in a game for the fifth time. All three came off Sain, a twenty-one-game winner the year before, and a winner on this day, too, because Mize's troika was wasted, as the Braves whipped the Giants, 14–5, in front of 5,876 Boston fans.

"Those three blows, along with one that [Walker] Cooper hit over the left field wall in the sixth, were completely buried under the mess of misfortune," wrote the *New York Times*' John Drebinger, who called Boston's twenty-one-hit attack "plain and fancy murder."[13]

The Braves never trailed, scoring 5 runs in the first two innings. After flying out to left field off Sain in the first inning, Johnny parked a two-run homer off the right-hander in the third, scoring Clint Hartung to make it 5–2. The Braves put the game out of reach in the fourth with 3 more runs. Mize added his next 2 homers, both solo shots, in the sixth and eighth innings. The wind in Boston was indeed at his back. But Sain scattered 8 hits and pitched a complete game for his first win of the year.

As Boston's players formed a conga line around the base paths (Danny Litwhiler led the onslaught with four hits, including a homer and triple), a three-piece band played music to taunt the Giants. Whenever things were going bad for the Giants, which was often, the band jumped on top of the New York dugout and played "Heartaches."[14]

Johnny added to his string of records as the balls kept flying off his bat and out of the park. In a 5–3 win over the Cubs in Chicago on May 16, he hit a two-run homer in the fifth inning, which brought him across home plate in his sixteenth straight game, setting a National League record for consecutive games scoring a run. The previous mark was shared by Max Carey of the Pirates (1924) and former New York Giant Fred Lindstrom (1927).

- - -

New York Daily News columnist Jimmy Powers asked an unnamed pitcher about the secret of Johnny Mize's success. This is the answer he got: "Johnny has great eyes. He seldom squawks to the umpires. And he has the fastest reflexes in the league. He can check his swing on a pitch quicker and better than anyone I know. He is mighty hard to fool."[15]

In 1947 Mize didn't seem to have a weakness at the plate. And the Giants looked like a gang of brutes in box scores. A perfect example was a 19–2 mauling of their archrival Dodgers in Brooklyn before a Ladies' Day crowd of 27,938 on July 3.

"This should be up on page 3, with the rest of the axe murders," Dick Young wrote in his *Daily News* game story, describing the Giants' hitting attack as "sadistic savagery."[16]

This was an ensemble massacre, featuring 2 home runs by twenty-three-year-old Bobby Thomson, a grand slam by Walker Cooper, and homers from Mize and Sid Gordon, as New York built a 19–0 lead. The stunned Brooklyn crowd let loose its biggest cheers for Jackie Robinson, whose bunt single in the fifth inning extended his hitting streak to twenty games.

The win left the Giants a half game behind the league-leading Dodgers. Both teams, along with Boston and Chicago, had been trading the lead over the first few months of the season. But the Dodgers won the pennant with a 94-60 record, a remarkable performance for a team that lost its manager, Leo Durocher, just before the season started. Commissioner Chandler suspended Leo for his "accumulation of unpleasant incidents," including his association with gamblers.[17]

Branch Rickey brought Burt Shotton out of retirement to manage the team, and the Dodgers rallied.

Robinson, who'd been a second baseman at Montreal, was converted to first base during spring training of '47. He had never played first, though, and soon rumors spread that the Dodgers were trying to find some insurance at the position. Mize was reportedly on the Dodgers' wish list.[18]

It didn't matter, because when the season started, the first base job belonged to Robinson.

\- \- \-

Johnny started at first base for the National League in the All-Star Game, July 8 at Chicago's Wrigley Field. His solo homer in the fourth inning, deep into the right-field bleachers, was his first and only round-tripper in the midseason classic.

Mize played in ten All-Star Games (nine for the National League) in his career, and he played on just one winning squad (1940). In 1947 Johnny's homer off the Yankees' Spec Shea gave the National League a 1–0 lead. But the American League rallied to win, 2–1.

He continued to hit home runs at a steady pace in July (11 homers) and August (13). By the end of July, he was already being mentioned in the same breath as the Babe. During an 8–3 win over the Reds on July 18, Willard Marshall matched Mize's feat of hitting 3 home runs in a row (numbers 22, 23, and 24 on the season for Willard). Also, Thomson hit his 16th homer, and Mize hit one completely out of the Polo Grounds, over the right-field roof, his 27th.

The Big Cat must have been smiling as he rounded the bases, because Cousin George was in the house to see the mighty wallop. And the Babe was overjoyed. In his game story, Hy Turkin of the *Daily News* wrote, "Babe paid his 'cousin' tribute by laying down a half-eaten hot dog to applaud Mize's jaunt around the sacks."[19]

No one really knew at the time that Ruth was dying. In January he'd gone through an extensive and delicate operation to remove a tumor that was wrapped around his carotid artery. Most of the growth was removed, and he followed that with radiation treatment and needed morphine to control the constant pain. Just three weeks before he watched Mize hit the long home run, Ruth embarked on new experimental therapy that had been effective in animal tests. On June 29 Babe Ruth became one of the first patients anywhere to receive a combination of the new drug pteroyltriglutamic acid (Teropterin) and radiation for nasopharyngeal cancer.[20]

The treatment seemed to improve Babe's condition, and in a few weeks, he felt well enough to cheer on the Big Cat at the Polo Grounds and, apparently, eat a hot dog. Soon, he and wife Claire (and a nurse) were traveling around the country, visiting American Legion baseball teams on behalf of the Ford Motor Company. During a stopover in Atlanta on July 24, en route to Montgomery, Alabama, Babe was interviewed by reporters who asked him about his single-season home run record. He expected someone to break it, and he hoped it would be Mize. "If Johnny does it, the record still will be in the family," he said.[21]

Not everyone was as supportive as the Babe while Johnny was threatening the hallowed record. After Ruth's death, Mize confided to Arthur Daley of the *New York Times* that there were plenty of people rooting against him.

"I kept getting more and more nasty letters," he said. "'Who do you think you are, you bum?' they'd ask."[22]

Some of the letters were filled with profanity. "They just scorched the hide off me," he added. "No one ever wrote to wish me luck. They all called me names." He concluded, sighing, "maybe they were right, though. I guess it would be sacrilege to hit more homers than the Babe."[23]

Although he was able to shrug off the hate mail, ducking trouble on the field was another matter. Johnny had a potential scare on July 22 when Cardinals pitcher Harry Brecheen hit him in the head. Harry (nicknamed "the Cat") was delivering some nasty retribution because Johnny hit a two-run homer off him in the top of the first inning. So, when Johnny led off the fourth, Brecheen hit him above the ear, and Mize crumpled.

"Harry the Cat was kind of a brushback pitcher," said St. Louis sportswriter Bob Broeg. "He'd throw the ball at the plate and shout, 'look out,' trying to drop a hitter. Well, this was a hot and muggy night in July, and Johnny was like Ted Williams. He didn't move out of the batter's box. He'd move his head, casually, away from inside pitches without moving his feet. This time, his reflexes were a little slow, and he got clunked."[24]

Mize's teammates rushed to him. He looked up at Blattner, who recalled, "He winked and said, 'Hey, Bud, tell Jene I'm all right, but I'm gonna take the rest of the night off.'"[25]

Diagnosed with a concussion, he didn't miss a game. The Giants were off the next day. But the day after that, he homered against the Cubs. He homered against them the day after that too. By late August he was ahead of the Babe's pace. He broke his own record for National League left-handed sluggers with his 44th homer on August 28 in a win over the

Cardinals at the Polo Grounds. That put him five games ahead of Ruth's 1927 pace. But the Babe smacked 17 homers in September to reach his 60. Johnny never really got close.

Kiner, meanwhile, mounted a mighty second-half charge, hitting clusters of home runs. He made up a lot of ground on Mize in June when he bashed 14 homers. By the All-Star break, Johnny had 24 and Ralph had 20. Heading into August, Johnny had 31, and Ralph had 25. By September, it was 44 to 39, Mize.

Then Ralph passed Mize with his 8 home runs in four-game explosion at Forbes Field, which began on September 10 against Johnny and the Jints. Ralph hit 2 that day, and Johnny hit none, giving Ralph 43 to Johnny's 46. The next day, Kiner hit 4 home runs in the Pirates' doubleheader sweep of the third-place Braves, including 3 in the second game. That same day, Mize hit 1 in Cincinnati, leaving them both with 47. The next day, September 12, Kiner took the lead, hitting numbers 48 and 49 in a win over Boston while the Giants had a day off.

"Pittsburgh's Kiner really stirred things up," wrote columnist C. M. Gibbs in the *Baltimore Sun*. "So much attention had been centered on Mize and his day-by-day pace as compared to Babe Ruth's big season gait that blokes like Kiner were overlooked entirely."[26]

Even the Babe weighed in again. My home run mark will be broken one of these years, if not this season," Ruth told reporters. "Mize, Kiner and [Ted] Williams all are worthy challengers for my record. They all are mighty hitters and for power, I'd rate them in this order, Mize, Williams and Kiner."[27]

Though Williams never approached Ruth's single-season record, Kiner took another crack in 1949, when he belted 54.

Mize tied Ralph at 49 with 2 homers on September 17 against the Cubs at Wrigley—one in each game of a doubleheader. The next day Ralph hit number 50 at home against Brooklyn, and two days after that, Mize matched him with a blast against the visiting Phillies in the Polo Grounds. At that point, Mize had nine games left to play in the season, and Kiner had seven. Ralph took the lead again on September 23 at home against St. Louis. Two days later in Boston, Johnny tied Kiner with a solo blast off his old Cardinals teammate and hunting buddy Si Johnson, helping the Giants beat the Braves, 3–1.

Both men had 51 homers, their final tally for the year, but they both kept swinging with gusto. In the last game of the season, to give him more at-bats, Ott placed Johnny first in the batting order, to no avail. Pirates' manager Billy Herman offered to put Kiner first in the order too, but Ralph refused. "I didn't want to jinx myself," he said.[28]

This was the second time that two Major Leaguers hit 50-plus homers in the same season (Greenberg and Jimmie Foxx did it in 1938). Incredibly, Kiner slammed 48 after June 1.

Besides sharing the home run championship, Johnny led the league in runs (137) and runs batted in (138), both career highs for him. He also topped the league with 79 extra-base hits. He was second to Kiner in slugging average and total bases (by one), and he performed well on defense, leading National League first basemen in putouts, assists, and fielding percentage.

He batted .302, the last time he'd bat .300 in a season, something he'd done every year since 1931. He had enough bat control now that he could focus on home runs in the Polo Grounds, with its intimate right-field fence.

Plus, he had more opportunities than ever to hit the long ball because he was surrounded by power throughout the Giants lineup. Pitchers couldn't afford to pitch around him, or anybody for that matter. Imagine the dilemma of facing the heart of the Giants' 1947 batting order: Bobby Thomson, batting third, had 29 homers and 85 RBIs. Cleanup hitter was Mize. Batting fifth was Walker Cooper (35 homers, 122 RBIs), with Willard Marshall (36 homers, 107 RBIs) in the sixth spot. Marshall, Cooper, and Thomson finished 2-3-4 in home runs in the National League. Even the light-hitting, bespectacled leadoff hitter, Rigney, hit 17.

The Window Breakers enjoyed themselves in 1947, even if they didn't challenge for the pennant. Rigney, who roomed with Mize, could be an imp, and the Big Cat was his favorite foil.

When they'd go out to dinner together, Mize would have a little scotch whiskey, while Rigney drank beer. But Johnny was shy about his drinking, according to Bill, who played a trick on him during an off day in August when Ott ordered the team to work out. It was a hot and muggy day, and Mize wore a long-sleeved wool shirt and a rubber shirt over that.[29]

After the workout, Johnny took off his clothes in the clubhouse, and the sweat falling from him formed a puddle. Rigney suggested to the Big Cat that this might be some of the whiskey coming out of him from the night before. Mize tried to shut him up and went to the shower. While Mize was gone, team trainer Doc Bowman poured lighter fluid into the puddle. When Johnny returned, Rigney and Bowman let him know there was just one way to find out if this was liquor on the floor. Bowman lit a match and flames burst from the puddle. Mize ambled over to Rigney and said, "Jeez, I didn't know that stuff comes out of your pores."[30]

- - -

Here's a trivial but perhaps interesting statistic for Mize in 1947: even though his home runs outnumbered his strikeouts, 51 to 42, he had more multistrikeout games (7) than multihomer games (4). Nonetheless, he had a Most Valuable Player–caliber year. He was the chief masher on a team of mashers and led the Giants from last place the year before to a respectable fourth place finish. Kiner, too, had the numbers to back up an MVP claim, but the Pirates had finished in last.

Instead, it was Bob Elliott of the third-place Braves who the Baseball Writers Association of America (BBWAA) honored as National League MVP. He'd been very good (22 homers, 113 RBIs, .317 batting average, .517 slugging average). But Elliott probably wasn't even the most valuable player on his own team. Warren Spahn won twenty-one games, led the league in ERA and innings pitched, and, latter-day statisticians have shown, had the best WAR of anyone in the National League, by far (9.4).

Over in Brooklyn, the Giants' archrival Dodgers had won the pennant, thanks mostly to their brilliant rookie first baseman. Jackie Robinson had excelled while dealing with the kind of extreme stress that shortens a man's life. He'd received threats, survived early team dissension, and dodged most of the baseballs aimed at his body. His 125 runs were second only to Mize. He brought a swashbuckling style of play to Brooklyn— bunting (he led the league in sacrifice hits), stealing, driving pitchers crazy, always displaying Ninja instincts between the lines, leading the Dodgers into a classic World Series against the Yankees, the first of six pennants Jackie would help Brooklyn win in his ten-year career.

The Yankees won in seven games, though Brooklyn won two of the most dramatic affairs (made famous by Dodgers broadcaster Red Barber's calls on the radio): Game Four, when pinch hitter Cookie Lavagetto broke up Yankees starter Bill Bevens's no-hitter with an RBI hit in the ninth, and

Game Six, when Al Gionfriddo's running catch at the left-field bullpen of Yankee Stadium robbed Joe DiMaggio of extra bases.

The Dodgers led in Game Seven at Yankee Stadium but couldn't finish the job. Phil Rizzuto, Bobby Brown, and Tommy Henrich had the key hits, and Joe Page (who had maimed Mize a year before) dominated the Dodgers, pitching five innings of one-hit ball, as New York won, 5–2, wrapping up one of the most extraordinary seasons anyone could remember.

Thankfully, the old ball game would never be the same again.

There was Robinson, of course. And on July 5 at Chicago's Comiskey Park, a twenty-three-year-old navy veteran named Larry Doby, who'd led the Newark Eagles to the Negro World Series title in 1946, debuted for the Cleveland Indians, becoming the first Black player in the American League.

About two weeks later, Negro League stars Hank Thompson (Mize's future teammate) and Willard Brown (Mize's former barnstorming foe) played for the St. Louis Browns. In the National League, pitcher Dan Bankhead also joined Jackie Robinson in action with the Dodgers.

The game had entered a new era—in fact, it had entered *the* era, according to author Roger Kahn, for whom the years 1947 to 1957 were "equally the most important and most exciting years in the history of sport." That's from his book *The Era, 1947–1957: When the Yankees, the Giants, and the Dodgers Ruled the World.*[31]

Before he was through, Johnny Mize would play for two of those epoch-defining clubs. And in 1947, he played a leading role in defining this new age of baseball.

Summing up the year, noting the integration of the game, the home runs, the exploding attendance, the breathtaking World Series, the *Sporting News* righteously gushed in its October 29 editorial, "What a year for the future to marvel at."[32]

18

Chasing Kiner

> There was no mutual admiration society
> among home run hitters. There was no
> animosity, either. I didn't have hatred or
> compassion for Mize in the three consecutive
> years we competed for the homer titles.   —Ralph Kiner[1]

The New York chapter of the Baseball Writers Association of America (BBWAA) held its twenty-fifth annual dinner on February 1, 1948, at the swank Waldorf Astoria ballroom, and 1,500 people in formal evening wear showed up to celebrate the 1947 season. They were treated to speeches from dignitaries on the dais, including Mayor William O'Dwyer; skits lampooning the poohbahs of baseball; a parody of pugilistic Larry MacPhail; a ballet featuring sports writers in drag mocking the woeful St. Louis Browns (John Drebinger of the *New York Times* broke his foot during this bit); a tacky minstrel show (an ironic choice given the historic nature of the 1947 season); and the evening's main event, the granting of awards for the best manager in baseball and the game's best player.[2]

Yankees manager Bucky Harris—the former "boy manager" of the Washington Senators—won the Bill Slocum Memorial Award. And with a clear-eyed view from their high horse, the writers gave Johnny Mize the Sid Mercer Memorial Award as the outstanding big league player of 1947.

New York Times sportswriter Roscoe McGowen presented the award to Mize, who "tossed off a few witty remarks, indicated that the plaque was a valued addition to his collection of baseball trophies, and made quite a hit with the gathering," according to Dan Daniel, writing for the *Sporting News*.[3]

Joe Trimble of the *Daily News*, taking a jab at the members of the

BBWAA who voted Boston's Bob Elliott the National League MVP, wrote that Mize "wasn't named Most Valuable Player due to the faulty voting system employed by the national association of baseball writers. But the scribes here in New York unanimously named him top athlete."[4]

Trimble wasn't the only one who shortchanged the Braves' slugging third baseman. When the *Sporting News* released its 1947 All-Star Team in January, Elliott didn't make the cut for the first team. Nearly three hundred sports writers from across the country voted on the eight top position players, and three pitchers—the newspaper's annual dream team.[5]

Mize was the easy choice at first base (one of three times he made the magazine's annual All-Star Team, with 1942 and 1948 being the others). Johnny's Giants teammate Walker Cooper was voted in as the All-Star catcher. Joining them was an outfield of Kiner, Joe DiMaggio, and Ted Williams, along with the Cleveland Indians' keystone combo—second baseman Joe Gordon and shortstop Lou Boudreau. At third base, instead of Elliott, the writers selected Detroit's George Kell. The All-Star pitchers were Ewell Blackwell (Reds), Bob Feller (giving the Indians three players on the team), and the Dodgers' young ace Ralph Branca. The runners-up comprised a second-string team, which included Jackie Robinson as Mize's backup at first and Elliott at third base.[6]

The Giants had already given Mize an award. In October, Stoneham increased his salary, signing him to a contract reportedly calling for $51,000 in 1948 or, a grand for every homer that he hit in 1947.[7] Other reports had Johnny earning as little as $30,000 in 1948, however.[8]

- - -

On March 21 Johnny Mize hit a pair of spring training home runs in Los Angeles that caused Giants fans across the continent to breathe a sigh of relief. These were his first homers of the exhibition season, and he did it against one of the best pitching staffs in baseball.[9]

The Giants and Indians had started training in Phoenix, Arizona, in 1947. But they left Arizona to play a series of exhibition games on the coast. With Bob Feller pitching on a Sunday, more than fifteen thousand fans flooded Wrigley Field in LA, which was the home of the Angels, a Chicago Cubs farm club in the Pacific Coast League. SoCal fans turned out to watch Rapid Robert, but they got an eyeful of the Giants' "Window Breakers."

In the top of the second with the bases loaded, Johnny parked a Feller fastball over the left-field wall, 350 feet away. He followed the grand slam with a two-run homer later in the game, also to left field, off lefty knuckleballer Gene Bearden, and the Giants rolled to a 14–5 win against the team that would win the 1948 World Series.

"All in all, it was most encouraging for hopeful Giant fans," the Associated Press reported. "That pennant might yet come back from Flatbush."[10]

The pennant would indeed leave Flatbush, but it bypassed Harlem and the Polo Grounds and went to Boston, where ace pitchers Warren Spahn and Johnny Sain would win big games and inspire poetry for the Braves in 1948. Meanwhile, the Giants struggled to break even that year, breaking Horace Stoneham's patience in the process.

Stoneham wanted to fire Ott, but Mel was the most popular Giant in the history of the team. If only Horace could find someone that made the fans forget the nice guy, Mel Ott.

He found such a creature in Brooklyn, where Branch Rickey was trying to unload Leo Durocher. The Dodgers were not responding well to the return of the Lip, who'd been suspended for all of 1947. Durocher didn't get along with Jackie Robinson, and the team was struggling to reach .500. Plus, Leo had just published his autobiography *The Dodgers and Me*, and it wasn't making him a lot of new friends.

New York Herald Tribune columnist Red Smith wrote that the book was "very poor reading because it is (a) in execrable taste and (b) dishonest," adding, "Durocher makes this tale a medium for the expression of private animosities, and his version is at all times one-sided. The literary Durocher is an author without sin, casting paving blocks in all directions."[11]

What Rickey wanted most was kindly old Burt Shotton back in the Dodger dugout. Stoneham thought that he wanted Shotton, too, but Rickey the great manipulator convinced him otherwise. "I happened to know with what high esteem Horace held Durocher as a manager," Rickey said. "Only recently I had heard him say Durocher was the greatest manager in the world."[12]

Rickey and Stoneham met on July 15, and Horace told Branch that Mel Ott had "resigned," and Horace asked for permission to talk to Shotton, who was working as Brooklyn's supervisor of Minor League managers. Rickey told Stoneham he had plans to make Shotton the Dodgers' manager again, but Horace could talk to Leo. A stunned but giddy Stoneham did so immediately.[13]

Leo met the Giants in Pittsburgh the day he was hired. The team was off, but he held a thirty-five-minute rap session with his new team, telling the Giants, "This is a good club, but give us a little life out there. If we could just catch fire, we'd go places."[14]

Then he singled out a few of the players, starting with Walker Cooper, who had already missed six weeks of action earlier in the season with a knee injury. "When you see a pitcher throw what I call a lay pitch, fire it back at him, wake him up," Durocher said.[15]

Then he turned to the Big Cat. "And you, Johnny Mize, you're no Hal Chase at first, but you're a great hitter and a good ball player, and it doesn't look nice for you to lob the ball around the infield. Fire that ball, knock over [Jack] Lohrke or Rigney with your throws. A team that's running to its position and snapping that ball around looks good from the stands and plays better on the field."[16]

It was basically the first indication that Cooper and Mize were not going to be part of Leo's plans for the Giants. He wanted speed, defense, and youth, and he already had the seedlings of a future pennant winner with players like Bobby Thomson, Whitey Lockman, Wes Westrum (Cooper's backup at catcher), Don Mueller, and Jansen on the roster. Therefore, even as Johnny was piling up home runs, it was evident that he and Leo were not on the same page.

"As soon as Leo became manager, the whole picture changed," Bill Rigney said. "He wanted a club that could operate better and not just rely on home runs."[17]

Mize already had become disenchanted with Durocher, his former Cardinals teammate, the same guy who wanted to bring Johnny to the Dodgers back in 1941. He basically shared Red Smith's opinion of Leo's recently published book. He refuted Durocher's published account of the Fitzsimmons strikeout episode in 1941 (when Fitz threw several pitches at Johnny's head and stormed around the mound like his hair was on fire).

"Johnny Mize insists that the account of an incident in a Dodger-Cardinal game in '41, an account which makes him the bewildered victim of a strikeout by Freddie Fitzsimmons, is not based on fact," wrote Bill Roeder of the *New York World-Telegram*.[18]

Nonetheless, in Leo's first game as Giants manager, Johnny welcomed his new boss with a triple and a home run in leading New York to a 6–5 win over the Pirates. Kiner also homered, and the two sluggers continued to pace the circuit again, competing for another home run crown.

A month later, August 16, the Giants were hosting the Yankees at the in a Mayor's Trophy game, the annual fundraiser for the city's sandlot baseball programs. Mize belted a home run off the Polo Grounds roof in the fourth inning to give the Giants a 1–0 lead. Shortly after that, everyone in the stadium who could stand was doing so, in silent tribute to Babe Ruth, who had just died at Memorial Hospital. Overcome by the moment and the loss of his friend and cousin-in-law, Johnny was allowed to leave the game early. It was fitting for the Babe that the Yankees came back to win the game, 4–2, in eleven innings.

A few days later, Johnny served as an honorary pallbearer at Ruth's funeral. Then it was back to work.

- - -

Major League teams collectively set another attendance record in 1948, as more than 20 million fans spun the turnstiles. The Giants saw a slight drop at the Polo Grounds to 1,459,269. Among the most devoted fans at the old ballpark in upper Manhattan, game after game, were the players' wives, who always sat together in assigned seats.

Jene Mize, though, was just a little bit different than the other women, noted Sid Gordon's wife, Mary.[19] Mostly, there was real camaraderie among the wives. But sometimes, not so much.

The assigned seating came about in response to a dispute between the wives. Jene always sat in an aisle seat next to Mrs. Gordon and Willard Marshall's wife, Maria, whom Mary described as "an attractive and feisty Italian girl from New Jersey."[20]

But Jene had a habit of showing up late to the games, which irritated Maria. One time, Jene still hadn't arrived by the third inning, so Maria took her seat. When Jene finally arrived at the ballpark in the fourth inning, Maria refused to give up the seat. A fight nearly broke out between the two women, and ushers had to intervene. According to Mary Gordon, Jene never came late again.[21]

The scrappiness that Giants wives showed in the stands is the kind of spirit Leo wanted to see on the ballfield. But the Giants were a peculiar bunch in 1948. Once again, this was a team with inconsistent pitching. Jansen was still the team's ace, winning eighteen games. Hard-throwing reliever Sheldon Jones emerged as a reliable and durable thrower, winning sixteen games. The team ERA was a little better than the league average, but the pitchers gave up more home runs than any other staff in the league (the Polo Grounds, with its short fences down the foul lines, could have that effect), and the Giants didn't get a lot of breaks in close contests, losing most of their one-run games.

New York had hoped for a big season from pitcher and outfielder Clint Hartung. But the six-foot-five bonus baby who broke in with the Giants in 1947 had a disappointing year. Stoneham had given him a $35,000 signing bonus after the "Hondo Hurricane" (Clint was from Hondo, Texas) posted a 25-0 win-loss record and batted .567 while serving in the army air corps on Pearl Harbor in 1946. He was 9-7 with an ERA of 4.57 and a batting average of .309 his rookie season of '47. But in 1948, his ERA went up and his batting average went way, way down (below .200).

Plus, the Giants had little speed, and their defense was average at best, the range of their large men (like Mize), somewhat limited. They were still the most powerful hitting team in the league, leading again in homers (a sharp drop to 164) and scoring. But some of their big bats from the year before wore silencers on the barrels now. Mize, with 40 homers, and Sid Gordon, with 30, were the main power suppliers.

- - -

The Dodgers were 35-37 and in fifth place when Durocher left the team. Under Shotton's calm guidance, they flourished. By the end of August, they were in first place, one game ahead of Boston. A loss to the Cubs on September 2 dropped them to a half game behind the Braves with the fifth-place Giants coming to Brooklyn for a critical four-game series.

This was a chance at sweet revenge for Leo, whose Giants took three out of four against the Dodgers. In the series, Mize collected seven hits, including two homers, with five RBIs and four runs. One of his hits, an RBI single in the first game of the series, a 6-5 Giants triumph, came against a talented Brooklyn twenty-one-year-old rookie named Carl Erskine, who had won his first five decisions since joining the club in July. Mize and Erskine would meet again with a lot more at stake in the years to come. Mize's two homers came in a twelve-inning, 4–3 loss in the fourth game of the series, giving him thirty-four for the season, tying him with Stan Musial for second place in the home run race, three behind Kiner.

The Dodgers and Giants met again the following week in another four-game series, this time in the Polo Grounds. Mize was ineffective, with one hit, but the Giants won three of four, sending the Dodgers to fifth place while the Giants took temporary possession of fourth, with a breath of hope. New York moved into third place, just five and a half games behind the Braves with a win over the visiting Pirates. But Pittsburgh won the next two games, and the Giants dropped to fifth, where they ended the season at 78-76. Meanwhile, Brooklyn finished third (84-70).

Kiner, who led in the home run race all season, hit his 39th on September 11, then went into his longest power outage of the season, finally hitting number 40 on September 26. Mize and Musial played catch-up.

Stan the Man, who was trying to hit home runs more than he had in the past because "he saw Ralph Kiner and Johnny Mize hitting home runs and getting paid for it," according to George Vecsey, was having one of the greatest seasons of any hitter, ever.[22] He finished one homer shy of a Triple Crown, as he led the National League with a .376 average and 135 RBIs. He hit his last homer of the year, number 39, on September 30.

Mize, who finished with the lowest batting average of his career to that point (.289), hit his 39th homer on September 23, then hit number 40, catching Kiner on the last day of the season, October 3, in an 11–1 rout of the pennant-winning Braves. While Johnny tied Ralph for the league homer championship, he edged out the Pirates' outfielder in RBIs, 125 to 124. And once again he had more homers than strikeouts (40 to 37).

No animosity among sluggers, Ralph said. This was just business, and business had been very good for him and Mize over the past few seasons. It would continue to be very good for both men going forward, though their job descriptions would diverge dramatically.

King Ralph would remain the National League's home run champion for four more seasons, putting up Hall of Fame numbers before a bad back ended his playing career at age thirty-two. Then he moved on to become an Emmy Award–winning broadcaster, working the booth for fifty-two seasons with the New York Mets.

The Big Cat would be thirty-six in January 1949, and his days as an everyday home run superstar were behind him.

But his days as a World Series hero were just ahead.

19

Big Cat Earns His Pinstripes

The bases are loaded, and the score is tied, 1–1, with two out in the top of the ninth in Game Three of the 1949 World Series.

Big Ralph Branca has been mowing down Yankees like daisies all afternoon, retiring fourteen straight batters until this inning, when Yogi Berra walks with one out, Joe DiMaggio pops up to third for the second out, Bobby Brown singles, and Gene Woodling walks. The bases are full of Yankees as right-fielder Cliff Mapes, due up next, steps toward the plate.

But Casey Stengel has a thought. The Yankees manager yells at the top of his lungs to be heard over the noisy Ebbets Field crowd, to get Mapes' attention, to call him back.

In the dugout, Johnny Mize already has a bat in his hand.

The Big Cat works the count to two and one and thinks, "Be smart, John. Pick your pitch. Take a walk if you can. Force in a run." His thoughts are interrupted by the jeers coming from the Dodgers' dugout and from Ebbets Field's foghorn fans: "Hey, John, Leo's watching you!"[1]

Then Mize spies Durocher, his former manager on the Giants, dressed sharp as usual, a spectator today, sneering at him from a box seat near the Brooklyn dugout.

"Pick your pitch," Mize thinks, a flat smile on his face.

Branca wants to throw a fastball high and inside, but he gets down in the strike zone and Johnny swings and connects. The ball flies toward the screen in right field, and for a giddy second, the Big Cat wonders if will leave the ballpark.

- - -

Johnny's future as a New York Giant was in doubt the minute Leo Durocher arrived in Pittsburgh to take charge of the ball club in July 1948. Leo met the team at the Schenley Hotel, took one look at the two beefy ballplayers lounging on the porch—Mize and Walker Cooper—and growled, "All that meat and no potatoes."[2]

Immediately following Leo's first season with the Giants, the trade rumors began. The Dodgers were supposedly planning to send Roy Campanella and Eddie Miksis to the Giants for Mize and shortstop Buddy Kerr.[3] In November, the Giants were supposedly trying to deal Cooper and Mize to Chicago, but the Cubs weren't interested.[4] Meanwhile, Durocher claimed the Cubs had been interested in Cooper, and denied that he had offered that club, or any other club, Johnny Mize.[5]

On the other hand, Leo made no secret of the fact that he was interested in acquiring Chicago's slick-fielding first baseman Eddie Waitkus, according to the *Daily News*' dogged Dick Young.

"His respect for Waitkus traces to the days when Leo would sit on the bench as Dodger pilot and watch the sharp-sticking first baseman beat the Brooks virtually by himself," Young wrote in December. "The vision of foul pops dropping like hailstones between Cooper and Johnny Mize gives Durocher off-season nightmares."

Nonetheless, when the Dodgers hosted the Giants on April 19 to begin the season, Mize and Cooper were in Durocher's starting lineup. Mize only hit one home run in April. Then he hit homers in three-straight games from May 4–6. In the middle game, May 5 against the Pirates, he broke a 2–2 tie in the bottom of the tenth with a blast into the right field bleachers to give the Giants a 3–2 walk-off win. It was a dramatic way for Johnny to hit the three hundredth home run of his career, but it wasn't enough to make Leo want to keep him.

But first, Durocher got rid of Walker Cooper during a game of catcher musical chairs on June 13–14: the Giants exchanged catchers with the Reds—Cooper for Ray Mueller; sent backup catcher Mickey Livingston to the Braves for $10,000; and brought Wes Westrum back up from Jersey City.[6]

The Giants were in fifth place at the time (a position they would basically hold all year), and Mize was living down to Leo's expectations. After Johnny's batting average plummeted to .237 following a 0-for-4 day in Pittsburgh, Durocher benched him for a week. Mize was relegated to pinch hitting duty, and he occasionally pitched batting practice.

On June 27 the Giants played the Yankees in their annual Mayor's

Trophy fundraiser. Before the game, Casey Stengel, in his first year as Yankees manager, asked Mize how he was doing.

"All right, but I'm not playing much," he answered.

Casey responded, "If you were over here, you'd play."

Mize told Stengel, "Well, make the deal."[7]

Leo put Mize back in the lineup, and for a few weeks he became the Big Cat of old, batting .491 with 11 RBIs in fifteen games before the All-Star break. Mize was voted an All-Star starter by the fans. The other leading vote getter at first base, Eddie Waitkus, the guy Leo coveted, had been shot by an obsessed female fan back on June 14.

Mize had a single in two at bats, made an error, and the American League won, 11–7.

- - -

A few days before the All-Star Game, on July 8, the Giants made franchise history when Monte Irvin and Hank Thompson became the team's first Black players. Thompson, who led off and played second base against the Brooklyn Dodgers at Ebbets Field, became the first Black player to integrate two different teams—he'd been the third Black player to integrate Major League Baseball in 1947, when he joined the St. Louis Browns. Irvin broke into the lineup later in the game, pinch hitting for Clint Hartung in the eighth inning. (Monte walked.)

"I was thrilled," Irvin said in an interview years later. "It was the greatest moment in my career at the time."[8]

Irvin and Thompson, playing for the Jersey City Giants the first half of the season, tore up the International League. Thompson was batting .296 with a .447 on-base average and 14 homers, and Irvin was hitting .373 with a .519 on-base average and 14 stolen bases when they were called up to the big club. Both men were more than ready and capable to play in the National League.

Though they were only teammates a short time, Irvin would say years later that the good-natured Big Cat was one of the Giant regulars who welcomed the new guys. "I played with Mize in 1949, and I would get with him and some of the other veterans," said Irvin, who respected Mize as a great player. "They would tell the younger players how to do certain things, give us little pointers, so we paid attention to that and learned fast."[9]

Not that they had a lot to learn. Both Irvin and Thompson were experienced big league ballplayers by then. Thompson had batted .315 in his one full season for the Kansas City Monarchs before going to war, then breaking in with the Browns. And Irvin had been one of the greatest stars to play in the Negro Leagues, a two-time batting champion before serving in the army during World War II. Monte, who would be elected to the Baseball Hall of Fame in 1973, was already thirty when he debuted with the Giants.

Mize only had about six weeks to get to know his new teammates. The Dodgers had shown interest in Johnny before the season started.[10] Later, the Detroit Tigers were in line to grab him.[11] When all of that blew over, Johnny figured he'd stay a Giant in 1949. But following the All-Star Game, he went into a tailspin, batting .211 over thirty-five games. On August 20, batting against Philadelphia Phillies reliever Jim Konstanty, Johnny popped up to shortstop in the top of the eighth. That was his last swing as a Giant. On August 22 the Giants sold the Big Cat to the Yankees.

The deal wasn't much of a surprise. One of the first things Durocher said after becoming Giants manager was, "We may sell Mize." But, according to a story by United Press International, "What did cause some raised eyebrows among baseball men is the fact that the Giants could get waivers on Mize from the rest of the National League clubs."[12]

Mize seemed more surprised than anyone. "Certainly came as a shock to me," he said, puffing on a cigar while waiting on a train to Detroit, where he was to join his new ball club. He didn't want to leave the Giants, but business was business, and he wasn't the kind to pine. "Hell, I've never been sentimental over anything," he said. "As far as I'm concerned, I'm making a clean start with the Yankees."[13]

They paid the Giants $40,000. The straight-cash deal came together after a short conference between Stoneham and Yankees co-owners Dan Topping and Del Webb.[14]

Casey Stengel did not sound thrilled about the deal, claiming he was as surprised as anyone and telling the press, "I don't know what I'm going to do with him."[15]

He was almost certainly playing it cute. Before the deal was made, Casey checked in on Mize through Chicago Cubs manager Frank Frisch. He told the Fordham Flash that he could get Mize on waivers and wondered if the Big Cat would be any help. Frisch said, "Grab him. Pay whatever you have to pay over the waiver price. He'll help you—big."[16]

While Johnny was surprised by the deal, Jene saw it coming. About a month earlier, Horace Stoneham told Mize, "Just so long as I have anything to do with this ball club, you will remain with it."[17]

Jene Mize wasn't buying it. Johnny said, "Mrs. Mize heard this and whispered, 'John, better start packing.' I thought she was joking."[18]

When the shock wore off—quickly—Johnny realized his great fortune and the potential ahead. "I face a tremendous opportunity with a club having a good chance for the flag," he said. "No ball player ever got sore because he was sent to the Yankees. I am not an exception."[19]

- - -

It didn't take Casey very long to figure out what to do with Mize. Joe DiMaggio was nursing a sore shoulder on the bench, so Johnny batted cleanup in his first game as a Yankee, in Detroit on August 24. He singled in four trips to the plate, but the Tigers routed the Yanks, 13–2, dropping New York's lead over the Red Sox to two games.

In his second game as a Yankee, August 25 in Cleveland, Johnny blasted the first pitch he saw from Bob Feller over the right-field fence in Municipal Stadium with Tommy Henrich aboard, giving New York a 2–0 lead en route to a 6–3 win.

Three days after the homer, Mize hustled his way onto the injured list. The seemingly unbeatable Yankees ran into double disaster. They lost Henrich in the first game of a doubleheader against the White Sox in Chicago when he ran into the Comiskey Park outfield wall chasing a fly ball and fractured two ribs. Mize doubled and scored in the winning rally as the Yankees triumphed, 8–7.

But he didn't last long in the second game (another Yankees win). In the bottom of the first inning, Chicago outfielder Dave Philley bunted toward first base. Mize fielded it cleanly, and dove back to the bag, tagging it ahead of the speedy Philley, but landing heavily on his right shoulder—the same shoulder he injured in 1941, in the same way. It was separated. Johnny spent the next three weeks as a spectator while the Yankees battled the Red Sox down to the final day of the season. He returned to pinch-hitting duty by late September but wasn't a factor until the World Series.

And once again, Mize inspired something akin to poetry (this time, he had a small but important role in John Vergara's parody of "Casey at the Bat" in the Daily News):

And then to add some power the Yanks bought Johnny Mize,
They'd put Henrich back in right; the move indeed seemed wise,
But soon thereafter in Chicago, Tommy hurt his back,
And they also lost Big John as he went diving for the sack.[20]

- - -

As luck would have it, the Yankees and Red Sox played each other five times over the last nine days of the season. Three straight wins by Boston (September 24–25) put the Red Sox all alone in first place for the first time that season. They still held a one-game lead as they prepared to play the last two games of the season in New York, Saturday and Sunday, October 1–2.

Nearly seventy thousand fans streamed into Yankee Stadium for the first game. And an air of doom descended on the ballpark as Boston took a 4–0 lead. Yankees starter Allie Reynolds was wild and left the game in the top of the third, giving way to reliever Joe Page, who was also wild at first. He walked in two of the runners he inherited, then settled down and held the powerful Red Sox to one hit the rest of the game. Johnny Lindell smashed a home run in the bottom of the eighth to furnish New York's 5–4 must-win, leaving the teams deadlocked at 96-57 with Sunday's game now a winner-take-all affair.

A slightly smaller crowd watched as the Yankees jumped out to a 5–0 lead, as a recovering Henrich homered, and Jerry Coleman hit a three-run double. The Yankees held off a Boston comeback in the top of the ninth to win, 5–3, clinching the pennant.

A subway World Series was in the offing because the Dodgers had won a pennant race in the National League that was just as intense as the Yankees–Red Sox clash. On the last day of the season, St. Louis trailed Brooklyn by a game after losing four in a row. The Cardinals beat the Cubs in Chicago, 13–5, on October 2, but the Dodgers kept their hold on first with a ten-inning, 9–7 win over the Phillies.

The Dodgers and Yankees, both 97-57, began their third World Series clash on October 5, a Wednesday afternoon, in Yankee Stadium. Johnny still couldn't throw, so he was relegated to pinch-hitting duty. Henrich would start at first base and Cliff Mapes had Tommy's usual spot in right field.

Allie Reynolds started Game One against the Dodgers big rookie right-hander, twenty-three-year-old Don Newcombe. He'd broken into big league ball as an eighteen-year-old with the Newark Eagles of the Negro National League, then posted a 50-14 record in the Dodgers' Minor League system over three seasons. In 1949 he led Brooklyn with seventeen wins and topped the National League with five shutouts.

Before a crowd of 66,224, Newcombe and Reynolds threw vapors. Allie pitched a two-hitter, striking out nine. Newcombe struck out eleven, surrendering five hits. It was the fifth hit that killed him. In the bottom of the ninth, "Old Reliable" Henrich led off for the Yankees and hit a Newcombe curveball into the lower right-field stands to win the game for New York, 1–0.

Johnny experienced the first World Series action of his career in the second game. It was another classic pitcher's duel, this time won by the Dodgers' cagey Preacher Roe, 1–0, who just barely outpitched Vic Raschi. The Dodgers scored in the second after Jackie Robinson doubled and scored on Gil Hodges's single. In the bottom of the eighth, Johnny batted for the weak-hitting catcher Charlie Silvera, and he gave the Yankees hope with a single to right field. Johnny was removed for a pinch runner, but New York couldn't push the run across. The Series was tied, one game each.

But Mize's hit served notice to the Dodgers. They had a chance to get him before the season started and considered making a move during spring training. "All of us had heard the rumors that the Giants were willing to sell Big Jawn," Al Campanis told George Kirchner of the *Lancaster (PA) New Era*, who was covering the World Series.

Campanis, who was manager of the Dodgers' Minor League club in Lancaster, told a story about a meeting that took place during spring training, when Branch Rickey called everyone together—players, coaches, everyone. Rickey said, "Boys, we have a chance to pick up a hard-hitting first baseman. A man, whom many people believe, could well mean the difference between us winning or losing the pennant." He closed with, "If you fellows think we need him to win, we'll get him. I'm leaving it entirely up to you."[21]

According to Campanis, no names were mentioned, but everyone in the room knew Rickey was talking about Mize. In a show of confidence in their young first baseman, Gil Hodges, the team voted unanimously to pass on the deal.

"And that's how the Dodgers passed up the chance to get Mize," wrote Kirchner, who asserted that Brooklyn would "continue to regard him with some fear in this series and the chances are that they'll be hoping that his service to the Yanks is limited."[22]

The Big Cat's service was limited but spelled disaster for Brooklyn. His big moment came in Game Three on Friday against Ralph Branca, with the score tied and the bases loaded in the top of the ninth. "Up went John Mize, who has devoted a long and blameless life to the abuse of National League pitchers," wrote *New York Herald Tribune* columnist Red Smith. "John is a guy they didn't want in Brooklyn. The Dodgers and six other clubs waived him out of the National League this summer and let the Giants sell him across the Harlem River."[23]

Then Johnny delivered what he later called "big thrill number one" of his career.[24] As he stood there and took two balls and a strike from Branca, the Dodgers kept up a barrage of "Hey, John, Leo's watching you." Later, Mize said, "I could hear them. Especially that Gene Hermanski. He's got a foghorn in his throat."[25] It never bothered him, though. He swung at Branca's fourth pitch and hit it well. But it stayed in the ballpark, banging off the screen above the Esquire Boot Polish sign in right field—a very long single, driving in Yogi Berra and Bobby Brown to give the Yanks a 3–1 lead and driving Branca from the game.

"Mize made no attempt to break down a fence," wrote Grantland Rice. "He swung smoothly and easily, and the ball left his big bat like a rifle bullet."[26]

The damage was done. As Mize left the game to be replaced by pinch runner Hank Bauer, he received an ovation from the American League rooters on hand in the enemy ballpark "and doubtless, too, drew many a hearty cheer from National Leaguers with whom the good-natured Georgian had been an idol throughout his career," wrote the *Times'* John Drebinger. "Just what Durocher's thoughts may have been as he watched it all from a box seat alongside the Brooklyn dugout may be conjectured."[27]

With Gene Woodling still on third, Jerry Coleman followed with a single to center to make it 4–1, and the Yankees withstood solo homers by Luis Olmo and Roy Campanella off reliever Joe Page in the bottom of the ninth for the 4–3 win. The rain, which held up all afternoon, began to fall on Brooklyn, sending the 32,788 fans scattering for cover.

"Tickled? I'll say I'm tickled," Mize said later in the jubilant visitors' clubhouse at Ebbets Field, his big face red with joy. "Say, it's one of the happiest moments of my life."[28]

And with that, Johnny clocked out for the season. Yes, he had slipped to nineteen home runs during the regular season and yes, his batting average had been a career-low .263. But the thinking man's hitter had entered a new phase of his career. He was a role player on a championship team. He'd batted 1.000 in his first World Series and was done for the year. And so were the Dodgers. Mize watched the rest of the Series from a vantage point he was familiar with, the visiting dugout in Ebbets Field.

The Yankees won Saturday's Game Four on the strength of Bobby Brown, the young doctor smashing a double and a triple to drive in three runs. Mapes and Yankees lefty starting pitcher Ed Lopat also hit RBI triples—all these triples coming against the hard-luck Newcombe.

The fifth and deciding game was never very close. Dr. Brown, who batted .500 for the Series, had 3 hits, including another triple and 2 RBIs. Coleman had 2 hits and 3 RBIs, and Woodling had 3 hits. Ailing Joe DiMaggio blasted a fourth-inning homer, and the Yankees won, 10–6, winning their twelfth World Series title and beginning a new championship era under old Casey Stengel.

Stengel had managed the team like an artist in 1949, mixing and matching lineups and players the way a painter mixes colors, winning it all despite seventy-one injuries to various Yankees. Casey earned Manager of the Year honors in his first year as the Yankees boss, "which may have been his best managing job," wrote Marty Appel in *Pinstripe Empire: The New York Yankees from before the Babe to after the Boss*. "There could be no assumption that anyone else could have managed this team of walking wounded."

Bringing Mize aboard late in the season also marked the beginning of a new Yankee tradition of the nascent Stengel era. "Johnny's acquisition through the waiver route marked the first in a run of late-season Yankee pickups that would help fill a need and invariably seemed to produce strong results," Appel wrote. "Mize was the poster boy for the late-season pickup."[29]

Following the Mize precedent, in years to come, the Yankees would pick up veterans like Johnny Hopp, Enos Slaughter, Ewell Blackwell, and Johnny Sain, among others, to help them in their annual pennant push.

After the Series, Stengel explained his initial apparent doubt regarding the Mize acquisition: "Not one deal was made or even contemplated all season without me in on it. I knew about the Mize negotiations and was all for getting him. But I didn't know just when the deal was going to be completed."[30]

Nonetheless, when asked about his top thrill in his first season as Yanks manager, Casey was unequivocal: It was Mize's single against Branca in Game Three.

That blow represented a new era for the Big Cat, years when his legs and shoulder limited his playing time, minimizing his plate appearances but magnifying the impact of his hits. Mize learned that at his advanced age (thirty-six), he could experience new rites of passage.

"I've hit many a homer and every one has given me a thrill, but no hit that I ever got meant more to me than that single," Johnny said several months after Game Three. "It was like I was then officially a member of the organization."[31]

20

Minor Setback, Major Recovery

Oh Johnny Mize, oh Johnny Mize
It took them long to realize!
Your arm is gone; your legs likewise,
But not your eyes, Mize, not your eyes!   —Dan Parker[1]

The right shoulder was still a problem. Even though Johnny had been given a clean bill of health in January 1950 from the doctors at Johns Hopkins Hospital, the damn thing still bothered him during spring training.

He made a special trip from De Leon Springs to Baltimore to be examined by orthopedic surgeon and sports medicine pioneer Dr. George Bennett at Hopkins. And he was told to exercise his arm as much as he wanted—specifically, the doctor suggested Johnny do some rowing and play a lot of golf. If anything, Bennett was more concerned with Big Jawn's weight than his shoulder.[2] Back in Florida, Johnny followed doctor's orders. He did a lot of fishing, rowing out to his favorite honey hole. And he played plenty of golf.

In a letter to Yankees GM George Weiss (after signing his contract for 1950, reportedly for $30,000), Mize wrote, "I'm playing golf just about every day and I carry a baseball along. In between golf shots, I throw the baseball and my arm feels fine. P.S. Don't forget to order me some new bats. Same as usual—36 inches, 36 ounces."[3]

By this point in his career, the Big Cat, who used to swing forty-ounce bats, was now using thirty-six-ounce models almost exclusively, and occasionally thirty-four-ouncers, which he lent out with spectacular results in 1950.

As the world champion Yankees assembled in St. Petersburg for spring training, Mize's shoulder would be sore one day, fine the next morning, then sore again. He asked for extra time off, and Stengel was happy to comply.[4] He wanted a healthy Mize.

It would be another close pennant race for the Yankees in 1950, followed by another quick run through another National League challenger for another World Series title. As brilliant new heroes broke into the pinstripe fold, Mize would be temporarily shipped out to the Yankees' farm team in Kansas City. For the Big Cat, it was a season of pain, demotion, recovery, and breathtaking rebirth.

- - -

Johnny had plenty of time to think on the road to Kansas City. He drove due west, 1,200 miles, chasing the sun and the glimmer of hope that remained in his fading baseball career.

In May the Yankees had to cut five men to bring their roster down to twenty-five players, and Mize was one of the five, along with Johnny Lindell (picked up on waivers by the Cardinals), Clarence "Cuddles" Marshall, Duane Pillette, and a scrappy rookie infielder from Oakland named Billy Martin. Mize, Martin, and Pillette (a pitcher) were assigned to the Kansas City Blues, the Yankees' farm club in the Class Triple-A American Association.[5]

As a veteran of ten-plus seasons in the Majors, Mize could have vetoed the reassignment and asked for his unconditional release. If the Yankees granted it, he could become a free agent and deal with any other club.[6]

But the Yankees weren't any other club. Mize figured his best chance to get back into a World Series was to deal with this temporary reassignment philosophically.

"I guess it is the only thing Casey could do since I was not in playing form," Johnny reasoned. He'd seen limited playing time, and mostly as a pinch hitter. In Kansas City he'd play every day and work his shoulder back into shape. "I believe that someday you will see me back in big company again. Meanwhile, I'll give the Blues all I got."[7]

Mize arrived in Kansas City in time to suit up against the visiting Indianapolis Indians. His old pal Don Gutteridge was an Indians player-coach, and he offered some words of support for his old friend and teammate.

"To me Mize has been the perfect hitter," Don said while watching Johnny take batting practice before the game on Friday night, May 19. "He's the fellow who can serve as a model for all young ball players. There are other great hitters but not as many of them would be suggested as models. Stan Musial, for example. Stan has his own peculiar style. It fits him but wouldn't likely fit anyone else. Johnny has rhythm in his swing, style in his stance."[8]

But Johnny hadn't been able to throw well since the injury in August '49. On the way to Kansas City, he stopped in St. Louis, where he listened to an osteopath tell him there was nothing seriously wrong with the shoulder.[9] And yet it hurt and tightened up when he threw a baseball. He needed someone who understood how to treat the aches and pains of an athlete. It turned out that he was in the right place to find that person.

Dr. Forrest Clare "Phog" Allen is remembered as the "Father of Basketball Coaching," the protégé of Dr. James Naismith, who invented basketball. Allen, part of the inaugural class of inductees in the Naismith Memorial Basketball Hall of Fame, was the longtime coach at the University of Kansas, a national basketball powerhouse about forty miles from Kansas City. Allen was also an osteopathic physician. Parke Carroll, general manager of the Blues, suggested that Mize see the coach-physician, who was convinced that he could fix the Big Cat's ailing shoulder.[10]

"I've seen many such injuries," Dr. Allen said. "Actually this injury is the best of its kind and the easiest to cure. I have suggested a course of treatment for Mize which he can take in Kansas City. It will include diathermy."[11]

Diathermy uses high-frequency electric currents to generate heat in body tissues and had been effective in treating muscle and joint conditions, improving mobility, and relieving pain in patients. Allen explained that while Mize's pain was in the front of the shoulder, the trouble came from the back. "However, I have found the conditions favorable for a remedy," Allen said. "This is an injury which should respond to treatment."[12]

After several weeks of Allen's prescribed regime, Mize's shoulder did feel better, and he was playing regularly for the Blues, throwing naturally, batting around .300, and hitting home runs. He belted his first as a Blue on May 28 in the first game of a Sunday doubleheader, driving in four runs (he also hit a double), but KC lost to the visiting Columbus Red Birds. Billy Martin had four hits in the two games, as the Blues rallied to win the second game.[13]

- - -

He'd heard it all before—the jeers, the taunting. Hell, hadn't he played for the Giants in Brooklyn, for God's sake? Those people knew how to razz a visiting player. Johnny can take a little jeering in the bush leagues.

"Try this park on for size, Johnny," the guy bellows from behind the Kansas City dugout. "This ain't no Polo Grounds. They catch pop flies in right field here!"[14]

Mize settles into the batter's box, looking at the distant outfield fence in Lexington Park, home of the St. Paul Saints.

"You gotta hit 'em long for home runs now," the guy shouts, then nearly chokes on the words as the Big Cat swings and connects, the loud crack of inevitability, and the ball soars high over the right-field fence, 365 feet away.

As Johnny trudges around the bases, he can hear the guy's loud voice crank up again. But now he's cheering, he's yelling encouragement. As the Big Cat walks slowly to the dugout, the fan with the big mouth reaches out from the stands and stuffs a $5 bill into his hand.[15]

- - -

It had been a productive month in Kansas City. Mize batted .298 and hit 5 home runs. More important, he was throwing well enough to be recalled to the Yankees, along with Billy Martin. Tommy Henrich, in his last season as a player, was banged up, and Stengel needed a first baseman. Mize was it.

But while Johnny had been away, he'd left behind a gift for Phil Rizzuto—one of his bats, a talisman for the diminutive Rizzuto. In Mize's telling of the story, Phil was nursing a sore hand that hurt most when batting. Johnny's bats were heavier than Rizzuto's, and Mize used heavier bats in cold weather partly because, he said, it prevented the sting that comes with hitting at that time of year. Rizzuto tried his bat in late 1949, and the results were immediate. He got a couple of hits his next game. Whenever he slipped into a hitting slump, he'd switch to one of Mize's bats.[16]

In 1950 Rizzuto had his best year, with career highs in runs (125), hits (200), doubles (36), walks (92), and batting average (.324). He earned the American League Most Valuable Player Award, helping the Yankees win a pennant race against the Tigers, Indians, and Red Sox. In *How to Hit*, Mize proudly noted, "He had switched to my bat almost exclusively. This came about in Boston where we opened the 1950 season. Phil had gone hitless the first two days and was fit to be tied. The following day he asked to try my bat again and with a great deal of satisfaction, I watched Phil spray hits to all fields."[17]

When Mize returned to the Yankees in June, it was almost a repeat of the first time he broke in with the Bombers, back in August '49. In his second game back, June 22, 1950, the Yankees were in Cleveland facing Bob Feller. And once again, Johnny took Feller deep for a home run. But this time the Indians won, 6–2, gaining some ground on the Yankees, who were in second place chasing the Tigers. Johnny added doubles on consecutive days in Detroit, but the Tigers won those games.

Johnny got very hot in July, including one four-game stretch (July 18–21) when he had 13 hits in 15 at bats, including 5 homers—two of which, along with 5 RBIs, were in a 14–5 win over the Tigers. Casey's boys became ruthless for a few weeks beginning in August, winning sixteen of eighteen games, including two out of three from Detroit in Yankee Stadium and a four-game sweep of Cleveland to end August, during which Johnny played the role of bully with 7 hits and 5 RBIs, including 3 home runs in three consecutive games (including another off Feller, who had become his whipping boy). By the end of that series, the Yankees were in first.

The Tigers kept battling back, trading the lead with the Yankees, who visited Detroit for a three-game series, September 14–16. The Yankees won two of the games, and when they bolted the Motor City, they were in first place for good.

But the most memorable game of that series is the one New York lost, 9–7, on September 15, a Friday afternoon. The 23,900 fans in Briggs Stadium attendance got a double bonus—a victory for their team in a tight pennant race and a historic performance from Johnny Mize. For the sixth time and final time in his career, the Big Cat hit three home runs in a game.

"Big Jawn Mize all but carried the Yankees over for a touchdown single-handed as the powerful Georgian exploded three tremendous home runs in Briggs Stadium to drive in six runs," John Drebinger of the *New York Times* wrote. "But the effort proved all for the naught."[18]

Johnny broke his own records for most times hitting three homers in a game, most times doing it in a losing effort, and most times hitting three in a row (this was the fourth time). He became the first player to hit three homers in a game in each league. As he sat in the visitor's clubhouse after the game, a cigar in his mouth, he told reporters, "You know, this was the sixth time that I hit three home runs in a game, and we won only one of them. I'm going to have to stop hitting three homers in a game."[19]

He hit all 3 homers off twenty-two-year-old right-hander Art Houtteman, a nineteen-game winner in 1950. He added 2 more four-baggers before the season ended, giving him 25 for the year (9 of the clutch variety against the Yanks' chief rival, the Tigers), third on the Yankees to Joe DiMaggio (32) and Yogi Berra (28). But Mize hit his homers in just 274 at bats. His 76 base hits accounted for 72 RBIs. Johnny was especially prolific in the second half of the season: in sixty-two games he hit 23 homers and drove in 59 runs. Also, while DiMaggio was the league leader in slugging average, Mize had a higher figure (.595) but not enough at bats to qualify in that department.

It was the second time within a week that a Yankee hit three home runs in a game—DiMaggio did it against the Senators on September 10 at Griffith Stadium.

The Yankees, which won the pennant with a 98-56 record, were trailed in the end by Detroit (95-59), Boston (94-60), and Cleveland (92-62). Mize was part of an efficient, hive-minded ensemble. DiMaggio added 114 runs, 122 RBIs, and a .301 batting average, and Berra had 116 runs, 124 RBIs, and a .322 average. Rizzuto, of course, was the team sparkplug. Besides the Scooter's career year at the plate with Mize's bat, he prevented a lot of runs with his great play at shortstop.

Raschi anchored the pitching staff with a 21-8 record. Ed Lopat (18-8, 3.47 ERA), Allie Reynolds (16-12, 3.74), and Tommy Byrne (15-9, 4.74) were the regular starters. The team also picked up some important pennant insurance by acquiring pitchers Tom Ferrick and Joe Ostrowski from the St. Louis Browns.

The best acquisition of the year might have been the waiver deal that brought first baseman Johnny Hopp over from Pittsburgh. He was hitting .340 at the time and was inexplicably unclaimed by all the National League teams. So, the Yankees picked him up on September 5. "He was, like Mize the year before, a perfect pennant-stretch pickup for New York," Marty Appel wrote in *Pinstripe Empire*.[20]

But the best surprise of the season for the Yankees was the emergence of rookie Whitey Ford into the regular starting pitching rotation in the second half of the season. Still known as Ed Ford when he broke in, he'd been Mize's teammate on the Kansas City Blues and was called up shortly after Mize and Martin. Ford won his first nine decisions and finished with a 9-1 record and team-best 2.81 ERA.

The rookie left-hander also pitched the most important game of the season for the Yankees, Game Four of the World Series against the Philadelphia Phillies. It was one of the closest sweeps in World Series history, with the Yankees winning each of the first three games by one run. Raschi outdueled National League MVP Jim Konstanty, 1–0, in the first game in Philadelphia's Shibe Park. Allie Reynolds earned the decision over Robin Roberts, as Joe DiMaggio hit a tenth-inning home run to lift the Yankees, 2–1, in Game Two. The Yankees won Game Three at home, 3–2, on Jerry Coleman's walk-off base hit with two out in the bottom of the ninth.

In Game Four, October 7, a Yankee Stadium crowd of 68,098 watched young Ford pitch with veteran poise, with an assist from Reynolds and some fine defense from Mize. Yankee heroes Berra, Brown, and DiMaggio provided the batting power in the 5–2 Series clincher. The Yankees were leading 4–0 when the Phillies threatened in the top of the fourth. With Del Ennis on third and Granny Hamner on first and one out, Andy Seminick shot a bouncing ball to Mize at first, a few steps off the bag. Johnny scooped it up cleanly and stepped on the bag, then fired the ball home to Berra, who tagged Ennis out, ending the inning.

Ford had a 5–0 lead through eight innings but got into trouble in the ninth when Gene Woodling dropped a fly ball and two runs scored. With two Phillies on base and the tying run at the plate, Casey called for Allie Reynolds, the "Chief," who struck out pinch hitter Stan Lopata, throwing heat in the afternoon shadows to give the Yankees their second straight World Series title.

"We could not have won without Johnny Mize," Casey Stengel said before the World Series.[21] It was among the many bouquets he tossed out after the Yankees had won the pennant. But it didn't mean job security.

A few days after the Yankees wrapped up the Series, Mize was barnstorming through New England with a team of big leaguers led by Washington Senators pitcher Mickey Harris. Gene Woodling, Warren Spahn, and Luke Appling were some of the other team players. During a rainout in Portland, Maine, Johnny spoke with Rollie Wirths, a sportswriter with the *Portland Press Herald*, responding to reports coming out of New York that his future with the Yankees was undecided.

"I'll play baseball for someone next year but I don't know yet who it will be," he said. "If [the Yankees] don't want me, I want to find out what you have to do to stay with the club."[22]

He didn't have to wait long to find out.

21

Sitting in Casey's Lap

The legends of baseball gather in an Atlanta–Fulton County Stadium clubhouse following a 3–3 tie in an old-timer's game between geriatric squads called the Lumber and the Leather. It is late August 1974. The room stinks of liniment, sweat, and cigarette smoke. Mickey Mantle is riffing on pitchers who throw harder in these games than they did during their careers. He teases his old Yankees pal Bob Turley about his control and how its better now than when Bullet Bob was playing. The subject turns to hitting. Stan Musial points across the room and says, "See old John Mize over there? There was a fellow who could hit. He had a great eye, a great stroke and stance. He never tried to kill the ball." Mantle, the king of trying to kill the ball, nods and says, "He was a long ball hitter, but you could hardly ever strike him out. He was the best— really something."[1]

- - -

After wondering aloud to the press about his future in pinstripes following the 1950 World Series, Johnny became one of the first Yankees to sign a contract for 1951, agreeing to a salary of $26,500.

But the big news in 1951 as spring training began taking shape was about departures and arrivals. On March 2 Joe DiMaggio announced that he was retiring following the season. Meanwhile, Yankees training camp was buzzing with the smashing arrival of the Commerce Comet, nineteen-year-old Mickey Mantle. The blonde bomber, who batted a league-leading .383 as an eighteen-year-old shortstop with the Joplin Miners of the Class C Western Association in 1950, was now sending baseballs into orbit above the Arizona desert.

The Yankees, which moved their spring training headquarters to Phoenix, also planned about a dozen exhibition games in California, where Mantle, the heir apparent to Joe DiMaggio, "excited keen interest wherever we went," according to Dan Daniel in the *Sporting News*. "At Wrigley

Field in Los Angeles on March 17, Mantle hit one of the longest homers yet achieved in that park." The ball shot like a laser to the center field wall, 430 feet away, traveling so fast the men in the press box and the befuddled center fielder lost sight of it.[2]

"The tour of California became a showcase of Yankee power with Mantle, DiMaggio, Mize, Hank Bauer, and Gene Woodling all hitting excellently," Peter Golenbock wrote. "But it was Mantle who drew the most attention."[3]

Mickey batted .402 with 9 home runs and 31 RBIs during the exhibition season. After some coaching from retired outfielder Tommy Henrich, Mantle opened the regular season as the starting right fielder, alongside DiMaggio in center.

Mize, after playing well in limited action during spring training, started at first on opening day, with Joe Collins backing him up as a defensive replacement. But this was the season that Mize's hitting numbers fell way off—he had 10 home runs and 49 RBIs in 113 games.

He didn't hit his first home run of the season until June 17, in a win over the visiting Tigers. Four days later he hit two more home runs in a loss to the league-leading White Sox.

Mize admitted to feeling every minute of his thirty-eight years, and his use of lighter bats reflected that. "With the Cardinals before the war, I used to hit four or five homers into the left field bleachers at Sportsman's Park," he told Dick Young. "I've been unable to hit a ball that far [354 feet] in the last couple of years with the Yanks."[4]

The Yankees started strong in 1951, winning twenty-six of their first thirty-five games. But the White Sox charged into the lead, at one point winning fourteen-straight games, eleven of them on the road, including games in Boston, New York, and Cleveland. Those four clubs stayed within a few fraction points of each other most of the season.

After a blazing start, Mantle cooled off. By mid-July another rookie in New York was grabbing most of the headlines. Willie Mays had arrived in May to patrol the Polo Grounds' spacious center field. Mickey was sent to Kansas City for a few weeks. Meanwhile, twenty-three-year-old infielder Gil McDougald was having a Rookie of the Year season for the Yankees, a perfect player in Stengel's platoon system. Gil played second and third, batted anywhere in the lineup (leadoff, second, sixth—all over), had good power (14 homers), hit for average (.306) with a strange batting stance, and scored runs.

McDougald was the only regular who batted .300, and only Berra hit more than 20 homers (27, with a team-leading 88 RBIS). Rizzuto's batting average dropped fifty points, but he was a great setup man at the plate, leading the league in sacrifice bunts. And Mantle was an improved player down the stretch, contributing to a strong outfield corps that included Hank Bauer, Gene Woodling, Jackie Jensen, and the fading DiMaggio.

The pitching staff was hampered by the loss of Whitey Ford to military service for two years. But Vic Raschi and Ed Lopat each won twenty-one games. Allie Reynolds won seventeen, including two no-hitters (July 12 against Cleveland and September 28 against Boston). And a twenty-one-year-old rookie named Tom Morgan emerged as a fine number-four starter, posting a 9-3 record. The bullpen was anchored by a couple of lefties, Joe Ostrowski and Bob Kuzava, as Stengel used nineteen different pitchers during the season.

Nary a maestro in the bunch that year—just a bunch of players performing with orchestral precision, and Stengel conducting it all. Mize contributed to Casey's growing reputation as a genius, with dramatic hits on consecutive days against the Cleveland Indians, who were in a three-way tie for first with the Yankees and Red Sox when they came to Yankee Stadium for a three-game series, July 24–26. The first game was tied with two out in the bottom of the eighth when Johnny lined a ball into the right-field stands off Early Wynn, and the Yankees won, leaving them in a tie for first with the Red Sox.

The next day, Wednesday, Johnny won the game for the Yankees with a two-out, two-run double in the bottom of the ninth. Cleveland's Mike Garcia and New York's Ed Lopat seemed unbeatable. The Indians led 1–0, but McDougald and Berra singled, and Mize sliced a line drive to left field for the come-from-behind, walk-off win, giving the Yankees solo possession of first place.

A small but energized Yankee Stadium crowd of 26,833 was still buzzing a half hour after the Big Cat's double. It was Johnny responding to the heat of the moment, or the heat of the summer.

"I'm your little hot weather baby," he told columnist Jimmy Powers. "The hotter it gets, the better I like it. I was born in Demorest, Georgia. I live in De Leon Springs, Florida. I can really time that ball when I'm cooked."[5]

By August the Big Cat was almost overcooked. His batting average plummeted to .259 by season's end. But he contributed the occasional timely hit, and the Yankees outlasted the Indians, which had a one-game lead on New York when they came to Yankee Stadium, September 16–17. This was the teams' last meeting of the season. The Yankees won Sunday's game, 5–1, as Reynolds outpitched Feller in front of 68,760 fans. Ed Lopat pitched a three-hitter to win Monday's game, 2–1, and the Yanks took over first place. The Yankees clinched the pennant on September 28, the day Reynolds threw his second no-hitter. That was the first game of a doubleheader against the Red Sox, an 8–0 win. The second game, won by Raschi, nailed down the Yankees' third straight flag with a 98-56 record.

But the drama of the Yankees' season-long battle with almost half of the American League paled in comparison to what was happening in the National League, where the Giants and Dodgers were involved in the greatest pennant race of all time.

The Giants trailed the Dodgers by thirteen games on August 11. Then the team went 39-8 (an otherworldly winning percentage of .830) to finish the season in a tie with Brooklyn, forcing a three-game pennant playoff. After splitting the first two games, Bobby Thomson hit the "Shot Heard Round the World." His three-run homer with one out in the bottom of the ninth lifted the Giants into their first World Series since 1937. In a repeat of that Series, their opponent would be the guys in pinstripes who played in the big ballpark across the river.

- - -

This was the sixth subway series between the Giants and Yankees. For Mize, here was a chance to meet his old team—managed by Leo Durocher—with everything on the line. And the Big Cat did okay in the Series, batting .286 (2 for 7, with 1 double, 1 RBI, 2 walks, and 2 runs).

The Giants, still flying on a magic momentum carpet, won two of the first three games. But the Yankees suffered their biggest loss in the game they won—Game Two, when Mantle went down with a knee injury in the fifth inning while chasing a fly ball struck by Willie Mays. Mickey had been the lead-off hitter in Casey's postseason batting order.

With the Giants leading 2–1, the Yankees won the next four contests to take the Series in six. Mize's double came in the 13–1 Game Five blowout. And he played a key role in the Yankees' Game Six clincher in the Bronx.

The score was 1–1 in the bottom of the sixth with one out when Berra singled off Giants starter Dave Koslo and took second as right fielder

Hank Thompson fumbled the ball. Koslo walked DiMaggio intentionally, then threw a wild pitch to Gil McDougald, and the runners advanced. McDougald lined out to Thomson at third, bringing Mize up with two out and runners on second and third.

What happened next was the turning point of the game and, according to Bobby Thomson, the World Series.

"Johnny Mize is at the plate. And Koslo isn't challenging him, he's nibbling," Thomson claimed years later. "I'm at third base screaming at Dave to get the ball over the plate."[6]

Thomson, who had played several seasons with Mize on the Giants, didn't believe the Big Cat could get around on a good fastball anymore. Koslo should challenge him, Thomson thought, because Johnny wouldn't swing at anything off the plate.[7]

"He really knew the strike zone," Thomson said. "Players like that get a reputation with umpires. They get a lot of close pitches called in their favor."[8]

And Johnny did. Koslo walked him to load the bases, bringing up Hank Bauer, who blasted a three-run triple over Monte Irvin's head in left field. Johnny rumbled home behind his teammates as the Yankees took a 4–1 lead. Old Johnny Sain, pitching in relief, gave up three straight singles in the bottom of the ninth, loading the bases for Monte Irvin, who had eleven hits in the Series.

Stengel brought in lefty Bob Kuzava to take on the heart of the Giants batting order. He threw heavy pitches—Irvin flew out to drive in one run, Bobby Thomson flew out to drive in another, making it 4–3. Then Sal Yvars lined out to Hank Bauer in right, and the season was over.

For Johnny Mize, who had scored what proved to be the winning run in the World Series against his old team, this championship stuff was something he could get used to.

- - -

Johnny Mize and Casey Stengel got along like old pals. According to Phil Rizzuto, "Some of the players used to say that Mize sat in Stengel's lap. They were two National League rejects and so on."[9]

Casey remembered back when Mize would pulverize his Dodgers and Braves teams in the 1930s, and he had great respect for Johnny's insights on the mechanics of hitting. When he wasn't starting at first base, Mize often sat next to Stengel on the Yankees bench and acted like a batting coach, offering tips and occasionally annoying teammates "who didn't particularly desire his criticism, especially right after they made an out and were returning to the dugout," Peter Golenbock wrote. "But Mize could help, because he knew how to analyze what they were doing wrong and could tell what the batter should expect from a particular pitcher. Often, he gave his teammates clues as to what they should be looking for at the plate."[10]

In 1952 Johnny was one of the oldest active players. If there had been a designated hitter at the time, he would have been the prototype. After all, Stengel had called him "the best pinch-hitter in baseball."[11]

Now he would have a chance to prove it. On his thirty-ninth birthday, January 13, 1952, Johnny signed a contract with the Yankees for a reported $25,000, and it wasn't for his glove. Johnny got into just twenty-seven games at first base in 1952, but he led the league in pinch-hitting appearances with fifty-one.

This was the beginning of the post-DiMaggio era, which also marked the beginning of Mantle's rise as a superhero. It also was the fiftieth season of the Yankees franchise. So, winning a fourth-straight championship to match the team's already established record (1936–39) would be a perfect way to celebrate the team's half-century legacy.

War in Korea was raging, and some players had been called back into action, most notably Ted Williams from the Red Sox and the Yankees dependable second baseman Jerry Coleman, both marine corps aviators. Losing Coleman meant the Yankees would be without a good hitting, wide-ranging infielder. Coleman was batting .405 after eleven games in '52 when he had to leave to fly combat missions over Korea.

So, Stengel played the scrappy kid from Oakland on a regular basis, and Billy Martin was up to the task. He had an excellent glove, was a clutch hitter, and was an intense competitor. The Yankees needed all of that and more because it was another close race in the American League, with New York battling Cleveland again. The Yankees ultimately clinched their pennant by winning fifteen of their last eighteen games. The Indians also blazed down the stretch, entering September two games behind the league-leading Yanks, and ending the season two games back.

- - -

The Yankees shared an ignominious slice of history before starting their September blitzkrieg. On August 25 against the last-place Tigers in Yankee Stadium, Casey's boys went oh-for-the-game against Virgil "Fire" Trucks, who made New York his second no-hit victim of the season. Trucks, a great pitcher in his best years who finished with a career-worst record of 5–19 in 1952, stifled the Senators on May 15. In both games, Trucks won a 1–0 decision.

The game against the Yankees came with a dose of controversy, thanks to John Drebinger of the *New York Times*, official scorer of that day's game. In the third inning, Rizzuto hit an easy grounder to shortstop Johnny Pesky, who had a hard time getting a handle on the ball, had to hurry his throw, and Rizzuto was safe. Drebinger called it an error immediately, and "E" flashed up on the scoreboard. Then he reversed himself and ruled it a hit. An immediate chorus of objections rose from the press box, but Drebinger wouldn't change his mind until he called Pesky down in the dugout. The shortstop said it was an error all the way, so Drebinger changed it back to an error, and Trucks had his historic no-hitter.

Mize had a chance to break it up when he pinch-hit for Rizzuto in the bottom of the eighth. Trucks overpowered the Big Cat, who popped up weakly to third base.

A few weeks later, Mize lifted the team with a record-setting home run against the Senators in Washington. It was Sunday, September 7, and the Yankees trailed, 1–0, in the top of the sixth when Washington starting pitcher Walt Masterson walked Billy Martin and Phil Rizzuto. Then Yankees starter Eddie Lopat bunted his way on, loading the bases.

"Casey Stengel told me to go up and hit for Gil McDougald," Mize recalled. "The only thing on my mind was to get the runner in from third and advance the runner on second to third, so that the next batter could drive him in. I would have settled for a long fly ball."[12]

He did hit a long fly ball, a very long one. On a 2-1 count, Masterson threw a slider that Mize timed perfectly and sent flying over the right-field fence, giving the Yankees a 4–1 lead en route to their 5–1 victory.

"After I returned to the bench, it was then that I realized I had hit a home run in every major league ballpark, including the old Baker Bowl," declared Mize, who had never even hit a ball out of Griffith Stadium in batting practice before.[13]

For the last two games of the regular season, in Philadelphia, Stengel started Mize at first base for the first time in five weeks. Casey was thinking ahead to the World Series. And it was good practice for Johnny, who went 3 for 5 with a double, a home run, and two RBIs in the Saturday game, September 27, playing flawless defense. He had a hit and an RBI in Sunday's game, won by the Athletics.

Johnny's final report card shows a .263 batting average, and his four home runs were an all-time low. But pretty soon he would add a few more in one of the great performances in World Series history.

- - -

The Brooklyn Dodgers grabbed first place in the National League on June 1 and never let it go, finishing at 96-57, four and a half games ahead of the Mays-less Giants. Manager Charlie Dressen had guided Brooklyn back into another subway series with the Yankees.

The Dodgers scored more runs than anyone else in the National League, powered by Gil Hodges (32 homers, 102 RBIs), Roy Campanella (22 homers, 97 RBIs), and Duke Snider (21 homers, 92 RBIs), with the explosive spark provided by Jackie Robinson (104 runs, 24 stolen bases, a team-high .308 batting average) and Pee Wee Reese (30 stolen bases, 94 runs). Carl Erskine led starting pitchers with a 14-6 record and a 2.70 earned run average. Billy Loes added 13 wins and a 2.69 ERA. The best pitcher on the team, though, was twenty-eight-year-old rookie Joe Black, who posted a 15-4 record coming out of the bullpen. Black, who played six seasons in the Negro Leagues, also had a 2.15 ERA, saved 15 games, and was named Rookie of the Year.

Black only started two games during the season, but he was Dressen's starter for Game One of the Series in Brooklyn on October 1, a Wednesday. Nearly thirty-five thousand fans squeezed into Ebbets Field to watch Black throw a complete game gem, holding the Yankees to six hits in winning, 4–2, as Robinson, Snider, and Reese homered for the Dodgers.

Snider and Reese were the hitting stars for Brooklyn in what was a classic seven-game World Series, both of them batting .345—Duke tied a Series record with 4 home runs (he added 2 doubles). Mantle emerged as an October star for the first time, smashing 2 homers among his 10 hits and batting .345, and Woodling batted .348. But the surprising star of this World Series was old Johnny Mize.

Vic Raschi stopped the Dodgers and Erskine in Game Two, knotting the Series at a game apiece. The third game, at Yankee Stadium, featured two off-speed lefties, Brooklyn's Preacher Roe against the Yankees' Ed Lopat. Roe was cagey and brilliant, holding the Yanks to six hits in a 5–3 win. Mize made it close in the bottom of the ninth. With one out and the Dodgers leading 5–2, he pinch-hit for pitcher Tom Gorman and blasted a Roe curveball into the right-field stands. Roe retired the next two batters, and Brooklyn had a 2–1 lead in the Series.

The next day, Mize started at first base and provided all the offense his fellow geezer, Allie Reynolds, would need to beat Joe Black, 2–0. Reynolds gave up four hits and struck out ten Dodgers (including Jackie Robinson three times). Black only gave up three hits in seven innings of work, but two of them were to Mize, and one of them was disastrous.

Johnny led off the fourth inning and whacked a high fastball from Black into the right-field seats. That was all the Yankees needed. Mantle added the insurance run in the eighth when his lead-off triple was misplayed into a home run—Reese's throw to third base was wild, and Mickey raced home. Mize added a ground-rule double to right field to lead off the bottom of the sixth, but the Yankees couldn't push him across. He also walked and played solid defense.

"His home run and double represented 50 percent of the Yankees' attack," wrote Red Smith. "Brooklyn batsmen sliced three balls his way and, naturally, he handled them all like George Sisler."[14]

The Series even at 2–2, the rivals met in Yankee Stadium next for one of the most thrilling games ever in a World Series. A Sunday crowd of 70,536 fans packed Yankee Stadium to watch Erskine take on New York's Ewell Blackwell, a late-season pickup for the Yanks. Erskine was all guts, and thanks to his roommate, Duke Snider, he also was the victor. But Mize did his best to change all of that.

Brooklyn held a 4–0 lead after a Snider home run in the top of the fifth. In the bottom half of the inning, the Yankees started nibbling at Erskine. Hank Bauer walked, and Billy Martin bounced a single over second base. Irv Noren, hitting for Blackwell, singled to drive in Bauer. Gil McDougald hit a slow roller to Reese at short, forcing Noren at second and scoring Martin, and now it was 4–2. Rizzuto followed with a single to right, putting Yankees on first and second for Mantle.

Batting left-handed against the right-handed curveball artist, Mickey popped up to third baseman Billy Cox in foul territory. Now there were two out with two on for the Big Cat. Instead of throwing his potent overhand curve, Erskine challenged him with his fastball and Johnny sent it on a 425-foot ride to the right-center-field bleachers. His three-run homer gave New York a 5–4 lead, and Yankee Stadium erupted in an explosion of noise.

U.S. senator Richard Nixon of California, the vice-presidential candidate on the Eisenhower ticket that fall, was also in the ballpark. He'd received a loud reception from the stadium crowd, but nothing like the cheers raining on Mize.

"When John Robert socked that three-run wallop for his third World Series homer in three successive days, the whole joint trembled," wrote Red Smith. "When he reappeared from the dugout to play first base, a noisier tumult saluted him."[15]

But there was still plenty of game left. The question was, could Erskine keep pitching?

"One thing a manager looks at that the average fan doesn't necessarily think about is how hard are the balls being hit," said Erskine, who was ninety-four when he clearly recalled Game Five, almost seventy years later. "Sometimes you get scored on with high bouncers and scratch hits. A good manager is more tuned in to *how* they are hitting the ball."[16]

So, when Dressen went out to the mound to check on his pitcher after Mize's home run, Erskine told him, while looking at the scoreboard, "I'm not in great shape right now. But Charlie said, 'The only ball they hit hard off you was the Mize home run.' So, he left me in the game," Erskine said. "It surprised me and probably everyone else."[17]

Following the Mize blast, 165-pound Carl became Superman, retiring the next nineteen men he faced, winning the game 6–5 in eleven innings, thanks to his roomie Snider's game-tying single in the seventh and game-winning double in the top of the eleventh.

Erskine faced Mize again in the bottom of the eleventh with one out, clinging to his one-run lead, and he challenged the Big Cat again with a fastball. Johnny hit it on a low line toward the right-field seats. Right fielder Carl Furillo, who'd entered the game in the fifth inning, turned and sped to the wall, gripped it, propelled himself up, and, at the apex of his leap, snared the ball, robbing Mize of another home run.

"I thought the ball was gone," Mize declared in his syndicated column. "I knew it was going to reach the stands. The only question in my mind was whether or not Furillo could reach it. He did."[18]

After his heart slowed down, Erskine struck out Berra looking. Now the Dodgers were going home to Brooklyn with a 3–2 lead in the Series. One more win and they'd finally vanquish the Yankees. The old man sitting in Casey Stengel's lap would have a say in the matter before it was settled.

The Yankees overcame two home runs by Duke Snider in Game Six to win, 3–2, tying the Series. Mantle provided the winning margin in the eighth with a solo blast to left-center field. He was falling away from the plate when he hit the ball.

Joe Black's only starts before the World Series came six days apart late in the season against the seventh-place Boston Braves. Now Dressen asked him to start for the third time in seven days, in Game Seven against the Yankees. Meanwhile, Stengel went with Lopat, "despite the realization that starting a left-hander in Ebbets Field was usually disastrous," Peter Golenbock wrote.[19]

In the top of the fourth, after Rizzuto lined a double past Dodger third baseman Billy Cox, Mize faced his new friend Joe Black. He'd walked in the second inning. This time he sent "shockwaves through the crowd," when his long blast to right field went just foul. But he followed that by singling sharply to right field for the first run of the game.[20]

It was 2–2 in the sixth when the combination of Mantle and Mize drove the exhausted Black from the game. Mantle's blow was devastating, for the sheer size of it and because it meant the ball game. Batting left-handed, the switch-hitting twenty-year-old smashed Black's slider to the far side of Bedford Avenue. The drive, giving New York a 3–2 lead, was so majestic, Mantle was halfway to second base when it cleared the screen in right. Mize followed with a line drive single to right field, and Black was finished, giving way to reliever Preacher Roe. Mantle added an RBI single in the seventh, making it 4–2.

Martin's clutch play in the seventh ended Brooklyn's last threat. With two out and the bases loaded, New York's left-handed reliever Bob Kuzava threw a curve ball that Jackie Robinson popped up to the first-base side of the pitcher's mound. The three Dodgers runners bolted as soon as Robinson hit the ball. "Catcher Berra yelled for the first-baseman to make the catch," Golenbock wrote.[21] Collins had replaced Mize at first, but he stood his ground after losing the ball in the sun. But Martin saw it all clearly—Collins was blinded and the ball caught in the wind, drifting away him—so Martin made a last-second sprint and grabbed the ball two feet off the ground, ending the inning. Kuzava finished the game without giving up a hit, and the Yankees had their fourth-straight title. Stengel and his ragtag Yankees had equaled the record of Joe McCarthy and the Yanks of Gehrig and DiMaggio.

After the game, Yankees were celebrating so hard in the chaotic visitor's clubhouse, it was as if they'd never won a World Series before. Stengel was overjoyed. "Mize, he's like Babe Ruth come to life," a disheveled Casey said. "Mantle . . . well, what more can you say?"[22]

The old guy and the young guy had made the difference. The New York chapter of the Baseball Writers' Association of America gave its Babe Ruth Award for the best postseason player to Mize, who batted .400 in the Series, had those 3 home runs, and drove in a team-high 6 runs. Johnny was the worthy choice, but not everyone agreed.

"In this spectator's opinion, it was no contest," wrote the Gayle Talbot. "Mize, it is true, came in when things were not looking too good midway of the Series and made a number of tremendous contributions to the Yankee cause. But Mantle was in there all the way, scaring Brooklyn pitchers to death and fielding like an angel."[23]

Talbot and everyone else who paid attention to baseball had witnessed a performance that foretold the future—Mantle would become the best player on the planet.

Mize, on the other hand, was already projected as becoming a coach, or possibly a manager somewhere, maybe Birmingham, his playing days seemingly over in a blaze of World Series glory.[24] But after his performance against the Dodgers, he figured a few good swings were left in his bat. He wanted to reach two thousand hits for his career and just needed fifteen more.[25]

He was going to be forty years old, and Jene was tired of being a baseball player's wife. She wanted him to quit. Imagine her reaction when Johnny told a reporter, "I'll play next season, if I get what I want. If Casey wants me, I'll be back."[26]

22

How to Hit

> There was a time when he was one of the
> sights of the city and he appeared to be
> permanent and everlasting, a guy who
> would be walking up to the plate forever,
> taking his bat with him, to swing at a
> pitched ball in that graceful way. —Jimmy Cannon[1]

Long before Murray the K became the "Fifth Beatle"—the New York disc
jockey and rock-and-roll impresario who introduced millions of Americans to the Fab Four—he was simply Murray Kaufman, a public relations
man and song plugger, and an agent for several dozen baseball players,
including the New York Yankees' aging first baseman and pinch hitter,
Johnny Mize.

Kaufman's most notable project with Mize was *How to Hit*. He was the
"to" in the as-told-to instruction book that Johnny published through
Henry Holt, fortuitously released around Opening Day 1953.

"As of this Saturday, J. Robert Mize of DeLand, Fla., will become the
only author who has hit a home run in every major-league ballpark,"
wrote John Fox in the March 29, 1953, edition of the *Press & Sun-Bulletin*
in Binghamton, New York. "The Big Cat joins the endless parade of distinguished Southern literary men Saturday when his 'How to Hit' is
published by Henry Holt and Company. Johnny goes only 108 pages in
his first effort, a collaboration with Murray Kaufman, his agent. Brief
that may be, but full of good baseball sense and good baseball stories."[2]

The book got some positive feedback from Fox and elsewhere. "Told with
extreme simplicity and sprinkled with illustrative, amusing anecdotes,
this is a remarkably clear and concise series of easy-to-absorb lessons
on batting from a master of the hitting craft," read one typical review.[3]

Besides Mize's sincere belief that hitters are made and not born (and his hope to make a little extra cash), a big inspiration for the book apparently came from his teammates. According to a sportswriter Joe Reichler, "At times, when Big Jawn starts expounding on his theories on batting, his teammates wink at each other and rib the great hitter with such [comments] as, 'Aw, why don't you write a book?'"[4]

Some of the ribbings, or suggestions, involved more colorful language. But they had the same essential meaning. And some of the Yankees appreciated Mize's unsolicited advice.

"He taught me about pulling the ball into the hole with a man on first," said Dr. Bobby Brown, who batted .500 in the 1949 World Series, including an RBI triple to right field. "He said to open my stance a little more at the plate. When he tried to pull the ball, he moved his front foot a little to the right. That little adjustment allowed me to really pull an inside pitch with some power."[5]

Sports columnist Jimmy Cannon remembered Mize's impromptu skull sessions on hitting during train rides, "as if he were a professor discussing some important topic. . . . He made it seem as if he had all the advantages, as if only an accident could get him out."[6]

Brown, who became a cardiologist after his playing career and, later, president of the American League, said most of the team paid attention when Mize talked about hitting. "He could hit with two strikes. He didn't strike out very often. He could hit bad balls. He could hit the home run. He hit left-handers, He hit to the opposite field," Brown said. "He was a hitter's hitter. So yes, we paid attention to him."[7]

Mize hoped readers would pay attention too. The book was aimed toward "young fellows looking to make their way in baseball," Johnny said. "The book tells them all they want to know about hitting."[8]

That included how to pick and grip a bat, stand in the batter's box, hit a fastball or a curve, bunt, hit against lefties versus righties, and break out of a slump—with plenty of photos and illustrations.

"Not even Ty Cobb has made a closer study of hitting than Mize," Reichler wrote.[9]

That's an interesting point because, in addition to his rules of hitting, Mize shared stories about his life and career, including his kinship to Cobb and Ruth. In the book he mentioned his well-known relationship to the Babe through his cousin Claire, while also telling a story about his other relative, the Georgia Peach. Johnny was dressing before a game when, he said, "a familiar figure approached me. 'Hear you and me is cousins,' he said, extending his hand and smiling. The familiar figure turned out to be Ty Cobb. I had heard that Ty and I were kin for some time. When he approached me that day, I was mighty pleased because although I wanted to tell folks about our relationship, I didn't feel it right unless he first acknowledged the fact."[10]

How to Hit also features pages of statistics: Mize's year-to-year record to that point in his career, the records he held, and a list of annual home run champions. There's also a chapter on Mize's All-Star hitting team. He picked a team for both the American and National Leagues, limiting his choices only to players he'd played with or seen in their prime. He excluded himself:

Mize's All Star Hitting Teams

American League: Lou Gehrig (first base), Charlie Gehringer (second base), Jimmie Foxx (third base), Joe Cronin, (shortstop), Ted Williams (left field), Joe DiMaggio (center field), Earl Averill (right field), Bill Dickey (catcher), Red Ruffing (pitcher), Hank Greenberg (pinch hitter).

National League: Bill Terry (first base), Billy Herman (second base), Bob Elliott (third base), Arky Vaughan (shortstop), Paul Waner (left field), Stan Musial (center field), Mel Ott (right field), Ernie Lombardi (catcher), Bucky Walters (pitcher), Ralph Kiner (pinch hitter).

"It has been my intention to give you all the information at my disposal about the art of hitting a baseball," Mize wrote in his final chapter. Then, two pages of reminders follow, such as: "Don't forget to select a bat that feels just right"; "Don't forget to stand in there against any pitcher"; "Don't forget you have plenty of thrills in store for you in this game of baseball"; and "Don't forget that baseball is a way of life, and it only gives you back what you put into it."[11]

The best marketing for the book on hitting was Mize himself. In May, Johnny had base hits in five-straight at bats as a pinch hitter, which set an American League record, and he reached base in seven-straight plate appearances. After one of those hits in the streak blooped into right field against the Senators, he returned to the Yankees bench and said, laughing, "You won't find any chapters on bloopers in the book."[12]

Stengel used him almost exclusively as a pinch hitter in 1953 (he only played fourteen games at first base). And when he got a walk or a hit that didn't leave the ballpark, he was usually replaced by a pinch runner. He could hardly run at this point in his career. It didn't matter because he only needed to run ninety feet, and Joe Collins or some other fresh pair of legs was usually jogging up the dugout steps before Mize reached first.[13]

- - -

Johnny was one of the last Yankees to sign his contract for the 1953 season, holding out for as long as he could for as much as he could. Yankees GM George Weiss could be a tough negotiator.

"George Weiss was very astute and also very tight with a dollar," Bobby Brown said. "It was always a battle just to get what you deserve. He was a tough guy to deal with."[14]

Mize would reportedly be paid $20,000. Martin signed for $12,000. Woodling drove the hardest bargain and talked Weiss into giving him a $4,000 raise to $25,000. Rizzuto received a bump of $2,000 to $42,000.[15]

Duly fortified, Casey's men were ready to take on the world. With Ford returning from service to rejoin the trio of Raschi, Reynolds, and Lopat, "for the first time manager Stengel was working with a pat hand," according to Golenbock. "He had Joe Collins at first, Billy Martin at second, Phil Rizzuto at short, and Gil McDougald at third. Bauer, Mantle, Woodling, and Noren were the outfielders, and Yogi Berra was the catcher. John Mize provided the bench power."[16]

The 1953 Yankees were alone in first place on April 22 with a 6–2 win over Boston, powered by Loren Babe, who had two hits and three RBIs. It was one of Babe's five games with the Yankees that year. Then, perhaps as punishment, he was sold to the miserable Philadelphia Athletics a couple of days later. Nonetheless, Babe, who had a fine career in Class Triple-A ball ahead of him, lifted the Yankees into sole possession of first place, and they held it the rest of the season. The Yanks may have lost Loren Babe, but they had Mickey Mantle, and this was the year of the tape-measure home run.

On April 17, batting right-handed, Mickey hit a baseball out of Griffith Stadium that Yankees publicity man Red Patterson claimed went 565 feet.

The term *tape-measure home run* was born, even though Patterson didn't use a tape measure but reportedly paced off the distance. It became part of the growing Mantle legend. And the breathtaking blast was kind of symbolic of the powerful Yankees that season, a dynasty surging to a fifth-straight championship.

The Yankees were never threatened, reeling off eighteen straight wins, the longest of the baseball season, and one short of the team record, from May 27 through June 14.

Johnny contributed during the streak, at one point knocking RBI base hits in three straight pinch-hitting appearances. His base hit driving in McDougald in a win over Detroit on June 10 was base hit number 1,999 of his career.

Then he notched number 2,000 on a night when the season's longest winning and losing streaks ended simultaneously at Yankee Stadium, "where a surprising reversal of their usual roles saw the lowly Browns, who had lost fourteen straight games, register a 3–1 upset over the first-place Yankees, who had won eighteen in a row," wrote Joseph Sheehan of the *New York Times* following the game on June 16.[17]

Another streak ended that night. Yankees starter Whitey Ford, who'd won his first nine starts as a rookie before taking a loss in 1950, restarted his career following two years of military service by winning his first seven decisions of 1953. The St. Louis Browns ended that streak too.

But the game's historic moment came in the bottom of the fifth, with St. Louis leading 3–0. Browns starter Duane Pillette walked Woodling, then McDougald singled. Stengel sent Johnny in to hit for Rizzuto, and he roped a single to right field, scoring Woodling. It was fitting that number 2,000 would drive in a run.

Johnny received a long ovation from the Tuesday-night crowd of 30,362, and the ball was removed from the game and sent to the Baseball Hall of Fame in Cooperstown. Then Pillette settled down, and Satchel Paige completed the win for St. Louis with two solid innings of relief.

Johnny and Satchel's working relationship went back to 1936 and barnstorming days. Since then, Mize had faced him several other times when Paige pitched for the Indians or the Browns. Satch, forty-seven in July 1953, was one of the few guys left in the game older than forty-year-old Mize. An Associated Press photo feature made the rounds in newspapers across the country, with the four images of Mize, Paige, Bobo Newsom (forty-five), and Dutch Leonard (forty-four) under the headline "Not Bad for over 40!"[18]

It was easy to feel old when surrounded by guys like Mantle (twenty-one), Ford (twenty-four), and Martin (twenty-five). The young turks were generally not part of Johnny's social group. He was more inclined to spend time with one of the older guys, or alone. Ford and the younger fellas enjoyed teasing the Big Cat.

"John would go downtown with a dozen autographed baseballs, and if he needed a new suit, he'd trade the baseballs," claimed Ford, a native New Yorker who grew up admiring Mize as a slugger with the Giants. "Billy used to kid John about that. 'What did you get for a dozen baseballs today, John?' And John didn't always take it too well. Mickey and I used to tease him a little too. But we knew better than to take it too far. He was a big guy, and he was important to the ball club."[19]

This was a powerful, balanced Yankees team. Seven of the eight regulars hit double-digit home runs, with Berra (27) and Mantle (21) leading. Seven had 20 or more doubles. Woodling and Bauer both hit over .300, while Berra and Mantle hit .296 and .295, respectively. The Yankees were first in the American League in scoring, batting average, and slugging.

In his first full season, Ford became the team's ace, with an 18-6 record and 3.00 ERA, anchoring a staff of old men. The thirty-five-year-old Lopat was almost unbeatable at 16-4 and 2.47, and thirty-four-year-old Raschi was 13-6. The bullpen was led by a pair of senior citizens who both appeared in forty or more games: Allie Reynolds, at thirty-six, a reliever and spot starter now, won thirteen games and saved thirteen; Johnny Sain, thirty-five, won fourteen games as a reliever-starter hybrid, second on the staff in innings pitched to Ford.

It was all very impressive on paper, except when compared to Brooklyn. This finally looked like "next year" for the Dodgers, who set team records with 105 wins, 955 runs, and 208 homers. MVP Roy Campanella belted 41 homers and drove in 142 runs. Duke Snider hit 42 homers, had 126 RBIs with a .336 batting average, and led the league in runs and slugging average. Gil Hodges (31 homers, 122 RBIs), National League batting champion Carl Furillo (.344, 92 RBIs), Jackie Robinson (.329, 109 runs, 95 RBIs), and Rookie of the Year Jim Gilliam (125 runs and a league-leading 17 triples) rounded out a lineup that pitcher Carl Erskine rated as the best of any Brooklyn team.

Erskine had his best season in 1953, posting a 20-6 record with a respectable 3.54 ERA and a career high in strikeouts, 187. Russ "the Mad Monk" Meyer, picked up from the Phillies before the season, went 15-5, and Billie Loes won fourteen games. Both men had earned run averages over 4.50, but it didn't really matter because the Dodgers scored lots of runs. Clem Labine was the team's ace in the hole, winning eleven games, mostly in relief, with a team-leading ERA of 2.77, about a run and a half better than the rest of the league.

- - -

Mize said he was quitting after the 1953 season. Then he said maybe he wasn't. He wasn't very clear one way or the other. But during a September 5 rainout in Washington, the subject came up, and Johnny was asked to weigh in.

"This is my last season. I think I'm about through with baseball," he said. When someone teased him about it, Mize emphasized, "Nope, I mean it this time. Oh, I suppose I could go up and get a pinch-hit now and then. But it wouldn't be worth it. It's too tough to stay in shape."[20]

He continued, "I don't enjoy this business any longer. If I were playing every day, maybe I'd like to hang on for another year. But this idea of keeping in condition just to go up and bat once in a while is too hard to take."[21]

But in another report, he said that he didn't care about playing anymore, then added as an afterthought, "It isn't definite, you know. It all depends on what kind of a proposition they make me."[22]

Either way, Johnny wasn't destitute. He'd already begun investing in orange groves in Florida, where he had other business interests, including part ownership in a liquor store.

Several weeks of baseball were still left to play. And as the Yankees and Dodgers made mincemeat of their regular-season competition, a rematch of their 1952 battle was inevitable in the golden anniversary World Series.

For Mize, it was nice to play out the string for a championship ball club, and he also had one more personal goal in mind. He was within range of the American League record for pinch hits in a season, which was 20, set by Ed Coleman of the St. Louis Browns in 1936. The Major League record was 22.

Heading into a September 13 game against Cleveland at the Stadium, Mize had 18 pinch hits, according to newspaper reports. (His figures on

Baseball Reference show him with 2 fewer pinch hits that season.) He got number 19 in dramatic style, in front of a Sunday crowd of 48,492 that was there to celebrate the return of Jerry Coleman from his Korean War service. Coleman, who missed most of 1952 and 1953, got the hero treatment—U.S. Marine band and precision drill corps going through the paces, followed by a squadron of eight planes flying overhead in formation. And then, there was a great ball game.

Larry Doby homered twice, and the Indians led, 3–2 in the bottom of the eighth, when Woodling tied the score with a home run off Mike Garcia. Martin singled, and Rizzuto reached on Al Rosen's error, and the Big Cat was sent in to pinch hit for Raschi. He sent Garcia's first pitch into the right-field seats for a 6–3 lead and the final score.

That was the last pinch hit of Mize's career, and the last home run, number 359. He was sixth on the all-time list at the time. Cousin George, of course, was way out in front of everyone; the order was Ruth, Jimmie Foxx, Mel Ott, Lou Gehrig, Joe DiMaggio, and Mize. He was in noble company.

Johnny had nine more chances to get the pinch-hit record but didn't deliver. The last base hit and last RBI of his career came a few days after the game-winning homer against the Indians. Stengel gave some of the regulars a day off for a Wednesday twilight doubleheader against the visiting St. Louis Browns on September 16. In the 5:30 game, Johnny started at first for the last time in his career. His sixth-inning single drove in Andy Carey with the Yankees' first run in a 5–3 loss.

For Johnny Mize of the New York Yankees, it was his last year as a player, and he'd be forever proud to go out as a champion, part of an elite group—one of the dozen Yankees who played on all five championship teams from '49 to '53 (with Rizzuto, Reynolds, Raschi, Lopat, Berra, Brown, Coleman, Collins, Bauer, Woodling, and backup catcher Charlie Silvera).

"I knew when I joined the Yankees in August of 1949 I was going to make the most of it," Mize said. "It was a great way to finish my active life in baseball. You can hear how good Joe DiMaggio and Rizzuto are, but you don't know until you see them every day."[23]

But years later, when looking back on his final season, Johnny aired his disappointment that he'd missed out on the pinch-hit record. When someone asked Mize why he quit, he said that Stengel could have given him another chance to break the record but went with another hitter. He explained, "So I figured, if that's the way it is, I ought to quit. So, I did."[24]

- - -

Despite the obvious strength of the Brooklyn club, the Yankees entered the golden anniversary World Series as six-to-five favorites. Eighty-six-year-old Cy Young, who pitched in the first modern World Series in 1903, threw out the ceremonial first pitch in front of 69,374 cheering fans in Yankee Stadium.

The odds only got better for New York after wins in the first two games. Erskine and Reynolds squared off in the first game, but both were hit hard, and the Yankees triumphed, 9–5. Lefties Eddie Lopat and Preacher Roe both went the distance in Game Two. Home runs by Martin and Mantle made the difference in a 4–2 Yankees win.

Reeling after losing two straight, the Dodgers limped back to Ebbets Field for a proverbial must-win Game Three on Friday, October 2. Carl Erskine was glad to be getting another shot at the Yankees. Dressen asked him if he could go on two day's rest, and "Oisk" jumped at the chance. He'd gone 15-2 since July 2 and still felt the sting from Game One of the Series, when he was shelled and lasted one inning.

"I felt like I had something to prove," Carl said in a February 2021 interview. "And Charlie Dressen was a bit of a gambler. He knew what I could do with little rest. And he had a lot of faith in me. I told my teammates that I was going to throw every pitch like it was my last."[25]

And that was saying something for the skinny kid with the mighty heart from Anderson, Indiana. Erskine injured his right shoulder in his very first big league start, in 1948 against the Cubs. He was pitching to Bill Nicholson, a good home run hitter, and trying to put something extra on his fastball.

"Why did I hurt my arm? Here's why," Carl said. "I had pitched almost six hundred innings the previous year, between the Minors and a season of winter ball, then spring training. Anyway, that was the beginning of the pain. I fought it my whole career. I lost some velocity, but I became a better pitcher."[26]

In Game Three of the 1953 World Series in front of 35,270 fans, he was a mind-blowing pitcher. His opponent was Raschi, big and tough. The two right-handers had a shutout through four innings. Erskine hadn't given up a hit and had seven strikeouts by then. In the dugout, Mize was criticizing his teammates, "Hit a good pitch, for Christ's sake."[27]

They finally reached Erskine in the fifth. Singles from Martin, Rizzuto, and McDougald gave New York a 1–0 lead. The Dodgers made it 1–1 in the bottom of the fifth when Jackie Robinson doubled, took third on Raschi's balk, and scored on Billy Cox's bunt. In the bottom of the sixth, the Dodgers took a 2–1 lead on Robinson's RBI single.

The Yankees tied it in the top of eighth, and Erskine got the lift he needed in the bottom half of the inning from Campanella, because Raschi ignored Stengel's orders to stick it in Campy's ear. Campanella had been clipped on the hand earlier in the Series by Reynolds, and the hand still hurt, and he didn't appreciate Stengel's suggestion. So, when Raschi instead threw a fastball over the plate, the catcher lined it into the lower left-field stands for a 3–2 Dodgers lead.[28]

That's all Carl would need. When he struck out pinch hitter Don Bollweg on three fastballs to open the top of the ninth, he tied a twenty-four-year-old World Series record. It was his thirteenth strikeout, matching the mark set by the Philadelphia A's Howard Ehmke against the Cubs in 1929.

"I didn't know I'd tied a record, and didn't care, but I could tell the fans were excited," Erskine said. "I was busy thinking about Johnny Mize. He was tough, maybe the best hitter I've seen or faced. Didn't swing at bad pitches. And I remembered what he did to me in 1952."[29]

Erskine continued, "Johnny Mize was kind of a nemesis for me," then added after a slight pause, a happy lilt in his old voice, "So, I'd say it was poetic justice, striking him out to set the record."[30]

Mize had been sitting in the dugout getting annoyed as his teammates kept striking out. And some of them were getting annoyed with him.

"He kept telling the guys to stop swinging at that junk curve ball in the dirt," Whitey Ford remembered. "They looked at him like he was crazy."[31]

Erskine didn't want to give Johnny anything fat to hit. He placed two overhand curves on the outside part of the plate, and Mize didn't swing— two strikes. Then Carl almost made a mistake—a fastball up, and Mize swung viciously. He fouled it backward. Carl breathed. Then, he threw another curve, the same delivery, but he took a little something off the velocity. Mize swung hard and missed, and Erskine had the record. He knew the strikeout was special because of the noise. He didn't know he'd set a record until Preacher Roe told him in the clubhouse.

"I was so busy, so determined to beat a great Yankee team, that I wasn't counting strikeouts," Erskine wrote years later.[32]

After Mize struck out, a couple of the Yankees—particularly Mantle and Collins, who struck out four times each—felt vindicated. As Ford remembered, "After Mize swung at the curveball in the dirt, a couple of the guys snickered. We hated to lose, but you had to laugh when Billy [Martin] said, 'Hey, John, that low curve take a bad hop or what?'"[33]

The Dodgers took the early advantage in Game Four on Saturday, October 3, scoring three runs in the first and chasing Ford from the game. Brooklyn won 7–3 to tie the Series. Mize had a chance to make it close when Stengel sent him in to hit with the bases loaded in the top of the ninth. He flew out to Snider in center field. The game ended with a bang when Martin tried to run over Campanella to score, and the Dodgers' catcher tagged him out, sending Billy flying.

With each team running out of fresh-armed pitchers, Brooklyn started twenty-year-old lefty Johnny Podres in Sunday's Game Five. Stengel started right-hander Jim McDonald, who gave up twelve hits and six runs but still earned the win, as the Yankees rolled, 11–7. Mantle, hitting left-handed against Russ Meyers, ended a streak of five-straight strikeouts with a grand slam into the left-center-field bleachers of Ebbets Field. Six home runs were hit in the game, tying a World Series record, and the Yankees were a game away from the title.

Carl Erskine loved Charlie Dressen but also felt that Charlie overused him sometimes. Game Six in Yankee Stadium, with a Monday crowd of over sixty-two thousand, was one of those times. Pitching again with two days' rest, Carl faced Ford. It was clear from the start that this Erskine was not the same as he was in Game Three. He left the game after four innings, trailing 3–0.

Robinson put the Dodgers on the scoreboard in the sixth, doubling to left, stealing third, and hustling home on Campanella's grounder to short. Then the right-handed-hitting Furillo, who had a great Series after missing most of September with a broken finger (suffered in a fight with Leo Durocher), blasted a two-run homer that landed deep in the right-field bleachers in the top of the ninth, tying it, 3–3.

But there's a reason why Billy Martin won the Babe Ruth Award as the Series's outstanding player—several reasons, really. He batted .500, tying a World Series record with 12 hits, including 2 home runs. And perhaps the best reason of all, he singled in Hank Bauer with the winning run in the bottom of the ninth, making it 4–3, giving Stengel and the Yankees their record fifth-straight World Series.

Mize celebrated with his teammates in the Yankee Stadium home team clubhouse. In the last at bat of his career, he pinch-hit for Joe Collins with two runners on base in the bottom of the eighth. He grounded out to first, ending the inning.

In summing up the Series, Tommy Holmes wrote, "Saddest sight was Johnny Mize, failing three times in his Series swansong."[34]

- - -

He must have known he was finished. After the otherworldly heroics in the 1952 World Series, Johnny had to fight with George Weiss to get his $20,000. Mize hinted that this was another reason for him to retire. After the Series was finished, he went into Stengel's office to tell him personally.

"They tell me you're quitting, but I don't believe it," Stengel said.[35]

"That's right, Case, I'm all through," said Mize, who did not look forward to another round of salary negotiations. "After that Series I had [in 1952], they cut me $4,000. So you can imagine what they'd offer me for next year."[36]

The clubhouse was nearly empty by then. Besides Stengel, cleaning out his office, only Allie Reynolds and Gene Woodling were still there. Mize shook their hands, said goodbye. Woodling thanked him for the hitting tips. "I sure hate to see you go, John," he said.[37]

"I'd rather go while they're still applauding me than hang around until they start to boo," Johnny said, heading for the door.[38]

Stengel watched him leave and said, "Don't think he won't be missed. He made this clubhouse a happy place to be more days than I can count."[39]

Mize thought he'd get a job somewhere in baseball as a coach or a manager. So, he sent Yankees brass a letter asking for his freedom, and they released him in late November. But in truth, Mize's retirement became official right after the World Series, when he quietly turned over all of his favorite bats to Billy Martin.[40]

23

Out to Pasture

Sure, I would have liked to make a connection
in baseball, but there were never any offers.
One owner told me I had a job with his
team anytime I wanted it. When "anytime"
came, he said there were no openings.   —Johnny Mize[1]

Johnny turned down his first postretirement job offer: a Las Vegas hotel
under development asked him to be a greeter. He basically told the hotel
that he'd prefer to go fishing.[2]

That odd job aside, when Johnny retired as a player, the common
assumptions were that he would continue in baseball, probably as a coach
or manager, and that he was a sure thing for induction into the National
Baseball Hall of Fame.

Mize led the National League in home runs four times and finished in
the top five nine times, led the league in batting once and was in the top
five six times, led the league in runs batted in three times and was in the
top five eight times, and led the league in extra-base hits four times and
finished in the top five eight times. He batted .312 lifetime in an age when
the .300 hitter was sacrosanct. He had a .562 slugging average—better
than Musial, Mays, Mantle, Aaron, and Kiner. He hit lots of home runs
and, as an old player, became the best pinch hitter on a team that won
five-straight World Series.

He had all the right qualifications. But his road to Cooperstown was
long and bumpy. He did find a job in baseball soon after retiring, though.
In January 1954 he reunited with his old ball club, the New York Giants.
Instead of swinging a bat, he'd sling a microphone.

"Johnny Mize, the one-time Giant star before being traded to the Yankees, is returning to the Giants—as a SPORTSCASTER," wrote Sid Shalit in the *Daily News*. "WMCA has signed the baseball slugger to do a daily commentary preceding and following all Giants games."[3]

Mize knew the game, but he was never a big talker. So, it seems like an ironic career choice. Nonetheless, when the season began, Johnny was behind the mic, giving his opinion and notes on the game. Perhaps the Big Cat was a good luck charm for the Giants, who won the National League pennant in 1954, then swept the favored Cleveland Indians in the World Series. More likely, it was Willie Mays, returning from his hitch in the army to win a batting title and the Most Valuable Player Award at age twenty-three.

Before Johnny started the broadcasting gig, he put on a Richmond baseball uniform again for the first time in twenty years. This time it was the Richmond Virginians, a Class Triple-A team in the International League (IL). They had been the Baltimore Orioles through the 1953 season. But the St. Louis Browns moved to Baltimore and renamed themselves the Orioles for the 1954 season.

Managing the Virginians was a fellow Georgian and future Hall of Famer, Luke Appling, former shortstop for the Chicago White Sox. Johnny was a spring training coach for Appling or, as Shelley Rolfe of the *Richmond Times-Dispatch* wrote, "Spring training professor of hitting arts and sciences."[4]

At least one student remembered his professor fondly. Larry Ciaffone, a pickup from the Rochester Red Wings, was the hitting sensation of spring training. He credited Mize's tips.

"He stands behind the batting cage for two, three minutes. He tells you a few little things, and the results are automatic," Ciaffone said. "He's getting $6,000 for the spring training, then reports to New York for his radio work on Giants games."[5]

Johnny was hired to cover the Giants again on WMCA for the 1955 season, this time with a cohost, Boston Celtics legendary voice Johnny Most. Their show was called *Johnny on the Spot*, and it would precede and follow Giant games on WMCA.[6]

He also got back into a Giants uniform in 1955 as a part-time batting coach.[7] That fall, the *New York Daily News* reported that Mize would replace Bill Rigney as manager of the Minneapolis Millers in the American Association because Rigney had replaced the deposed Durocher in New

York. "Mize has long been recognized as one of the real students of the game and potential managerial material," read the story. "He has said all along he would be willing to take a job piloting a minor league team and now he has that chance."[8]

Willing or not, this was far from a done deal. Mize had not yet been offered the job, according to Rosy Ryan, the Millers' general manager. "I heard Mize's name mentioned as a possibility since he finished the season as a batting coach with the Giants," Ryan told the *Saint Paul Star Tribune* in a story published on October 2. "But I haven't discussed it yet with [Giants owner Horace] Stoneham. There will be a lot of names dropped into the hopper in conversation about the Miller manager, but I don't think any decision has been made yet."[9]

Mize, it turned out, was not Ryan's preference. The Millers also were interested in Eddie Stanky and Joe Gordon, but particularly Stanky, who had been fired as manager of the St. Louis Cardinals. Rigney, never very close with Mize (except for the fact that they slept a few feet from each other as Giants roommates), apparently lobbied for Stanky, who was a lot like Rigney—nervous energy, aggressive. Eddie, who detested his nickname "the Brat," was named Millers manager on October 3, and Ryan was pleased, saying, "Stanky was my No. 1 candidate."[10]

Mize kept mum about the Millers job that didn't happen and served as a part-time batting coach for the Giants again in 1956. But he added some new, bigger responsibilities to his life. In February, Johnny and Jene completed the $150,000 purchase of 120 acres, including 80 acres of citrus grove, along State Route 44 in Lake County, Florida. Central Florida had long become home for the couple during the off-season. Now it was their full-time home when Johnny wasn't working in New York. Mize also was co-owner of a liquor store in DeLand, where he kept memorabilia from his baseball career on display, including signed photos of his former Yankees teammates.

Ewell Blackwell recalled, in Donald Honig's book *Baseball between the Lines*, visiting Johnny's liquor store. First Blackwell told Honig that Stan Musial, as great as he was, never hit a home run off his side-winding delivery, adding that "neither did Johnny Mize."[11] And he told Honig about the liquor store, its shelves lined with baseballs autographed by all the pitchers Mize had hit home runs against.

"I walked in there one day and stood gazing at all those baseballs,"

Blackwell recalled. "'John,' I said, 'where's my baseball?' He growled a little and said, 'You don't have one.'"[12]

- - -

Over time, as Johnny devoted more time to his different postbaseball jobs, he and Jene grew increasingly apart. For years, Jene had enjoyed the lifestyle of being a ballplayer's wife. Supportive of his career, she attended most home games and kept scrapbooks filled with newspaper clippings of his heroics. But she wasn't happy that he played for as long as he had. By 1957 they were living apart, and Jene was spending more time with her mother. Her father had died in 1954. Then her mother, Gladys, died on June 16, 1957. More despondent than ever, on the evening of July 10, Jene fell asleep on a living-room couch while smoking a cigarette. She was severely burned in the resulting fire. She was thirty-nine when she died in the hospital on Sunday, July 14. Funeral services were held in the same chapel where Gladys had been memorialized a month earlier.[13]

- - -

Johnny didn't spend much time grieving—he had fallen in love again. Her name was Marjorie Harper Pope, a classy, popular Florida gal described as "a pretty radio station women's editor" in a wire story about their marriage on October 23. Following a simple ceremony in the home of Marjorie's parents, the new couple drove to New York for their honeymoon, then settled in Johnny's home in DeLand.[14]

This was also Marjorie's second marriage, and she had two children, Jim and Judi, twelve and eight. Overnight, Johnny had a family.

Not long after marrying Marjorie, Johnny sold his interest in the liquor store and focused on managing the eighty acres of orange grove, about a thirty-minute drive from his home in DeLand. "There was a house on that property, and we spent time there in the summers, tending the groves," Jim Mize recalled.[15]

In his book, *How to Hit*, Mize offers advice to fathers and sons, but it's from an abstract perspective. At that point in his life, he had zero experience as a parent and no consistent father figure to base his perspective on. Even with that, Mize's advice is sound: "Don't force your son to play baseball. Encourage him every way you possibly can, but don't try to make him love the game," he writes in the first chapter. In most cases, he adds, the boy will fall in love with the game in time, and it will be Dad "who will have to holler quits from shagging flies and throwing the ball too much."[16]

There is an almost wistful undertone to the sentiment. Johnny didn't have a daddy to introduce him to baseball or play catch with. Then, when he had a chance to be a father to his stepson, he probably should have stuck closer to his own advice.

As a youngster, Jim Mize typically was one of the best players on his baseball teams, but much of the time, that didn't seem enough to please Johnny, who had literally written the book on hitting. Even after a good game, which was most games for Jim back then, he might hear negative criticism from the Big Cat. Jim could have three solid base hits, but Johnny often would ask him why he swung at that pitch outside the strike zone.

"He was a tough, old-school guy," Jim said reflectively. "He grew up in the twenties and thirties, didn't really have parents in his life, and made it on his own, in his own way."[17]

While young Judi had Johnny wrapped around her finger, it was not always easy for Jim.

"We had very different personalities," Jim Mize said. "I was growing up, moving into my teen years. In retrospect, I think he was being a disciplinarian to make sure I knew the value of hard work. He had a good work ethic, and that's something I probably got from him, and it has served me well."[18]

Jim has some good baseball memories from boyhood: Johnny helping to get Major League scouts to come and watch him play as a high school kid. They liked what they saw. Jim played one season of pro ball for Middlesboro (Tennessee), a Cubs rookie team in the Appalachian League. He batted an impressive .284 as an eighteen-year-old outfielder but was released, so he switched gears, went to college, and had a long and successful career as a bank executive in Florida.

- - -

"Mize is like Ted Williams," Dick Young wrote after the Big Cat offered some pointers to a slumping Mickey Mantle in 1959. "When he talks, they listen; anybody who listens can learn. He was a master with a bat, in full command of the strike zone. When they fired close to Big Jawn, he'd tilt his head back casually and let the ball buzz by his stubble. His feet wouldn't budge. He saw the pitch, every pitch, all the way."[19]

So far, he'd landed part-time jobs as a hitting coach here and there, with the Giants for a couple of years, with Braves rookies during winter league ball in Florida, but nothing permanent. His situation changed in 1961, when an old Yankees teammate came calling. Soon, Johnny was in the big leagues again. Hank Bauer was managing the Kansas City Athletics, and one of his first orders of business was to tell owner Charlie Finley that the team needed a hitting coach.[20]

"The man I had in mind was Mize," Bauer said when the hiring was announced on July 1. "I think John was one of the best hitters I ever saw. He never moved his bat unless he was going to swing. When he'd come back to the bench, he could tell you whether a ball as an inch inside or an inch outside."[21]

Mize had helped Bauer with his hitting when they were both Yankees, and Hank liked the way Johnny worked with some of the younger guys in Yankees training camp. Bauer was, no doubt, also aware of how he'd helped Mantle. Mize was attending an old-timer's game at Yankee Stadium when he suggested Mantle lower his bat a little in his stance. After smacking a few balls in batting practice, Mize asked him how it felt. "Felt good," Mantle said. "Real good."[22]

Bauer wanted someone of Mize's temperament to coach his players on the finer points of hitting. "John has a lot of patience and that's what it takes to be a good instructor," Bauer said. "A lot of players who were good hitters don't have that patience and they can't get things across to younger players."[23]

Once Johnny got someone to take care of the citrus groves, he was on his way to Kansas City. Jim Mize remembered it as a fun summer.

"As a young ballplayer myself, I was really eager to be there," Jim said. "I'd warm up some of the players, even got in a little batting practice. It was a fun summer. Some of the players became friends with both Judi and me."[24]

Judi's fondest memory of that summer in Kansas City was probably Lew Krausse Jr., the teen pitching phenom for the Athletics. Many years later she said, smiling, "Lew Krausse stole my heart. I had a such a crush on him when Daddy was the Kansas City batting coach."[25]

Krausse was eighteen when he went from high school ball to the Athletics and pitched a shutout in his first game, on June 16, 1961. He was the son of Lew Krausse Sr., former Athletics pitcher and now a scout. The right-handed Lew Jr. never could live up to his brilliant debut but had a twelve-year Major League career.

"I always respected what Johnny had to say, because you can learn a lot about how hitters think by talking to smart hitters, and that was Mize," Krausse said in a 2000 interview. At the time, he was running an aluminum and steel distributorship in Kansas City.[26] Lew died in 2021.

"Johnny's son was just a few years younger than me, but he was a good ballplayer, and I remember Johnny had a cute, young daughter," Krausse said. He added with a laugh, "You have to remember, I was just out of high school."[27]

Judi, who described herself as "a pretty, blonde teenybopper," said that Marjorie "would dress me to the tens, in cashmere. I remember Lew's father saying, 'Here comes that cashmere cutie pie.' And I remember Mom saying, 'God, don't let her marry a ballplayer.' We would visit Charlie Finley when we stayed out there. He had a house on a lake, and I remember thinking that this was how everybody lives."[28]

- - -

Johnny wasn't a miracle worker, and that's what it would have taken to improve the 1961 Kansas City A's. Owned by Finley and run by Frank "Trader" Lane, this was a truly horrible ball club with a horrible history. When the team moved from Philadelphia to Kansas City in 1955, it finished in sixth place under Lou Boudreau. Since then, the A's had hobbled between seventh and eighth in the eight-team American League. In 1961 Hank Bauer became Kansas City's fifth manager when the previous skipper, Joe Gordon, was fired after sixty games and a 27-33 record.

The A's made the managerial move a few days after young Krausse's three-hit shutout of the Los Angeles Angels, an expansion team in its first year of existence. The addition of the Angels and a new version of the Washington Senators (the old version having moved to Minnesota to become the Twins) gave the American League ten teams in 1961.

While the Yankees, led by Roger Maris (61 homers) and Mickey Mantle (54), hit 240 home runs—crushing the record Mize's Giants had set in 1947—the Athletics hit a league-low 90 dingers. And only the Angels and

Senators had a lower team batting average than the A's, which also had the highest team earned run average. The Athletics finished in a tie for last place with the new Senators (61-100). The following season, Bauer was back but Mize was not.

That was Johnny's last full-time job in big league baseball.

"After that, he pretty much focused on the orange grove, and that was a pretty good source of income for a while, until we had several freezes," Jim Mize said. "My folks didn't want their income to be dependent on the elements anymore, so they sold the property."[29]

Johnny wasn't entirely through with baseball. He was a frequent invited participant in old-timer's games, particularly at Yankee Stadium, where these pregame exhibitions would routinely be televised nationally.

He also spent few months in 1965 as a batting instructor for the Mexico City Reds. Mize, former Brooklyn Dodgers slugger Babe Herman, and several other former big leaguers had been recruited to the Mexican League. This was part of a campaign by league president Antonio Ramirez to improve the quality of play, so that U.S. teams would start bidding for the services of Mexican players.[30]

After working in Mexico City for a few months, Mize's next foray into baseball, besides old-timer's games, was a ground-floor opportunity of an ambitious project that never got off the ground. It was called the Global League, the stillborn brainchild of huckster Walter Dilbeck, part owner in a couple Minor League ball clubs and a two-time failed mayoral candidate in Evansville, Indiana, where his real estate license had been revoked. The idea was to field two teams from the United States and one each in Japan, Puerto Rico, Venezuela, and the Dominican Republic. Or maybe it was three teams from the United States, one in Mexico City, and four in Japan. The alignment kept changing.[31]

He hired former Major League umpires. He tried to hire big league stars like Brooks Robinson and Don Drysdale and Henry Aaron. It was all bluff and bluster. But he somehow got Mize, Enos Slaughter, former baseball commissioner Happy Chandler, and other big league folk to climb aboard his train to nowhere.[32]

Johnny met Dilbeck in December 1968 and listened closely to the man's spiel, and he liked what he heard.[33] With the growth in popularity of the World Baseball Classic in the 2020s, perhaps Dilbeck had a slightly prescient notion. He didn't have any resources, though.

Mize was the highest paid manager and even received some of his promised $35,000—sometimes Dilbeck paid him in bills peeled from a money roll. In April 1969 Mize directed spring training as 150 players converged on Daytona Beach.

It was not an easy job.

"I think I have an ulcer," Mize complained to a reporter, then admonished, "You write something nice, not any of that other stuff."[34]

He was referring to the stories that had already been written, ridiculing the developing league, which scheduled its Opening Day for April 24 with all its games being played in Latin America. The games in Puerto Rico and the Dominican Republic took place in virtually empty ballparks.[35] And the teams in Venezuela faced a complete disaster—eighty-seven players were stranded in Caracas, unable to get hotel rooms or meals because the league owed about $100,000. The Japanese team was basically held for ransom—their players were blocked from leaving until hotel bills were paid. Some players were stuck in Venezuela for months.[36]

"It is hard to describe the confusion that existed when we arrived in the Caribbean," said Johnny, who returned home (as did Slaughter) after not getting paid for a few weeks.[37]

The Global League had disintegrated and taken Johnny Mize's baseball career with it.

In the summer of 1961, Johnny Mize was elected to the Hall of Fame—the Elmira Baseball Hall of Fame.[38]

But he never came close to being elected to the National Baseball Hall of Fame by the Baseball Writers Association of America. A player needs 75 percent of the vote from the BBWAA, and the closest he ever got was 43.6 percent in 1972.

He had the misfortune of retiring just before an epoch that author Joe Posnanski described as "the dark period of Hall of Fame voting." That is, 1957 to 1971, when the BBWAA voted just nine players into the Hall. Four of those were allowed through the hallowed doors only after Hall of Fame leadership strongly suggested the BBWAA hold special runoff elections. At the time, Posnanski wrote, "The writers seemingly didn't want anybody in the Hall of Fame."[39]

When Mize retired in 1953, Hall of Fame elections were held every year, and ballplayers became eligible for election after being retired for a year.

But in 1954, the eligibility rules changed—a five-year waiting period was installed for players. And from 1957 through 1965, elections were held every other year (returning to annual elections in 1966).

The BBWAA, acting as the guardians of high standards, weakened the Hall of Fame, Posnanski indicated. When the writers wouldn't vote for players, the Hall empowered its Veterans Committee, which elected thirty-six players from 1957 to 1971, "including some of the most questionable choices in the Hall today," wrote Posnanski, who used 1971 as the telltale year.[40]

That year, the writers didn't elect anyone, even though superstars like Yogi Berra, Duke Snider, and Mize were on the ballot. Meanwhile, the Veterans Committee elected some dubious inductees, such as Rube Marquard, Chick Hafey, Dave Bancroft, Harry Hooper, Jake Beckley, Joe Kelley, and former Yankees exec George Weiss.

"The BBWAA thought it was protecting the Hall of Fame much the way the people who created Prohibition thought they were protecting American values," Posnanski wrote. "And all either did was open up the back door."[41]

As each Hall of Fame voting season passed and Johnny wasn't elected, writers called him for reactions. He didn't hide his increasing bitterness.

"I'm getting too old now and it doesn't help me one way or another," Mize said following the 1971 vote. "Sometimes a guy puts his record down and lays it beside some of the others and gets a little disgusted about it."[42]

If a player wasn't inducted by the BBWAA within twenty years of retirement, he came off the ballot for five years, then he could be considered by the Veterans Committee. After failing to make the cut again in 1973, Johnny was disappointed the writers didn't think he was worthy of the Hall, while they'd elected some of his contemporaries, like Hank Greenberg, Ralph Kiner, Joe Medwick, and Lou Boudreau.

"I don't know why I'm not in there," Mize wondered a few years after the vote. "I was just never voted in."[43]

24

Going Home

His absence from the Hall of Fame
remains one of the larger injustices
perpetrated by the shrine's electors.　　—Hal Bock[1]

Mize was a shoemaker defensively,
quite disinterested in doing anything
at first base except catch a ball
thrown right to him or to reach for
an alibi. He was a selfish player.　　—Bob Broeg[2]

Bob Broeg, who claimed he was Johnny Mize's friend but was also brutally honest, wrote that the Big Cat was "strictly for No. 1." The longtime St. Louis sportswriter and BBWAA member also accused Mize of goldbricking while the St. Louis Cardinals were in a life-or-death struggle with the Brooklyn Dodgers for the 1941 pennant. These, Broeg explained, were just some of the reasons why he had consistently voted against his good friend Johnny Mize for all of those years.[3]

The baseball writers passed on Mize in the following Hall of Fame elections: 1960, 1962, 1964, then 1966 through 1973. The Big Cat, a batting champion who had hit home runs off Bob Feller, was 0 for 11 with the keyboard jockeys. After that, he was no longer eligible to appear on the writer's ballot.

But in February 1973 he was inducted into the Georgia Athletic Hall of Fame. Even then, however, he received the Rodney Dangerfield treatment—no respect.

Emcee Milo Hamilton, introducing Mize, mentioned that he was an All-Star nine times (it was ten), that he had played on four World Series championship teams (it was five), and that he hit 358 home runs (it was 359). On top of that, Mize was introduced last in the order, following a lineup of inductees that included a college track coach, college golf coach, and high school football coach.[4]

Mize responded with humor, taking it all in stride in front of 650 guests at the gala affair in downtown Atlanta. With laughter in his eyes he said, "Not only did they hit me in the ninth spot and cheat me out of those other things, but Milo said I hit three home runs in a game four times instead of six. That takes a big-league record away from me!" Moved by the recognition, he added, "I'm very appreciative of this honor. I'm very happy I was raised in Georgia."[5]

He also missed Georgia.

After selling their orange-grove property, Johnny and Marjorie left DeLand and lived for a while in Daytona. In 1974 they made Demorest their permanent residence, moving into Mize's boyhood home, the white cottage with the picket fence at 393 Oak Avenue, across from the city park and just down the street from the Piedmont College campus. They named it after their longtime home in DeLand: Diamond Acre.

Back in Demorest, Johnny tended his garden (he always had a green thumb, his mother said), smoked his pipe, walked down the street to the post office, went to church dinners, watched ball games on TV, mellowed out, and befriended some of Georgia's most influential politicians. And the little college town welcomed him back with open arms. In 1975 the city erected a decorative sign welcoming visitors to "Demorest, Home of Johnny Mize," and that same year, Piedmont established the Johnny Mize Athletic Award, given annually to the college's top all-around athlete.

The mountain folk were glad to have him back in the fold, and the mountains suited his laid-back demeanor.

But he was just a Delta flight away from the old-timer's reunions that still beckoned back in bustling New York. It was during one of these gatherings that Johnny met author Donald Honig for an interview that landed in *Baseball When the Grass Was Real* and helped bring more notoriety to the Big Cat, because the book was a hit.

It is a splendid sequel to Lawrence Ritter's classic *The Glory of Their Times*—Honig, a novelist and short story writer, took on the project at his friend Ritter's urging. The result is another classic, every bit as good as Ritter's groundbreaking book of oral baseball history.

Honig presents edited interviews from men who played the game in the '20s, '30s, and '40s. He captured the stories of Lefty Grove, Charlie Gehringer, Billy Herman, Pete Reiser, Bob Feller, Wes Ferrell, Cool Papa Bell, and Mize, among others. Decades later, Honig clearly remembered his impressions of the aging Big Cat.

"What I sensed in Mize was a deep pride and an unusually deep inner being," Honig said. "I don't want to sound presumptuous about what was, after all, a ninety-minute conversation. But I felt he was a man who kept a tight hold on his emotions, who shrewdly took in what was said to him and measured his responses carefully."[6]

When the book was published a year later and Honig sent Mize several copies to his home in Demorest, Mize wrote to the author "not one but two letters, praising the book with an effusion of complimentary phrases I would not have suspected of him," Honig said.[7]

This is very much like the Johnny Mize that former U.S. senator and Georgia governor Zell Miller got to know: the thoughtful, gracious Big Cat.

"He was just the most gentle, unassuming guy you'd ever find," said Miller, a rabid baseball fan from Young Harris, another small college town in the Northeast Georgia mountains, about forty-five curvy miles from Demorest.[8]

"When we first met, he was really surprised that I knew so much about his career," said Miller, lieutenant governor when he befriended Mize in the late 1970s.[9]

Miller, who died in 2018, grew up hearing stories about the Big Cat from his uncle, Hoyle Bryson, "who played semipro ball against Johnny, up here in Towns County, then played three years of Minor League ball before his arm gave out. My uncle remembered how good Johnny was as a teenager."[10]

Georgia State Senator John Foster, who introduced Miller to Mize, called Johnny "one of my dearest friends."[11]

Owner and operator of wcon, a radio station based in Cornelia, Foster had lived next door to Ty Cobb for a while. "He was my next-door neighbor when we both lived in apartments in Cornelia," Foster said. "We'd sit outside on the steps and chat about this and that. I never even asked him for his autograph."[12]

This was a point of pride for Foster—he didn't ask Mize for his autograph. Doing so seemed like a gauche thing to do, and he never wanted to come across as a fanboy. Besides, Foster was never a big pro sports fan. But he was a big fan of Johnny and Marjorie Mize, the celebrity couple in Habersham County.

"Around here, he was just John," said Foster, who made sure to brush up on his baseball history after meeting Mize. "After learning what I learned, I was absolutely stunned that he wasn't in the Hall of Fame."[13]

So, Foster got busy writing letters to every member of the Veteran's Committee in support of Mize's induction. Eventually, he spearheaded installation of a granite monument in Demorest Springs Park, commemorating Mize's baseball career.

"Johnny really appreciated the effort, and that made us very close friends," said Foster. "But I have no idea if my letters had any influence at all."[14]

- - -

Diamond Acre was a hive of activity on March 11, 1981. Marjorie hosted her weekly prayer meeting. And carpenters' tools could be heard buzzing upstairs on the second-floor porch, where they were building the "Dear John Room."[15]

Marjorie wanted a place to display the letters Johnny had received and his mementos "so the high school kids can come around and look at them," Marjorie said. "If it were up to John, he wouldn't show off anything. He's not very demonstrative, and I'm exactly the opposite."[16]

At 3:00 p.m., the construction crew, with Johnny helping, decided to quit for the day. There were too many work interruptions because the phone wouldn't stop ringing and Johnny had to keep answering it. Everyone in the country wanted to talk to the Big Cat about his election to the National Baseball Hall of Fame.

He received the news about half past noon, breathing a sigh of relief while expressing some regret.

"I knew if it didn't come this year, then I wasn't ever going in," Johnny told Ken Picking of the *Atlanta Constitution*. "I'm just a little disappointed they didn't see to vote me in earlier. My mother is 87 years old and in the hospital after having both of her legs removed after five operations. She always had looked forward to me getting in the Hall."[17]

After spending about five hours on the phone talking to the press and well-wishers, Mize told Picking, "I'm talked out." Then, as the phone rang again, he added, "So this is what it's like to be in the Hall."[18]

For his induction in August, Mize had an entourage: Marjorie; Judi and her husband; Jim's oldest son Darren; friends from Northeast Georgia, including Foster and Miller, who sat on folding chairs and cheered their friend; and the others receiving plaques that day, former Cardinals pitcher Bob Gibson and the late Negro Leagues founder, pitcher, and manager Rube Foster.

The quiet giant from Demorest had to stand up in front of three thousand people and make a speech. As he did so often when he was a ballplayer, he hit it out of the park.

"Baseball finally rectified one of its most glaring oversights this week with the induction of Johnny Mize into the Hall of Fame," wrote Larry Eldridge, sports editor of the *Christian Science Monitor*.[19]

Hal Bock, an AP sportswriter who grew up in New York watching Mize swing for the fences in the Polo Grounds, wrote, "It was an honor long overdue and it brought back memories of the man who used to hit all those home runs."[20]

Now that he was a Hall of Famer, new doors opened for Johnny—invitations to the White House, meetings with presidents and vice presidents, and annual visits to the Hall of Fame to see old friends, be celebrated, or have David Eisenhower recite poetry to him: "Not your eyes, Mize, not your eyes."[21] He was a member of baseball's most exclusive fraternity and grew closer to some of his old peers, like Ralph Kiner and his third wife, DiAnn. After both of her parents had died, Judi Mize kept in touch with the Kiners and some of her father's other baseball pals.

"DiAnn Kiner is precious to me—she was very close to my mother," Judi said in 2000. "Stan Musial is hilarious, maybe the craziest man I've met in my life. And Ted Williams—" She hesitated a second before adding with a smile, "Well, Ted put a move on me. Then he realized who I was and said, 'Wait, you're Johnny's daughter?'"[22]

The last Hall of Fame function Judi attended, she saw her father hanging out with Joe DiMaggio and Ted Williams. "Joe was a very private man," she said, adding with a chuckle, "Daddy and Ted surrounded him, the big guys trying to protect him."[23]

After his induction, Johnny was in greater demand. He traveled across the country, an invited guest at countless baseball-card and memorabilia shows, funneling about $40,000 of his autograph income to the local Boy Scout troop.[24] Along the way, the Big Cat became a pussycat.

Mize was usually the grand marshal of the annual Fourth of July parade through Demorest, soft-tossing baseballs and batting gloves that he had signed to the cheering crowd that lined Old U.S. 441. Local resident Richard Erwin was about sixteen when he met Johnny at the annual celebration, the city's marquee event.

"He was signing autographs, and my uncle told me to ask him to sign my baseball 'Johnny "Big Cat" Mize.' So, I did, and he, Johnny, got a big kick out of that, said he knew someone would ask him to sign it that way," Erwin said. "He was a nice guy."[25]

Stephanie Chitwood was a student at Demorest Elementary School when she walked to Diamond Acre with her class for a field trip. "He let us ring his doorbell, and it played 'Take Me Out to the Ballgame.' He was such a sweet person," she said.[26]

Lots of parents now were kids when Mize was alive, many of them with similar stories of just walking up to the front door at Diamond Acre, being greeted by Marjorie or Johnny, and leaving with a cookie, an autograph, and a story.

Mize found that wherever he went now, people were interested in what he had to say. Didn't matter if it was a baseball card show, an old-timer's game, or the highest office in the game. He left an impression.

"Listening to Johnny Mize at age eighty talk about hitting like he would be ready if called on was one of my joys as commissioner," said Fay Vincent, commissioner of baseball from 1989 to 1992.[27]

As he got older, Mize's large body betrayed him—he had both of his knees replaced, and the legs always bothered him. He had cataracts removed. He beat prostate cancer. And there was his heart. About two weeks before Christmas 1982, he had open-heart surgery and spent about two weeks in an Atlanta hospital.[28]

On October 26, 1985, Emma Mize died, after battling a series of illnesses the last six or seven years of her life. She was buried in the Loudermilk family cemetery. While they'd never enjoyed a traditional mother-son relationship, Johnny had looked after her needs, and when he was a player made sure to bring her to watch him play in the World Series.

Johnny was now the last living member of his immediate family—older brother Pope died in 1973 at age sixty-two in Knoxville, where he'd raised his family and operated a coin laundry.

A few years before his mother's death, Johnny approached Rev. Tom

Mewborn, pastor of Demorest Baptist Church, and told him he wanted to be a Christian. "I tell you," Mewborn said, "with those old knees of his, it wasn't easy getting in and out of the baptistry, but he did it."[29]

Mewborn remembers Marjorie as a graceful, outgoing woman who was easy to love. Because of her, the couple attended monthly fellowship dinners at the small church, and "they were the life of the party," Mewborn said. "John mellowed out quite a bit and began to feel more like a part of the community. Marjorie was his alter ego. She was loquacious, outspoken. That's probably why she had a radio show down in Florida when she was younger—she was a natural."[30]

The natural hitter and natural talker made for a cute old couple in Demorest. Johnny was the quiet giant, and Marjorie was his lively beauty. And theirs was a genuine love story.

"It tells you a lot about Johnny that she loved him so much," Mewborn observed. "She was a good judge of character and that, in itself, says a lot about Johnny."[31]

She was his constant companion. They went together to New York in May 1993 for a black-tie dinner to raise money for a Hall of Fame expansion. Johnny and Marjorie made a classy couple, socializing with old friends and teammates like Joe DiMaggio, Stan Musial, Yogi Berra, and Enos Slaughter.

But it wasn't as easy to travel these days—the damn knees. Before they got too painful, Johnny enjoyed going to Atlanta Braves games with his pal John Foster. The shy and quiet giant, who told Foster, "It's when they forget you that you have to start worrying," didn't even mind being mobbed by fans.[32]

He was eighty now and enjoyed watching the Braves on TV. They had become an exciting, winning ball club, and Johnny saw plenty of excitement that must have reminded him of old times as Atlanta won National League titles in 1991 and 1992 in thrilling pennant races. In 1993 the Braves were on their way to another division title and a team record 104 wins. But on June 1, a Tuesday night, they lost, 2–1, to the visiting San Diego Padres, wasting a great effort by starting pitcher John Smoltz. Johnny flicked the game off, went to sleep, and didn't wake up. It was a heart attack in the night.

Johnny Mize's sudden death made headlines in sports pages across the country, as former teammates and opponents weighed in on the Big Cat.

"If you could go back in time and just sit in the dugout again between Medwick and Mize," Marty Marion said wistfully. "They were such great rivals, even when they were on the Cardinals. Mize and Medwick were such tremendous competitors, and now they're both dead. It's a shame."[33]

Ralph Branca, the Dodgers' pitcher that Mize feasted on, called him "the toughest out in baseball."[34]

"He was the best hitter I ever saw," said Mize's fellow Hall of Famer Duke Snider, the great Dodgers center fielder.[35]

Enos Slaughter, one of the guys who kept in contact with Mize through the years, called his old friend "one of the best curveball hitters I ever saw. He had such a great batting eye."[36]

The funeral packed little Demorest Baptist Church. Marjorie had her children with her. Rev. Mewborn presided. Boy scouts in their uniforms filled six pews. Zell Miller was there. Most of Demorest was there. After the service, the Big Cat was buried at Yonah Memorial Gardens, on a green hill about a mile from the college campus where he once hit gargantuan home runs as a boy.

Epilogue   Extra Innings

I never copied any hitter. —Johnny Mize[1]

Long after Babe Ruth died, his wife Claire and her daughters kept receiving fan mail. Everyone loved the Babe and had memories or knick-knacks to share.

In 1980 Claire's daughter, Julia Ruth Stevens (who was adopted by Ruth) received a photo of her daddy from a fan, who also asked about her other baseball relative, her cousin Johnny Mize. Julia's letter to the fan, dated May 27, 1980, addressed, with great clarity, Mize's long absence from the Cooperstown elite: "Mother had always hoped that he'd be elected to the Hall of Fame, as of course so did I. However, I understand it's a question of politics and somehow Johnny is not too popular with the sports writers. Too bad, he sure deserves to be there."[2]

Julia was right—her cousin did not enjoy a great relationship with the press. Mize didn't help himself, his discomfort with reporters often coming across as disinterest or slowness, when actually he was a deep thinker. A man of few words, he could talk for hours about baseball.

"He was basically a quiet guy," said Enos Slaughter.[3]

A quiet guy who played in an era of great first basemen. Lou Gehrig was still playing when Mize broke into the big leagues. Bill Terry was active with the Giants. And of course, there was Hank Greenberg, a man Mize greatly respected.

Both large men, neither Mize nor Greenberg was a gazelle around first base. While Mize had a slight edge in fielding percentage, Greenberg had a slightly better range factor. Also, Greenberg was a full-time left fielder some years. Both men led their league in errors, range factor, assists, and fielding percentage at different points.

Hank was a two-time Most Valuable Player and helped lead the Tigers to four pennants. Mize never won an MVP Award but deserved at least one and possibly two. And when Johnny helped the Yankees win five straight pennants, he was past his prime, a role player in Casey Stengel's platoon system.

Greenberg came closer to Ruth's 60 homers than Mize, with 58 blasts in 1938, compared to Mize's 51 in 1947. Mize hit 359 home runs in fifteen seasons. Greenberg hit 331 in thirteen seasons.

Bill James—author, historian, baseball executive, and analytical guru—rates Mize as the better player. He ranked him as the sixth-best first baseman of all time in *The New Bill James Historical Baseball Abstract*; Greenberg is ranked eighth.[4]

James believes it's there in the numbers. In addition to his insightful, often hilarious writing, the author introduced new approaches to measuring a player's value. He called it sabermetrics, which he defined as "the search for objective knowledge about baseball."[5]

Two key sabermetric stats are WAR (wins above replacement) and win shares. WAR rates a player's value, deciphering how many more wins he's worth than a replacement player at the same position. Win shares calculates the number of wins a player contributes to his team.

"Mize has been tremendously underrated in history," James noted. "He probably should be rated ahead of Greenberg, but not only is he generally not remembered as being in a class with Greenberg, but people will actually be offended if you even suggest that he might be greater than Greenberg, although he easily has more WAR and Win Shares."[6]

Mize's lifetime WAR is 70.6, and Greenberg's is 55.4. Mize's total win shares is 338, Greenberg's 267. Greenberg has a higher lifetime slugging average (.605 to .562), higher on-base average (.412 to .397), and slightly higher batting average (.313 to .312). But Mize struck out a lot less. The career numbers are affected somewhat by the length of their careers, and both men lost significant time to service in World War II.

With the benefit of modern metrics, most rankings in recent years place Mize ahead of Greenberg. For example, the website Baseball Egg ranks the Big Cat fifth among first basemen and Greenberg tenth. But Hank was elected to the Hall of Fame in 1956 by the baseball writers, Mize twenty-five years later by the Veterans Committee. When you add it all up, Greenberg doesn't look twenty-five years better than Mize. But then, it doesn't really matter, because both men wound up where they belong, even if they got to Cooperstown by completely different routes.

- - -

Following Johnny's death, Marjorie kept getting invitations to the summer induction weekends at the Hall of Fame. She'd become a beloved fixture in Cooperstown, but she couldn't bear to go alone. So, she asked her son. Jim Mize had missed Johnny's induction in 1981, though his oldest son from his first marriage, Darren, represented the family well. Nonetheless, Jim was not going to miss out this time. He took his mom.

"We went together a few times, and those were some of the best, most exciting times of my life," said Jim. "Absolutely wonderful experiences— because of where we were, why we were there, and who I was with."[7]

The last time they went together was July 1995, for the induction of Mike Schmidt, Richie Ashburn, Leon Day, William Hulbert, and Vic Willis. Jim and Marjorie celebrated the new inductees. Jim played golf with Ralph Kiner and other baseball legends. He and Marjorie enjoyed the dinners, the reunions, the fellowship. It was a grand finale to what had become a fun tradition for Marjorie.

In February 1996 she was diagnosed with pancreatic cancer. She handled the news with the grace she was known and beloved for. "The doctor told her she had about six weeks to live, and it was almost six weeks to the day," Jim recalled.[8]

Marjorie spent most of that time in Demorest saying goodbye to friends who came to Diamond Acre, then moved into hospice care in Jacksonville, Florida, to be closer to her extended family. Jim had been flying up every weekend from Florida—the flight to Atlanta was quicker than the time it took to drive from the airport up to Demorest.

"She was just incredible during those final weeks," Jim said, "smiling at every one of her friends, reassuring them, telling them she was going on a vacation and she would see them all again in heaven. This was right before we left for Jacksonville. Seeing the joy in her, knowing what she was facing—my love for her was always strong, but in those days, it was bursting. Her example had a profound impact on me."[9]

Marjorie died on April 3 at Hadlow Center for Caring in Jacksonville. She was buried close to her roots, in Mount Zion Primitive Baptist Cemetery, back in Volusia County, Florida.

Once again, the invitations to the Hall of Fame induction weekend arrived. Marjorie had hoped to take Jim again. Now, Jim wasn't sure he could go alone. So, he let himself forget about it. "Then Ralph Kiner's wife, DiAnn, called," he said. "She said, 'There are a lot of people who loved your mother and would like to pay condolences—I think you'd better come.' She convinced me."[10]

He went to Cooperstown. One of the traditions of induction weekend, Jim remembered, included a gathering at the Baseball Hall of Fame and Museum following the banquet at the Otesaga Hotel. All the guests took limo rides to baseball Valhalla, where the mingling and the stories continued among the ancient relics, statues, plaques, and memorabilia.

The first thing Jim and Marjorie used to do upon arriving for this postbanquet soiree was make their way to the Plaque Gallery, where Johnny Mize's likeness hangs on a wall among all the other immortals. This time, Jim was by himself, and as he walked into the gallery, he saw several people observing the plaque of a new inductee, Ned Hanlon.[11]

Old "Foxy Ned" made his fame as the manager of the great Baltimore Orioles teams of the 1890s, though his playing career goes back to the 1880s. He is sometimes called "the Father of Modern Baseball" for his strategic innovations, such as the platoon system.

None of that really mattered to Jim. He was less interested in Foxy Ned's bronze plaque and baseball pedigree than he was in the woman standing there admiring it. Her name was Carolyn Hanlon—Ned's great-great-granddaughter. Jim and Carolyn started talking and they soon hit it off.

Today, Jim and Carolyn Mize live in Florida. Their marriage of more than twenty-five years has given the couple two children. While Johnny Mize may have been an awkward parent, Jim has unhesitatingly embraced fatherhood, with four children, including two sons from his first marriage.

But it's easy to imagine the spirit of Johnny Mize in some Elysian Fields clubhouse or perhaps an Iowa cornfield, a satisfied ghost in diaphanous cleats smiling at the thought of his son sharing his life with the descendant of another Baseball Hall of Famer, a pioneer of the game, another link in the family baseball tree: Cobb, Ruth, Mize, and now Hanlon.

- - -

Judi Mize lived in Diamond Acre for more than twenty years and became almost as well known in Demorest as her parents had been. A schoolteacher when she lived in Florida, she found a job as an English instructor at a local technical college after moving to Northeast Georgia.

When Piedmont University (then, Piedmont College) dedicated the Johnny Mize Athletic Center & Museum in the fall of 2000, Judi was there for the ceremony, leaning on a baseball bat for a cane. Big brother Jim was there with his family. Special guests from the baseball world included retired Braves knuckleball ace Phil Niekro and former New York Giant infielder Alvin Dark.

The museum, with its display cases holding artifacts and photos that the Mize family had donated, was placed in the front lobby of the facility, home of the college basketball teams and headquarters for the athletic department. There are bats, trophies, uniforms, photos of Mize with different presidents.

"Daddy would be proud of all this," Judi said that day.

Like her mother, she also was actively involved in her church. A devout Christian, she nonetheless wondered out loud if her father might be better off spending eternity in an ethereal cornfield—she loved the movie *Field of Dreams*.[12]

"That doesn't sound so bad, does it, as a kind of heaven," she mused. "I have a feeling that's where I'll find Daddy when I die."[13] By then Judi was using the cane all the time to get around slowly, due to her multiple sclerosis. Fortunately, because of the deal the Mize family had made with Piedmont College, she would always have a place to live.

In the end, Judi needed full-time care. She was seventy-three when she died on January 13, 2022. Judi's ashes were scattered at her father's grave, where there is a plaque listing all his baseball accomplishments. She would be Daddy's girl for all time.

- - -

The Big Cat is seventy-six and feels every bit of it. He feels it in his arthritic fingers, in his wrecked knees, and in his artificial hip, and he feels it with every breath since the heart bypass surgery seven years ago. And he couldn't be happier.

Here is Johnny Mize, Baseball Hall of Famer, comfortable in his own, worn skin, visiting a place that he knows and loves, central Florida, where he once grew oranges and sold liquor and enjoyed the sun and endured the tragic death of one wife and fell madly in love with another.

He's here to sign his autograph on baseball cards and anything else, selling his name to raise money for a local school system. Right now, the pen is in his pocket and a thirty-six-inch, thirty-three-ounce Louisville Slugger is in his hands. It's lighter than the tools he used when he was seventeen and thirty-five, but it still feels good. It feels right. It feels natural. And for a minute, he is seventeen, and he is thirty-five.

He tells a reporter there to cover the event, "Like my wife said, it's when they forget you that you start feeling something's wrong."[14]

Nothing is wrong here. He assumes the stance that once terrified the best pitchers on the planet, demonstrates the swing that was admired by the best hitters on the planet. A group of fans gathers around him, kids, and older folks who remember the Big Cat in his prime. Standing there, the center of everyone's attention, he swings his menacing swing and says, as much to himself as to them, "I loved hitting."[15]

- - -

After Judi Mize died, Piedmont University put Diamond Acre on the market. The property was sold in 2023, but the historical marker is still there in the front yard.

Administered by the Georgia Historical Society, it's typical of the metal roadside markers that can be seen throughout the country, on battlefields and birthplaces from coast to coast, three dimensional footnotes to the nation's history.

Erected and unveiled in 2000, seven years after Johnny died, it reads, "Home of Johnny Mize," along the top with "The Big Cat" in slightly smaller letters below that. And then, the marker text—Johnny's accomplishments were all there: his teen years at Piedmont, his seasons with the Cardinals, Giants, and Yankees, interrupted by service in World War II, his World Series heroics, his Hall of Fame induction, lifetime statistics.

And the one thing Johnny Mize would have seen right away if he'd been alive when the marker was unveiled: "In 1947, he hit 50 home runs while striking out only 42 times."

They wrote "50" (instead of 51) and cast it in metal! When the marker was unveiled it's easy to imagine the ghost of Johnny Mize shaking his spectral head, drawling, "Well, that figures."

- - -

Donald Honig's meeting with Johnny Mize for *Baseball When the Grass Was Real* was a reunion of sorts for the two men. Mize was the first Major League ballplayer he ever saw. A ten-year-old Brooklyn Dodgers fan in 1941, young Honig, with his brother, Stanley, and their father, were swept along with the crowd into the brilliant sunlight with a long, green field glittering in the distance like a mirage. Coming into focus, right in front of them, was the St. Louis Cardinals' dugout.

"There standing, unmistakably, was the imposing, broad-shouldered person of slugging first baseman and future Hall of Famer Johnny Mize, already with batting and home run championships to his name, his large, narrow-eyed moonface gazing impassively directly at us," Honig wrote in his autobiographical *The Fifth Season*. "'Johnny Mize,' I whispered breathlessly, taking hold of my brother's arm. 'I know,' he said as we gaped at our first big leaguer."[16]

So, yes, Johnny Mize always occupied a special place in Donald Honig's baseball-loving heart. Many years later, when he interviewed Mize in 1974, Don told him the story of this profound experience at Ebbets Field long ago. Mize's reaction? "He merely stared at me, patently unmoved, as impassive as that first time," Honig wrote, "waiting for me to say something more interesting."[17]

Honig, who has written more than thirty books—fiction, nonfiction, and most famously about baseball—built a fruitful career for himself being interesting. And he summed up Mize as well as anyone ever has.

"With his quiet voice, his keen, narrow eyes, his easy athletic grace, he was a memorable presence," Honig said. "He was not just a feared slugger, but also highly respected by his peers as a student of hitting. In his prime the very sound of his name, like the names of Babe Ruth and Jimmie Foxx, evoked strength, and power. Being a quiet and undemonstrative man only added to his menace at home plate."[18]

Impassive. Quiet strength. Grace and power. Narrow eyes. Undemonstrative. Menacing. Just like a big cat.

ACKNOWLEDGMENTS

This project began twenty-three years ago, then I put it down for about twenty years, then picked it up again. It's a long story. But if you've come this far, you already know that, and I am truly grateful that you've come this far. My sincerest thanks to you, dear reader.

Because this is a book with old, deep roots, some contributors have taken their backstage passes to the universe (a lovely euphemism for death that a dying friend gave me). While these people are beyond caring about acknowledgment, they should be remembered out loud, or in print, or pixels. For starters, there is Judi Mize, Johnny's stepdaughter, who welcomed me into her home and loved the idea of a book about her daddy. She was supportive, open, and gracious.

Also gone and deserving recognition are Buddy Blattner, Bobby Brown, Whitey Ford, Don Gutteridge, and Bill Werber, all of whom played baseball with Johnny Mize; Bob Broeg, who covered the St. Louis Cardinals for forty years; and Zell Miller, who served Georgia as lieutenant governor, then governor, then U.S. senator. These people all shared stories. Not wanting to have wasted their time, along with other reasons, I returned to Johnny Mize and tried to write the book that he deserves.

The book also has the beautiful cover that it deserves thanks to the late Edward Hastings Ford, vaudeville comedian, radio star, and under-appreciated artist. Ford presented the painting that the cover is derived from to Johnny Mize in 1947. The Mize family then donated the painting to Piedmont University. It is one of the first things a visitor now sees when entering the university library.

Special thanks go to these amazing writers who compose a Mount Rushmore of baseball authors: Donald Honig, Tom Stanton, Marty Appel, and Peter Golenbock. I have loved their books and learned from all of them. Donald and Peter helped start me on this journey, submitting to phone interviews way back when. And both were incredibly supportive when I contacted them again twenty years later to continue the Johnny Mize conversation.

Thank you, Joe Posnanski, Neal Hynd, and Gary Bedingfield for sharing your wonderful, insightful words, and thank you, Shawn Hennessey for generously sharing your knowledge and photographs.

Mighty thanks go to Carl Erskine, who picked up the phone one day and spoke with a stranger. So began a conversation about Johnny Mize, the Brooklyn Dodgers, Carl's son Jimmy, and Carl's own remarkable career. Meeting Carl, even over the phone, has been one of my greatest joys.

Bob Glass, dean of libraries at Piedmont University, was incredibly helpful, pointing me toward great photos and arranging visits to the Arrendale Library to sift through the Johnny Mize archives. Thanks also go to Cassidy Lent and John Horne at the National Baseball Hall of Fame and Museum, to Gary Mintz of the New York Giants Preservation Society, to Joseph Webb for his editing wizardry, to Sara Springsteen for shepherding this project at the University of Nebraska Press, and to her colleague Rob Taylor for giving the Big Cat a chance.

I'm also fortunate to have such great friends who have been tolerant and supportive and who have listened to me drone on about Johnny Mize and other mad projects through the years: Lisa Mount (who knew that a six-letter Hall of Famer was Mel Ott) and M. K. Wegmann and their Home for Wayward Girls, a wellspring of creativity; my fellow Wayward "Girls," Billy Chism, Jack Etheridge, and Jon Schwartz, who helped me on the path; and Andy Estes, my brother from another mother, whose spare room and advice have been both free and priceless.

Thank you, Bob Lundegaard and Steven Weiner for sharing your priceless baseball memories. Thank you, Paul Hemphill (a slick-fielding, light-hitting Class D infielder and a Major League author who wrote the greatest baseball novel of all time, *Long Gone*, and left the world too soon) and Susan Percy for gifting me Paul's old, dog-eared copy of *How to Hit*—signed by Johnny Mize—which has helped give *this* book a pulse.

Also, big thanks to former Georgia state senator John Foster and to the Reverend Tom Mewborn, who knew Johnny Mize not as a baseball legend but as a friend and a member of the community. And I am deeply grateful to Jim Mize, Johnny's stepson and Judi's big brother.

Thanks, always and forever, go to my family: Joe, the coolest son on the planet; Sam, daughter extraordinaire who kept saying, "Dad, write a baseball book" and then pitched in with her editing eyes and indexing expertise; and my best friend and wife and partner for life, Jane, as beautiful today as when we married (George Foster was playing for the Mets, to give you some context) and who continues to surprise me and enrich the world.

Finally, this book is dedicated to my parents, Anna and Tony, who grew up and fell in love in New York at a time when the city had three baseball teams.

Dad, who took his backstage pass to the universe in 1987, is the reason that I'm a baseball fan. But it was his appreciation of the game's improvisational drama and action, his love of the characters and humanity—the heroes and the villains—that kept him interested and continues to keep me interested.

And Mom may not be a devoted baseball fan, but she loves *The Pride of the Yankees* and *Field of Dreams*, and she always supported my passion for a ridiculous game. When I was thirteen or fourteen, Mom surprised me with a lovely thing she quietly made. She took the Hank Aaron autograph that I'd recently acquired, cut out magazine photos of Aaron and other players, and built a collage around the signature, then framed it. I'm looking at it now, hanging on the wall above my computer screen, while typing these words.

Thank you, Mom and Dad for always making me feel so loved, lucky, and inspired.

NOTES

Preface

1. Wheaties Champions List, Wheaties.com, n.d., http://www.wheaties.com /history/champions_list.aspx (webpage removed). For pictures of the seventy-fifth anniversary box, see https://mearto.com/items/75th-anniversary-box-of -wheaties.
2. Goliatero Pizancinio, "El 'Concordia' encabeza la Serie Coronel Trujillo Martinez, al blanquear por la mañana al 'Licey' y vencer también en la tarde de Ayer al 'Escogido,'" *Listin Diario* (Santo Domingo, DR), February 5, 1934.

Prologue

1. Jimmy Powers, The Powerhouse, *Daily News* (New York), July 6, 1953.
2. Posnanski, *Baseball 100*, 235.
3. Cohen, *50 Greatest Players in St. Louis Cardinals History*, 90.
4. Bill Werber, in discussion with the author, January 2001.
5. Peter Golenbock, in discussion with the author, May 2001.
6. Joe Lattanzi, in discussion with the author, May 2000.
7. Buddy Blattner, in discussion with the author, April 2000.
8. Blattner, discussion.
9. Durocher and Linn, *Nice Guys Finish Last*, 14.
10. Henrich, foreword, vi.
11. Bobby Brown, in discussion with the author, May 2001.
12. Donald Honig, in discussion with the author, September 2000.
13. Scott Pitoniak, "Bob Gibson Stars at Hall of Fame," Gannett News Service, *Courier News* (Bridgewater NJ), August 3, 1981.
14. Don Gutteridge, in discussion with the author, August 2000.
15. Furman Bisher, "Mize Was a Mountain of a Man," *Atlanta Constitution*, June 6, 1993.
16. "Johnny Mize," National Baseball Hall of Fame, n.d., https://baseballhall.org /hall-of-famers/mize-johnny.
17. Grantland Rice, The Sportlight, *Tampa Times*, July 25, 1951.

1. Hills of Habersham

1. Honig, *Baseball When the Grass Was Real*, 86.
2. J. S. Hartsfield, "Old Memories Recalled by Mize, Georgia," *Atlanta Journal*, February 27, 1921.
3. Hartsfield, "Old Memories."
4. Hartsfield, "Old Memories."
5. Hartsfield, "Old Memories."
6. Elizabeth B. Cooksey, s.v. "Habersham County," New Georgia Encyclopedia, last modified July 7, 2022, https://www.georgiaencyclopedia.org/articles/counties -cities-neighborhoods/habersham-county/; Margie Williamson, "Clarkesville and 'the Hills of Habersham,'" Now Habersham, last modified August 26, 2022, https://nowhabersham.com/clarkesville-and-the-hills-of-habersham/.
7. John C. Inscoe, s.v. "Unionists," New Georgia Encyclopedia, last modified June 8, 2017, https://www.georgiaencyclopedia.org/articles/history-archaeology/unionists/.
8. Cooksey, "Habersham County."
9. Cooksey, "Habersham County."
10. Lane, *History of Piedmont College*, 2.
11. Gwen Pope Mize, in discussion with the author, March 2001.
12. Furman Bisher, "Emma Mize's Son John," *Atlanta Constitution*, June 17, 1952.
13. Gwen Pope Mize, discussion.
14. Bisher, "Emma Mize's Son."
15. "Our History," Piedmont University, n.d., https://www.piedmont.edu/about -piedmont/history/.
16. Gwen Pope Mize, discussion.
17. Honig, *Baseball When the Grass Was Real*, 88.
18. Honig, *Baseball When the Grass Was Real*, 88.
19. Honig, *Baseball When the Grass Was Real*, 88.
20. Posnanski, *Baseball 100*, 236.
21. Mize and Kaufman, *How to Hit*, 5.
22. Mize and Kaufman, *How to Hit*, 5.
23. "Interview with James Davis (Spec) Landrum," by Thomas Allan Scott, February 12, 2004, Kennesaw State University Oral History Project, https://soar.kennesaw .edu/handle/11360/367.
24. Mize and Kaufman, *How to Hit*, 6.
25. Jack Ellard, in discussion with the author, March 2000.
26. Ellard, discussion.
27. "Christians Lose to Georgia Team," *News and Observer* (Raleigh NC), April 25, 1930.
28. "Atlanta League," *Atlanta Constitution*, April 27, 1930.
29. Eddie Allen, "Grandma, I'm Goin' with This Man," *Charlotte Observer*, June 11, 1950.
30. Allen, "Grandma, I'm Goin'."
31. Allen, "Grandma, I'm Goin'."
32. Allen, "Grandma, I'm Goin'."

33. J. G. Taylor Spink, "Nobody Gets Sore on Being Sent to the Yankees," *Sporting News*, August 31, 1949, 12.

34. Honig, *Baseball When the Grass Was Real*, 88.

35. Birtwell, "Yankees' Top Pinch Hitter in First Series After 20 Years of Pro Ball," *Boston Globe*, October 8, 1949.

36. Honig, *Baseball When the Grass Was Real*, 88.

2. High Drama in the Low Minors

1. Frank Graham, "They All Love the Big Cat," *Sport*, January 1953, 80.

2. "Interview with James Davis (Spec) Landrum."

3. "Interview with James Davis (Spec) Landrum."

4. "Interview with James Davis (Spec) Landrum."

5. "Interview with James Davis (Spec) Landrum."

6. Greenberg and Berkow, *Hank Greenberg*, 22.

7. Greenberg and Berkow, *Hank Greenberg*, 21.

8. "Bedders Take Atlanta Loop Diamond Title," *Atlanta Constitution*, September 28, 1930.

9. Associated Press, "Patriots Lick Collegians, 8–7," *Charlotte Observer*, April 16, 1931.

10. "Pats Sign Mize, Former Collegian," *Charlotte News*, June 1, 1931.

11. Associated Press, "Dixie's Baseball Territory Is Gradually Taking Form," *Charlotte News*, January 3, 1931.

12. Associated Press, "Charlotte and Asheville Admitted to Piedmont, Forming 8-Club Loop," *Greenville (SC) News*, March 5, 1931.

13. "William Bramham," Baseball Reference, last modified November 28, 2011, https://www.baseball-reference.com/bullpen/William_Bramham.

14. "William Bramham."

15. "William Bramham."

16. "William Bramham."

17. "The History & Function of Minor League Baseball," Milb.com, n.d., https://www.milb.com/milb/history/general-history.

18. United Press International, "Minor Czar Approves Deal for Negro Star," *Daily News* (New York), October 26, 1945.

19. "Johnny Kane Claims He'll Quit Baseball," *News and Observer* (Raleigh NC), September 15, 1931.

20. "Pats Promote Pair to Rochester Red Wings," *News and Observer* (Raleigh NC), September 13, 1931.

3. Scenic Route in the Bushes

1. Golenbock, *Spirit of St. Louis*, 213.

2. Joe Mathes to Johnny Mize, telegram, March 31, 1932, Johnny Mize Collection, Arrendale Library, Piedmont University Archives, Piedmont GA.

3. "Pats Promote Pair to Rochester Red Wings," *News and Observer* (Raleigh NC), September 13, 1931.

4. "1939 St. Louis Cardinals Affiliates," Stats Crew, n.d., https://www.statscrew.com /minorbaseball/a-SLN/y-1939; 1939 St. Louis Cardinals Minor League Affiliates, Baseball Reference, n.d., https://www.baseball-reference.com/register/affiliate .cgi?id=STL&year=1939.

5. Bobby Norris, "Teachers Defeat Piedmont, 29 To 22," *Macon Telegraph*, March 6, 1932.

6. "Piedmont Beaten by Norman, 6 to 4," *Macon Telegraph*, April 3, 1932.

7. "Rams Defeated by Piedmont, 9–7," *Macon Telegraph*, April 5, 1932.

8. Jim McCulley, "Mize Acclaimed Lone Hitter without Single Weakness," *Daily News* (New York), June 29, 1947.

9. Christensen, "Take Me Out."

10. Associated Press, "Triplets Rally to Beat Out Elmira," *Standard-Sentinel* (Hazleton PA), May 5, 1932.

11. Don Seeley, "Lefty Heise Captures 12th Contest for Red Wings," *Star-Gazette* (Elmira NY), July 13, 1932.

12. Don Seeley, "Wings Are Close to .500 in Standings," *Star-Gazette* (Elmira NY), July 15, 1932.

13. "Mize Injured, Lost to Team about 10 Days," *Star-Gazette* (Elmira NY), June 16, 1932.

14. Associated Press, "Johnny Mize Is Returned to Greensboro," *Herald-Sun* (Durham NC), December 25, 1932.

15. Associated Press, "Mize Stars as Pats Cop Opener," *Asheville Citizen-Times*, April 25, 1933.

16. Edward Mitchell, "Mize Leads Attack as Locals Take Slugfest," *News and Record* (Greensboro NC), April 28, 1933.

17. John Herndon, "Insects Trim Pats by 4–3 When Frank Delivers in Clutch," *Charlotte Observer*, August 4, 1933.

18. "Red Wings Break Even in Double Bill with Jersey Skeeters," *Democrat and Chronicle* (Rochester NY), August 6, 1933.

19. "Red Wings Break Even."

20. Henry Clune, "Wings' Home Debut under Lights Finds Them Looking Like Nervous Chorus Girls," *Democrat and Chronicle* (Rochester NY), August 8, 1933.

21. Clune, "Wings' Home Debut under Lights."

22. Clune, "Wings' Home Debut under Lights."

23. "The Play-Off Experiment," *Democrat and Chronicle* (Rochester NY), September 12, 1933.

24. Joseph T. Adams, "Spec's Men Primed for Tough Fight," *Democrat and Chronicle* (Rochester NY), September 12, 1933.

25. "Shires Gets Shave," *Buffalo News*, September 20, 1933.

4. Beisból with El Maestro

1. O'Neil, Wulf, and Conrads, *I Was Right on Time*, 3.

2. McNeil, *Black Baseball out of Season*, 114.

3. David Lidman, "Barnstorming Colts Return," *Richmond Times-Dispatch*, February 17, 1934.

4. Lidman, "Barnstorming Colts Return."

5. Rollo Wilson, "Baseball in Puerto Rico," *Pittsburgh Courier*, December 16, 1933.

6. Paul Ramos, "As We Celebrate This Historic Centennial, Why Puerto Rican Baseball Truly Matters in Negro League History," Conbasesllenas.com, August 16, 2020, https://conbasesllenas.com/as-we-celebrate-this-historic-centennial-why-puerto-rican-baseball-truly-matters-in-negro-leagues-history/.

7. Posnanski, *Baseball 100*, 664.

8. Lidman, "Barnstorming Colts Return."

9. Guilfoyle, *National Baseball Hall of Fame and Museum Yearbook*, s.v. "Martin Dihigo," 106.

10. Cora, prologue, 11.

11. Cora, prologue, 12.

12. Torombolo, "Los Rubios Continentales del Richmond alconzaron la Victoria en los dos juegos celebrados ayer Domingo contra las nevenas capitaleñas Licey y Escogido," *Listin Diario* (Santo Domingo, DR), November 13, 1933.

13. Dihigo, *My Father Martin Dihigo*, 98.

14. Guilfoyle, *National Baseball Hall of Fame and Museum Yearbook*, s.v. "Martin Dihigo," 106.

15. Jim Mize, in discussion with the author, March 2022.

16. Wilson, "Baseball in Puerto Rico."

17. Doc Silva, "Hockette, Hannahoe, Homan Back from Tropics," *Reading (PA) Times*, January 26, 1934.

18. Silva, "Hockette, Hannahoe, Homan."

19. "Llegó ayer a esta capital el potente team 'Richmond,'" *Listin Diario* (Santo Domingo, DR), November 9, 1933.

20. Roorda, "Wreck of the USS *Memphis*."

21. Roorda, "Wreck of the USS *Memphis*."

22. Torombolo, "Rubios Continentales."

23. Goliatero Pinancinio, "Los Leones del 'Escogido' vencen al 'Richmond' por la mañana y éste al 'Licey' por la tarde," *Listin Diario* (Santo Domingo, DR), November 20, 1933.

24. Pinancinio, "Los Leones."

25. Revel and Munoz, *Forgotten Heroes: Juan "Tetelo" Vargas*.

26. Gómez, "Tetelo Vargas en Venezuela."

27. Golioataro Pinancinio, "El 'Concordia' encabesa la Serie Coronel Trujillo Martinez," *Listin Diario* (Santo Domingo, DR), February 5, 1934.

28. Torombolo, "Martin Dihigo y Pinzón sobre el center," *Listin Diario* (Santo Domingo, DR), February 12, 1934.

29. Torombolo, "Sensacional fue el juego de la tarde," *Listin Diario* (Santo Domingo, DR), February 19, 1934.

30. "Ayer partio para los Estados Unidos el famoso player Mize," *Listin Diario* (Santo Domingo, DR), February 21, 1934.

31. Ty Cobb [pseud.], "El 'Concordia' ganó la Serie Cor. Rafael Trujillo Martínez," *Listin Diario* (Santo Domingo, DR), February 28, 1934.

32. Dihigo, *My Father Martin Dihigo*, 99.

5. Can Mize Field This Year?

1. Joe Adams, "Dodgers Get 7 Tallies in First Game," *Democrat and Chronicle* (Rochester NY), March 19, 1934.

2. Joe Adams, "John Mize Stars with Four Blows," *Democrat and Chronicle* (Rochester NY), April 19, 1934.

3. "Melton Hit off Mound in Seventh," *Democrat and Chronicle* (Rochester NY), April 22, 1934.

4. "Carey's Fifth Hit Nets Victory for Wings," *Democrat and Chronicle* (Rochester NY), April 29, 1934.

5. Henry Clune, "Marshal Rutz, Maranville Give Opener Proper Setting," *Democrat and Chronicle* (Rochester NY), May 3, 1934.

6. Joe Adams, "Wings Down Orioles in Home Debut," *Democrat and Chronicle* (Rochester NY), May 3, 1934.

7. Joe Adams, "Mize, Winsett and Lewis Hit Homers as Wings Defeat Orioles Again, 6–2," *Democrat and Chronicle* (Rochester NY), May 5, 1934.

8. Joe Adams, "Mize Hurt on Sack in Third Frame," *Democrat and Chronicle* (Rochester NY), May 7, 1934.

9. "Umpire Has Last Say on Final Pitch," *Democrat and Chronicle* (Rochester NY), May 31, 1934.

10. "Wing First Baseman May Be Out for Year," *The Gazette* (Montreal), June 9, 1934.

11. "Mize Out at Least Another Month as Examination Shows Pelvis Growth," *Democrat and Chronicle* (Rochester NY), June 9, 1934.

12. Mead, "Surgeon General of Baseball," 95.

13. Mead, "Surgeon General of Baseball," 96.

14. Byrd, "Femoroacetabular Impingement."

15. Joe Adams, "Double Win for Wings over Leafs Yields Second Place, Gain on Newark," *Democrat and Chronicle* (Rochester NY), July 5, 1934.

16. "Red Wings Defeat Albany to Capture Playoff Series," *Democrat and Chronicle* (Rochester NY), September 19, 1934.

17. "Blake Hurls Wings into Submission," *Democrat and Chronicle* (Rochester NY), September 20, 1934.

18. Joe Adams, "Red Wings Break Out in Rash of Hits to Trip Leafs," *Democrat and Chronicle* (Rochester NY), September 24, 1934.

19. Joe Adams, "Leafs Gain Right to Play Association Flag Winner," *Democrat and Chronicle* (Rochester NY), September 25, 1934.

20. "Mize, Rochester Star Will Join Birds Tomorrow," *St. Louis Post-Dispatch*, September 28, 1934.

6. The Temporary Red

1. "This Johnny Mize Has Bat of Big League Size," *Cincinnati Post*, March 21, 1935.
2. Arch Ward, Talking it Over, *Chicago Tribune*, September 17, 1934.
3. W. H. James, Reflections from the Sidelines, *Globe-Democrat* (St. Louis), September 19, 1934.
4. Tom Swope, "Big League Clubs Have Swap Fever," *Cincinnati Post*, December 5, 1934.
5. "Larry MacPhail," National Baseball Hall of Fame, n.d., https://baseballhall.org/hall-of-famers/macphail-larry.
6. Tom Swope, "Bosses Buy Lew Riggs, Goodman," *Cincinnati Post*, November 22, 1934.
7. Jack Ryder, "Cincinnati Club Offers $55,000 for First Sacker Mize," *Cincinnati Enquirer*, December 14, 1934.
8. Jack Ryder, "Mize Deal Completed; Red Infield Now Is Set," *Cincinnati Enquirer*, December 25, 1934.
9. Ryder, "Mize Deal."
10. Ryder, "Mize Deal."
11. Ryder, "Mize Deal."
12. Jack Ryder, "Mize Attracts Kelly by Natural Actions," *Cincinnati Enquirer*, February 23, 1935.
13. "Mize's Hitting Features Reds' Training Work," *Tampa Tribune*, February 27, 1935.
14. Red Newton, "Red Rookies Slam Homers in Game Here," *Tampa Tribune*, March 5, 1935.
15. Newton, "Red Rookies."
16. *Cincinnati Post, When Mize Catches 'Em They Ought to Stay Caught*, March 13, 1935, photograph.
17. "Mize's Leg Is Ailing Again; Manager Dressen Worried; Bottomley Is at First Base," *Cincinnati Enquirer*, March 25, 1935.
18. Associated Press, "Veteran Declares Club's Terms Are Not Satisfactory," *Dayton Daily News*, March 30, 1935.
19. Joe Aston, "Is Mize Worth $55,000?" *Cincinnati Post*, April 6, 1935.
20. Associated Press, "Injury to Keep Howell in Hospital for Two Weeks," *Dayton Daily News*, April 12, 1935.
21. Associated Press, "Mize Returned to Cards; Bottomley Plays First Base," *Dayton Daily News*, April 15, 1935.
22. Grantland Rice, "Gehrig's Slugging Supremacy to Face Challenge, Says Rice," *Baltimore Sun*, April 15, 1935.
23. Associated Press, "Mize Returned."
24. Honig, *Baseball When the Grass Was Real*, 89–90.

7. All the Way Back

1. "Johnny on the Spot," *Democrat and Chronicle* (Rochester NY), April 25, 1935.
2. Honig, *Baseball When the Grass Was Real*, 90.
3. Honig, *Baseball When the Grass Was Real*, 90.
4. Matt Jackson, "Mize Returned to Wings for First Base Berth," *Democrat and Chronicle* (Rochester NY), April 23, 1935.
5. Jackson, "Mize Returned."
6. "Johnny on the Spot."
7. "1935 Rochester Red Wings Roster," Stats Crew, n.d., https://www.statscrew.com/minorbaseball/roster/t-rw14128/y-1935; "1930 Rochester Red Wings Roster," Stats Crew, n.d., https://www.statscrew.com/minorbaseball/roster/t-rw14128/y-1930.
8. "Giles to Accept Blame, Not Dyer," *Democrat and Chronicle* (Rochester NY), May 2, 1935.
9. "Giles to Accept Blame."
10. "Mize's Butterfly Net Glove Gets Wild Ones," *Democrat and Chronicle* (Rochester NY), May 4, 1935.
11. "Mize's Butterfly Net Glove."
12. "Mize's Butterfly Net Glove."
13. "Lyons' Five-Hit Twirling Stops Newark Bears, 5 to 0," *Democrat and Chronicle* (Rochester NY), May 3, 1935.
14. "Carey, Mize Lead 15-Hit Barrage off Bird Hurlers for 12–5 Win," *Democrat and Chronicle* (Rochester NY), June 19, 1935.
15. "Revived Wings Hand Bewildered Bisons Pair of Setbacks, 6–4, 8–2," *Democrat and Chronicle* (Rochester NY), June 25, 1935.
16. "Wings Return Johnny Mize to St. Louis; Wilson Signs," *Democrat and Chronicle* (Rochester NY), July 23, 1935.
17. Honig, *Baseball When the Grass Was Real*, 90.
18. Ralph McGill, "An Atlanta Doctor Sent Mize to the Majors," Break o' Day, *Atlanta Constitution*, May 17, 1936.
19. McGill, "Atlanta Doctor."
20. "Johnny Mize Doing Well, after Operation," *St. Louis Post-Dispatch*, November 18, 1935.
21. Mead, "Surgeon General of Baseball," 96.
22. "Mize, Through Exercise, Will Try To Prove Cards Got a Break When $55,000 Deal for Him Fell Through," *St. Louis Post-Dispatch*, December 8, 1935.
23. "Mize, Through Exercise."

8. Cardinals Rookie

1. W. H. James, Reflections from the Sidelines, *St. Louis Globe-Democrat*, April 15, 1936.
2. Martin J. Haley, "Cardinals Lose Protested Battle to Cubs, 5–3," *St. Louis Globe-Democrat*, April 17, 1936.
3. "Frisch Holds 1.000 Record in Fielding," *St. Louis Globe-Democrat*, April 14, 1936.

4. Golenbock, *Spirit of St. Louis*, 214.
5. Associated Press, "Stengel Offers Two Players and Cash for First-Sacker," *St. Louis Post-Dispatch*, February 5, 1936.
6. Jack Troy, "Johnny Mize, of Cards, Sought by Big Teams," *Atlanta Constitution*, January 26, 1936.
7. J. Roy Stockton, "Chance for Rookies," *St. Louis Post-Dispatch*, February 21, 1936.
8. Associated Press, "Paul Dean Leaves for Camp after Agreement," *St. Louis Globe-Democrat*, March 24, 1936.
9. J. Roy Stockton, "Cardinals Use Five Pitchers in Losing to Pirates, 12 to 5," *St. Louis Post-Dispatch*, April 26, 1936.
10. Associated Press, "Dizzy Turns Back Pirates, 3–2," *Star Tribune* (Saint Paul MN), April 27, 1936.
11. Mize and Kaufman, *How to Hit*, 92.
12. Mize and Kaufman, *How to Hit*, 92.
13. Mize and Kaufman, *How to Hit*, 92.
14. Thad Holt, "Mize and Cards Talk Salary Terms Monday," *Atlanta Constitution*, January 23, 1938.
15. Martin J. Haley, "Mize Leads Cards to 3–2 Triumph over Giants," *St. Louis Globe-Democrat*, May 1, 1936.
16. Martin J. Haley, "Parmelee Allows Only Six Safeties, Hubbell Yields 11," *St. Louis Globe-Democrat*, April 30, 1936.
17. Don Gutteridge, in discussion with the author, August 2000.
18. Gutteridge, discussion.
19. Ernest Mehl, Sporting Comment, *Kansas City Star*, August 18, 1961.
20. Gutteridge, discussion.
21. Ray J. Gillespie, "Recruit Mize, in Batting Slump, to Be Benched Today by Cards," *St. Louis Star-Times*, May 29, 1936.
22. J. Roy Stockton, "Dizzy Dean Doubles to Gain His Eighth Victory of Year," *St. Louis Post-Dispatch*, May 30, 1936.
23. Gillespie, "Recruit Mize."
24. Gillespie, "Recruit Mize."
25. Durocher and Linn, *Nice Guys Finish Last*, 144.
26. J. Roy Stockton, "More Hitting Needed If Cards Are to Retain Chance for Flag," *St. Louis Post-Dispatch*, September 10, 1936.
27. Ray J. Gillespie, "Banishment of Mize by Umpire Paves Way for 3 Chicago Runs," *St. Louis Star-Times*, September 28, 1936.
28. Frank Graham, "They All Love the Big Cat," *Sport*, January 1953, 80.
29. Gillespie, "Banishment of Mize."
30. Gay, *Satch, Dizzy & Rapid Robert*, 161.
31. Gay, *Satch, Dizzy & Rapid Robert*, 159–66.
32. Peterson, *Only the Ball Was White*, 242.
33. Peterson, *Only the Ball Was White*, 242.

34. Gay, *Satch, Dizzy & Rapid Robert*, 166.
35. W. H. James, Reflections from the Sidelines, *St. Louis Globe-Democrat*, April 10, 1936.

9. Johnny and Jene

1. Jene Mize, "Yell of 'Hit Him in the Head!' Worst Worry of Player's Wife," From the Feminine Viewpoint, *Sporting News*, November 19, 1942, 16.
2. Broeg, in discussion with the author, March 2000.
3. "Johnny Mize Weds," *St. Louis Post-Dispatch*, August 9, 1937.
4. Bill Boring, "Babe Boosts Mize's Ambition," *Shreveport Journal*, January 29, 1937.
5. Boring, "Babe Boosts Mize's Ambition."
6. Martin J. Haley, "Paul Dean at Cards' Camp Opening Rites," *St. Louis Globe-Democrat*, March 2, 1937.
7. Scotty Reston, "Cincinnati Also Interested in Buying Hurler," *St. Louis Globe-Democrat*, February 6, 1937.
8. Honig, *Baseball When the Grass Was Real*, 92.
9. Jimmy Cannon, Jimmy Cannon Says, *Newsday* (New York), December 17, 1958.
10. Broeg, discussion.
11. Gutteridge, in discussion with the author, August 2000.
12. Gutteridge, discussion.
13. Broeg, discussion.
14. Gutteridge, discussion.
15. J. Roy Stockton, "First-Baseman Hit on Head by One of Gumbert's Pitches," *St. Louis Post-Dispatch*, September 2, 1937.
16. Mize, "Yell of 'Hit Him in the Head!'"
17. "Tiger Manager Battles Death after Accident," *News Messenger* (Fremont OH), May 26, 1937.
18. Honig, *Baseball When the Grass Was Real*, 92–93.
19. L. C. Davis, "The Passing Show," *St. Louis Post-Dispatch*, September 5, 1937.
20. Golenbock, *Spirit of St. Louis*, 214.
21. Golenbock, *Spirit of St. Louis*, 214.
22. Golenbock, *Spirit of St. Louis*, 214.
23. Honig, *Baseball When the Grass Was Real*, 92.
24. Cannon, Jimmy Cannon Says.
25. John O'Donnell, "Major Leaguers Put on Real Show to Beat Colored Stars Before 4,000 Fans," *Davenport Democrat and Leader*, October 6, 1937.
26. O'Donnell, "Major Leaguers Put on Real Show."
27. "It'll Be Golf, Hunting and Fishing for Most Cardinals after Season Is Completed," *St. Louis Star-Times*, September 29, 1937.

10. Rule of Three

1. Sid Keener, "Mize Is Now Best First Baseman in Game," *St. Louis Star-Times*, April 1, 1938.

2. W. Vernon Tietjen, "Johnny Mize Equals League's Home Run Mark as Cards Lose," *St. Louis Star-Times*, July 14, 1938.

3. Sid Keener, Sid Keener's Column, *St. Louis Star-Times*, July 2, 1938.

4. Mize and Kaufman, *How to Hit*, 81.

5. Mize and Kaufman, *How to Hit*, 80.

6. Tietjen, "Johnny Mize."

7. Tietjen, "Johnny Mize."

8. Gutteridge, in discussion with the author, August 2000.

9. Tietjen, "Johnny Mize."

10. Tietjen, "Johnny Mize."

11. Haley, "John Belts Three Homers in Finale," *St. Louis Globe-Democrat*, July 21, 1938.

12. Creamer, *Babe*, 411.

13. Hy Turkin, "Cards Tie Dodgers; Cuyler Hits Homer," *Daily News* (New York), August 4, 1938.

14. Hy Turkin, "Dodgers Thrash Cards in Double Bill, 6–2, 9–3," *Daily News* (New York), August 3, 1938.

15. "P.A. Forgets to Duck," *Brooklyn Daily Eagle*, August 3, 1938.

16. Gutteridge, discussion.

17. Sid Keener, "Frisch Believes High Salary Caused His Dismissal by Cardinals," *St. Louis Star-Times*, September 12, 1938.

18. Keener, "Frisch Believes."

19. "New Cardinal Boss to Follow Policies of Frankie Frisch," *St. Louis Star-Times*, September 12, 1938.

20. Golenbock, *Spirit of St. Louis*, 218.

21. Associated Press, "'Watch the Gas' and Pope Mize Crashes Back into Baseball," *Montgomery Advertiser*, March 10, 1938.

22. Margaret Turner, "Scatterings," The Woman's Angle, *Lubbock (TX) Avalanche-Journal*, June 19, 1938.

23. "Little Brothers," *Fort Worth Star Telegram*, May 2, 1938.

24. Joe LeBlanc, "Cards Reject $250,000 for Medwick and Mize," *Collyer's Eye and the Baseball World*, December 3, 1938, 3.

25. Martin Haley, "Rickey Says Cubs Never Made Offer for Mize," *St. Louis Globe-Democrat*, January 26, 1939.

26. Dick Farrington, "Pay Roll of Cards Close to $200,000," *Sporting News*, February 2, 1939, 8.

27. Farrington, "Pay Roll of Cards."

28. Farrington, "Pay Roll of Cards."

11. Best Hitter in the National League

1. Jimmy Powers, The Powerhouse, *Daily News* (New York), August 22, 1939.

2. "Mize's .360 Paces NL Batting Race," *Daily News* (New York), September 3, 1939.

3. Golenbock, *Spirit of St. Louis*, 221.

4. Golenbock, *Spirit of St. Louis*, 221.

5. Golenbock, *Spirit of St. Louis*, 221.

6. Dick Farrington, "Ducky Likely to Be Stubborn Bird," *Sporting News*, February 29, 1940, 3.

7. Martin Haley, "Medwick Protests Removal by Blades as Cards Nip Bees, 4–3," *St. Louis Globe-Democrat*, August 2, 1939.

8. Don Gutteridge, in discussion with the author, August 2000.

9. J. Roy Stockton, Extra Innings, *St. Louis Post-Dispatch*, November 8, 1938.

10. Sid Keener, Sid Keener's Column, *St. Louis Star-Times*, August 19, 1939.

11. Lou Smith, "Reds-Cards Split; One Win Needed," *Cincinnati Enquirer*, September 27, 1939.

12. Advertisement, *Baltimore Afro-American*, November 29, 1941.

13. "Sports Dope," *Journal Gazette* (Mattoon IL), October 20, 1939.

14. Associated Press, "Sees Cards, Medwick in 1940 World Series," *Spokesman Review* (Spokane), October 23, 1939.

15. Associated Press, "Sees Cards."

12. The Temperament of Genius

1. David Bloom, "The Last Out at Russwood," *Commercial Appeal* (Memphis), January 30, 1962.

2. Dave Anderson, "Man for Many Seasons, Butch Has Seen It All," *St. Louis Post-Dispatch*, October 26, 1982.

3. Mize and Kaufman, *How to Hit*, 14.

4. Mize and Kaufman, *How to Hit*, 14.

5. Sid Keener, Sid Keener's Column, *St. Louis Star-Times*, March 27, 1940.

6. Keener, Sid Keener's Column, March 27, 1940.

7. Keener, Sid Keener's Column, March 27, 1940.

8. Golenbock, *Dynasty*, 49.

9. Mize and Kaufman, *How to Hit*, 14.

10. Mize and Kaufman, *How to Hit*, 14.

11. Don Gutteridge, in discussion with the author, August 2000.

12. Gutteridge, discussion.

13. Mize and Kaufman, *How to Hit*, 88.

14. Tommy Holmes, "'He Hasn't Hurt Us a Bit,' Is Durocher's Guarded Praise of Dodger Rookie Catcher," *Brooklyn Eagle*, September 6, 1940.

15. Buddy Blattner, in discussion with the author, April 2000.

16. Blattner, discussion.

17. Art Spander, "1987 Baseball Preview," *Albuquerque Tribune*, March 30, 1987.

18. "Billy Southworth to Replace Blades as Cardinal Manager," *St. Louis Post-Dispatch*, June 7, 1940.

19. Sid Keener, "Blades Is Fired and Southworth Hired as Card Pilot," *St. Louis Star-Times*, June 7, 1940.

20. Golenbock, *Spirit of St. Louis*, 221.

21. J. Roy Stockton, "Southworth Happy over Change," *St. Louis Post-Dispatch*, June 7, 1940.

22. Dick Farrington, "Ducky Likely to Be Stubborn Bird," *Sporting News*, February 29, 1940, 3.

23. Martin Haley, "Cardinals Trade Joe Medwick and Curt Davis to Brooklyn," *St. Louis Globe-Democrat*, June 13, 1940.

24. Golenbock, *Spirit of St. Louis*, 227.

25. Gutteridge, discussion.

26. Golenbock, *Spirit of St. Louis*, 227.

27. Donald Honig, in discussion with the author, September 2000.

28. Golenbock, *Spirit of St. Louis*, 227.

29. Laurence Leonard, "Former Patriot Mize Mashing That Pellet Comparable to Ruth," *News and Record* (Greensboro NC), June 20, 1940.

30. Gutteridge, discussion.

31. James, *New Bill James Historical Baseball Abstract*, 201.

32. James, *New Bill James Historical Baseball Abstract*, 206.

33. James, *New Bill James Historical Baseball Abstract*, 206.

34. Honig, *Baseball When the Grass Was Real*, 91–92.

35. Honig, *Baseball When the Grass Was Real*, 92.

36. Honig, *Baseball When the Grass Was Real*, 92.

13. Goodbye, St. Louis

1. "X-Rays Reveal Bone Chips in Mize's Bruised Finger," *St. Louis Globe-Democrat*, June 8, 1941.

2. "X-Rays Reveal."

3. Dent McSkimming, "Redbirds Will Begin Series of Three Games with Cubs Tomorrow," *St. Louis Post-Dispatch*, July 2, 1941.

4. Durocher and Linn, *Nice Guys Finish Last*, 144.

5. De Kever, *Freddie Fitzsimmons*, 239.

6. Durocher and Linn, *Nice Guys Finish Last*, 143.

7. Durocher and Linn, *Nice Guys Finish Last*, 144.

8. Durocher and Linn, *Nice Guys Finish Last*, 145.

9. Durocher and Linn, *Nice Guys Finish Last*, 145.

10. Durocher and Linn, *Nice Guys Finish Last*, 146.

11. Golenbock, *Spirit of St. Louis*, 232.

12. Golenbock, *Spirit of St. Louis*, 231.

13. Durocher and Linn, *Nice Guys Finish Last*, 146.

14. Honig, *Baseball When the Grass Was Real*, 92.

15. Golenbock, *Spirit of St. Louis*, 237.

16. Steve Snider, "National League and Landis Vote No; All-Star Game to Raise Military Baseball Fund," *St. Louis Star-Times*, December 11, 1941.

17. Honig, *Baseball When the Grass Was Real*, 94.

18. Honig, *Baseball When the Grass Was Real*, 92.

19. Sid Keener, Sid Keener's Column, *St. Louis Star-Times*, December 11, 1941.

14. Land of the Giants

1. Donald Drees, "Mize Not Surprised at Deal Sending Him to Giants," *St. Louis Star-Times*, December 12, 1941.

2. "U.S. Planes Sink Jap Cruiser, Big Battleship and Destroyer," *St. Louis Star-Times*, December 11, 1941.

3. J. Roy Stockton, "Mize May Go to Dodgers for Camilli, Franks and Cash," *St. Louis Post-Dispatch*, December 8, 1941.

4. Drees, "Mize Not Surprised at Deal."

5. Drees, "Mize Not Surprised at Deal."

6. Honig, *Baseball When the Grass Was Real*, 94.

7. Hynd, *Giants of the Polo Grounds*, 321.

8. Hynd, *Giants of the Polo Grounds*, 321.

9. John Drebinger, "Giants' Camp Disturbed as Mize Is Treated for Recurring Shoulder Ailment," *New York Times*, March 6, 1942.

10. "'Not a Spring Hitter': Mize," *Daily News* (New York), April 7, 1942.

11. Werber, in discussion with the author, January 2001.

12. Hynd, *Giants of the Polo Grounds*, 323.

13. Hynd, *Giants of the Polo Grounds*, 324.

14. Werber and Rogers, *Memories of a Ballplayer*, 41, 43.

15. Werber and Rogers, *Memories of a Ballplayer*, 43.

16. Werber and Rogers, *Memories of a Ballplayer*, 43.

17. Werber and Rogers, *Memories of a Ballplayer*, 43.

18. Cannon, "Musial Recalls Glory Years," *New York Journal-American*, January 13, 1963.

19. Vecsey, *Stan Musial*, 99.

20. Harold Parrott, "Dodgers Doff Caps to Javery, Melton," *Brooklyn Eagle*, August 19, 1942.

21. Honig, "Kirby Higbe," in *Baseball between the Lines*, 17:50.

22. Jack Smith, "Dodgers Divide, Lead Slashed to 2½ Games," *Daily News* (New York), September 7, 1942.

15. War Clubs

1. Dan Polier, "The Great Lakes Ball Team Has a Major League Lineup," *Yank*, August 6, 1943, 23.

2. Lee Scott, "Navy Relief Game," *Brooklyn Citizen*, May 9, 1942.

3. "42,822 Give $58,806 to Navy," *Daily News* (New York), May 9, 1942.

4. Tommy Holmes, "Twas a Great Day for Navy and Dodgers," *Brooklyn Eagle*, May 9, 1942.

5. "42,822 Give \$58,806 to Navy."

6. Bedingfield, "Baseball in World War II."

7. Bedingfield, "Baseball in World War II."

8. Mike Eisenbath, "Managing to Win," *St. Louis Post-Dispatch*, June 21, 1992.

9. Hennessey, "Johnny 'Big Jawn' Mize."

10. Hennessey, "Johnny 'Big Jawn' Mize."

11. United Press International, "Mize Is Inducted, Is Lost to Giants," *Pittsburgh Press*, March 25, 1943.

12. Clifford, "Silas K. Johnson."

13. Willis Johnson, "Mize in Navy, Expected to Train at Great Lakes," *St. Louis Globe-Democrat*, March 26, 1943.

14. "Great Lakes Beats Indians in Ninth, 2–1," *Chicago Tribune*, June 22, 1943.

15. "Sailors Claim Forces' Title," *Stars and Stripes*, June 24, 1943, 3.

16. Dan Polier, "The Great Lakes Ball Team Has a Major League Line-Up," *Yank*, August 6, 1943, 23.

17. "American Giants Beat Great Lakes Navy Team of Ex-Major Leaguers," *Chicago Defender*, August 14, 1943.

18. Hennessey, "Morrie Arnovich."

19. "American Giants Beat Great Lakes," *Chicago Defender*.

20. Riley, *Biographical Encyclopedia of the Negro Baseball Leagues*, s.v. "Radcliffe, Theodore Roosevelt (Ted, Double Duty)," 649.

21. "American Giants Beat Great Lakes," *Chicago Defender*.

22. Dan Polier, "Critics Put the Blast on Navy Big Leaguers," *Yank*, February 6, 1944, 23.

23. Caswell Adams, "On the Line," International News Service, *The Tribune* (Scranton PA), October 4, 1943.

24. Associated Press, "Navy Doctors Deny Mize to Get Medical Discharge," *Chicago Tribune*, November 24, 1943.

25. Bedingfield, *Wartime Baseball in Hawaii 1944*, 2.

26. Bedingfield, *Wartime Baseball in Hawaii 1944*, 2.

27. Blues Romeo, "Hitting Three Homers in Game Was Biggest Thrill for Mize," *Honolulu Star-Bulletin*, March 29, 1944.

28. "Mize Will Try to Hit a Homer over Stands," *Honolulu Star-Bulletin*, April 27, 1944.

29. Carl Macado, "Majors Need Extra Innings to Win," *Honolulu Star-Bulletin*, May 1, 1944.

30. Bedingfield, *Wartime Baseball in Hawaii 1944*, 17.

31. Bedingfield, *Wartime Baseball in Hawaii 1944*, 8.

32. Bedingfield, *Wartime Baseball in Hawaii 1944*, 18.

33. Bert Nakaji, "Largest Big Island Sports Crowd in History Sees Million Dollars Worth of Baseball Flesh," *Hawaii Tribune-Herald*, October 8, 1944.

34. Bedingfield, *Wartime Baseball in Hawaii 1945*, 22.

35. Richard Camp, "Taking Tinian," *World War II Quarterly*, Winter 2019, 64.

36. Frank Graham, "They All Love the Big Cat," *Sport*, January 1953, 80.

37. Howard Norman Bornak, letter to the editor, *Berkshire Eagle*, July 6, 1945.

38. United Press International, "Records of World Series Shattered in Tiger Victory," *Pittsburgh Press*, October 11, 1945.

16. Agony of Defeat

1. Dan Daniel, "Let It Snow! Clubs Set for Rush to Sunkist Zone," *Sporting News*, February 7, 1946, 3.

2. "1946: It's Good to be Home," This Great Game, n.d., https://thisgreatgame.com /1946-baseball-history/.

3. Daniel, "Let It Snow!"

4. "Record Attendance at Training Camps," *Sporting News*, February 7, 1946, 3.

5. Joe Reichler, "Mize Should Be Help to Giants," *Muncie Evening Press*, February 12, 1946.

6. John Drebinger, "51 Giants Drill in Miami Camp, with 21 Still to Be Heard From," *New York Times*, February 12, 1946.

7. John Drebinger, "Job at First Base Clinched by Mize," *New York Times*, February 17, 1946.

8. Hynd, *Giants of the Polo Grounds*, 336–37.

9. Jimmy Powers, "Maglie Cast in Giant Villain Role," *Daily News* (New York), April 3, 1946.

10. Hynd, *Giants of the Polo Grounds*, 337.

11. Hy Turkin, "Yanks Top Giants, 3–2, Win Series, Mize Hurt," *Daily News* (New York), August 6, 1946.

12. "Elliott's Power, Kiner's Bat, Head for Record," *Pittsburgh Post-Gazette*, September 26, 1946.

13. Jack Troy, "Broken Bone Robbed Mize of League Home Run Crown," *Atlanta Constitution*, September 30, 1946.

14. Troy, "Broken Bone."

17. Chasing the Babe

1. "Bill Rigney," in Peary, *We Played the Game*, 27.

2. "Bill Rigney," in Peary, *We Played the Game*, 27.

3. J. G. Taylor Spink, "Nobody Gets Sore on Being Sent to the Yankees," *Sporting News*, August 31, 1949, 12.

4. Spink, "Nobody Gets Sore."

5. Spink, "Nobody Gets Sore."

6. Hynd, *Giants of the Polo Grounds*, 342.

7. Hynd, *Giants of the Polo Grounds*, 343.

8. "Ralph Kiner," Bob Feller Act of Valor Award, n.d., https://www.actofvaloraward .org/ralph-kiner-profile.

9. "Ralph Kiner," in Peary, *We Played the Game*, 32.
10. "Ralph Kiner," in Peary, *We Played the Game*, 32.
11. "Ralph Kiner," in Peary, *We Played the Game*, 32.
12. "Ralph Kiner," in Peary, *We Played the Game*, 32.
13. John Drebinger, "Ottmen Fall, 14–5, to Braves' 25 Hits," *New York Times*, April 25, 1947.
14. Drebinger, "Ottmen Fall."
15. Jimmy Powers, The Powerhouse, *Daily News* (New York), July 4, 1947.
16. Dick Young, "Giants Massacre Flock, 19–2, on 15-Hit Barrage; Gain 2d," *Daily News* (New York), July 4, 1947.
17. "Leo Durocher," National Baseball Hall of Fame, n.d., https://baseballhall.org/hall-of-famers/durocher-leo.
18. Harold C. Burr, "Dodgers Back in U.S. from Foreign Junket," *Brooklyn Eagle*, April 7, 1947.
19. Hy Turkin, "3 Marshall HRs Rip Reds, 8–3; Giants in 2d Place," *Daily News* (New York), July 19, 1947.
20. Leavy, *Big Fella*, 447.
21. Associated Press, "Babe Ruth Hopes Mize Is One to Break Mark," *Evening Sun* (Hanover PA), July 26, 1947.
22. Arthur Daley, "Still More on the Babe," *New York Times*, August 18, 1948.
23. Daley, "Still More."
24. Bob Broeg, in discussion with the author, March 2000.
25. Buddy Blattner, in discussion with the author, April 2000.
26. C. M. Gibbs, Gibberish, *Baltimore Sun*, September 13, 1947.
27. Associated Press, "Six Awarded Scholarships," *Baltimore Sun*, September 13, 1947.
28. "Ralph Kiner," in Peary, *We Played the Game*, 32.
29. "Bill Rigney," in Peary, *We Played the Game*, 27.
30. "Bill Rigney," in Peary, *We Played the Game*, 27.
31. Kahn, *The Era*, 1.
32. "Home Runs a la Carte Surprising," editorial, *Sporting News*, October 29, 1947, 14.

18. Chasing Kiner

1. "Ralph Kiner," in Peary, *We Played the Game*, 69.
2. Dan Daniel, "Hilarious Skits Dent Game's Brass Hats at Gotham Writers' Dinner," *Sporting News*, February 11, 1948, 7.
3. Daniel, "Hilarious Skits."
4. Trimble, "Mize Player of the Year; Harris Honored," *Daily News* (New York), January 25, 1948.
5. Brands, "DiMag Only Yank on Writers' All-Star Club," *Sporting News*, January 28, 1948, 13.
6. Brands, "DiMag Only Yank."

7. Hy Turkin, "DiMag Signs 65G Yanks Contract," *Daily News* (New York), January 7, 1948.
8. "Mize Visits Stoneham—Then Signs for '49," *Daily News* (New York), November 25, 1948.
9. "Giants Hammer Feller; Mize Homers with 3 On," *Daily News* (New York), March 22, 1948.
10. Associated Press, "Mize Lifts Giants Pennant Hopes," *Star-Gazette* (Elmira NY), March 22, 1948.
11. Red Smith, Views of Sport, *New York Herald Tribune*, May 14, 1948.
12. Golenbock, *Bums*, 204.
13. Golenbock, *Bums*, 205.
14. Hy Turkin, "'Give Us Some Life,' Lippy's Talk to Giants," *Sporting News*, July 28, 1948, 7.
15. Turkin, "'Give Us Some Life.'"
16. Turkin, "'Give Us Some Life.'"
17. "Bill Rigney," in Peary, *We Played the Game*, 67.
18. Bill Roeder, "Lip's Books Startles Brass Hats," *New York World-Telegram*, May 26, 1948.
19. Cahn, *Sid Gordon*, 157.
20. Cahn, *Sid Gordon*, 157.
21. Cahn, *Sid Gordon*, 157.
22. Vecsey, *Stan Musial*, 200.

19. Big Cat Earns His Pinstripes
1. Associated Press, "Mize Hears Jeers at Big Moment," *Baltimore Sun*, October 8, 1949.
2. Vince Johnson, "Once Over Lightly," *Pittsburgh Post-Gazette*, September 15, 1948.
3. Dana Mozley, "Flock 3d, Bows, 4–2; Giants Lose, 11–1," *Daily News* (New York), October 4, 1948.
4. Associated Press, "Giants Offer Cooper and Mize to Cubs, but Grimm Rejects," *Daily Times* (Davenport IA), November 2, 1948.
5. "Giants May Name 2 Coaches Today," *Evening Express* (Portland ME), November 3, 1948.
6. Dana Mozley, "Giants Call Westrum, Sell Livingston," *Daily News* (New York), June 15, 1949.
7. Honig, *Baseball When the Grass Was Real*, 94.
8. Monte Irvin, "An Interview with Monte Irvin," by Jeff Idelson, National Baseball Hall of Fame, n.d., https://baseballhall.org/discover-more/stories/baseball-history/interview-with-monte-irvin-2006.
9. Zachofsky, *Idols of the Spring*, 149–50.
10. Roscoe McGowen, "Dodger-Giant Deal Is Seen in Making," *New York Times*, April 14, 1949.

11. Frank Adams, "Yankees Purchase Mize; Joins Club Today," *Daily News* (New York), August 23, 1949.
12. United Press International, "Giants Sell Johnny Mize to Yankees," *Hopewell (VA) News*, August 23, 1949.
13. "Yanks Get Big First Sacker from Giants," *Press & Sun-Bulletin* (Binghamton NY), August 23, 1949.
14. Adams, "Yankees Purchase Mize."
15. Joe Trimble, "Buy Puts Sox in Hole," *Daily News* (New York), August 23, 1949.
16. Arthur Daley, "Mize for Hall," *New York Times*, January 21, 1971.
17. J. G. Taylor Spink, "Nobody Gets Sore on Being Sent to the Yankees," *Sporting News*, August 31, 1949, 12.
18. Spink, "Nobody Gets Sore," 12.
19. Spink, "Nobody Gets Sore," 12.
20. John Vergara, "Casey at the Helm," *Daily News* (New York), October 5, 1949.
21. George Kirchner, "Mize Scares Brooks," *Lancaster (PA) New Era*, October 7, 1949.
22. Kirchner, "Mize Scares Brooks."
23. Red Smith, Views of Sport, *New York Herald Tribune*, October 7, 1949.
24. Mize and Kaufman, *How to Hit*, 94.
25. Stan Baumgartner, "Yankees' Mize Hero of 3d Game," *Philadelphia Inquirer*, October 8, 1949.
26. Grantland Rice, "Joe DiMaggio Looks to Be Sick Man, Says Rice," *Boston Globe*, October 8, 1949.
27. John Drebinger, "Yanks Top Dodgers with 3-Run 9th, 4–3, for 2–1 Series Lead," *New York Times*, October 8, 1949.
28. James P. Dawson, "Mize, World Series Hero at Long Last, Likes Those Fences at Ebbets Field," *New York Times*, October 8, 1949.
29. Appel, *Pinstripe Empire*, 275.
30. Wolf, "Stengel Would Have Quit If Yankees Lost," *Sporting News*, October 26, 1949, 3.
31. United Press International, "Yank Uniform Does Things to You, Mize Says," *Winston-Salem Journal*, March 5, 1950.

20. Minor Setback, Major Recovery

1. Dan Parker, "Broadway Bugle," *Courier Post* (Camden NJ), July 25, 1950.
2. Jim McCulley, "Arm All Right, Yanks Sign Mize," *Daily News* (New York), January 31, 1950.
3. McCulley, "Arm All Right."
4. Joe Trimble, "Murderers' Row Reborn—Wakefield, Mize Added," *Daily News* (New York), March 10, 1950.
5. Louis Effrat, "Yankees Dispose of Five Players in Slash to Reach the Limit of 25," *New York Times*, May 16, 1950.

6. Lawrence Perry, "Bill Rigney and John Mize Prove a Credit to Baseball," *Kansas City Star*, May 19, 1950.
7. Perry, "Bill Rigney and John Mize."
8. Ernest Mehl, "Mize the Perfect Batting Model for a Boy to Follow," Between Innings, *Kansas City Star*, May 21, 1950.
9. Mehl, "Mize the Perfect Batting Model."
10. "In Series with Hens," *Kansas City Times*, May 24, 1950.
11. "In Series with Hens."
12. "In Series with Hens."
13. Associated Press, "Mize Socks First Home Run; Blues Split," *Star Tribune* (Saint Paul MN), May 29, 1950.
14. Ernest Mehl, "Mize Convinces a Skeptic with Home Run in St. Paul," Between Innings, *Kansas City Star*, June 6, 1950.
15. Mehl, "Mize Convinces Skeptic."
16. Mize and Kaufman, *How to Hit*, 13.
17. Mize and Kaufman, *How to Hit*, 13.
18. John Drebinger, "Tigers Overcome 3 Mize Homers in a Row to Top Yanks and Take First Place," *New York Times*, September 16, 1950.
19. Associated Press, "3 Homers in Game a Jinx," *New York Times*, September 16, 1950.
20. Appel, *Pinstripe Empire*, 282.
21. Dan Daniel, "Bombers to Boost Stengel to $65,000 for '51," *Sporting News*, October 11, 1950, 7.
22. Rollie Wirths, "Mize Ponders Status With Yanks," *Portland (ME) Press Herald*, October 13, 1950.

21. Sitting in Casey's Lap

1. Charlie Roberts, "Maris 'Protests' Starrette Pitch," *Atlanta Constitution*, August 25, 1974.
2. Dan Daniel, "Casey's Vets Look Like Champs Again—with Spring Color," *Sporting News*, March 28, 1951, 7.
3. Golenbock, *Dynasty*, 77–78.
4. Dick Young, Diamond Dust, *Daily News* (New York), September 6, 1951.
5. Jimmy Powers, The Powerhouse, *Daily News* (New York), April 25, 1951.
6. Lally, *Bombers*, 74.
7. Lally, *Bombers*, 74.
8. Lally, *Bombers*, 74.
9. Rizzuto and Horton, *October Twelve*, 73.
10. Golenbock, *Dynasty*, 51.
11. Jim McCulley, "Mize Signs for $25,000 At 39; Eyes HR Mark," *Daily News* (New York), January 9, 1952.
12. Mize and Kaufman, *How to Hit*, 94–95.
13. Mize, *How to Hit*, 94–95.

14. Red Smith, "Stengel Psychic; He Knows When to Start Mize," *New York Herald Tribune*, October 5, 1952.
15. Red Smith, "The Mahatma Made Sure," *New York Herald Tribune*, October 6, 1952.
16. Erskine, in discussion with the author, February 2021.
17. Erskine, discussion.
18. Johnny Mize, Johnny Mize Says, *Philadelphia Inquirer*, October 6, 1952.
19. Golenbock, *Dynasty*, 132.
20. Golenbock, *Dynasty*, 132.
21. Golenbock, *Dynasty*, 134.
22. Francis Stann, "Win, Lose, or Draw," *Evening Star* (Washington DC), October 8, 1952.
23. Gayle Talbot, "Mantle-Stengel Duo Credited with Yanks' Fourth Straight," *Star-Gazette* (Elmira NY), October 8, 1952.
24. Furman Bisher, "Mize Betrothed to Birmingham, in Rumor," *Atlanta Constitution*, October 21, 1952.
25. Associated Press, "Johnny Mize Will Get Chance to Wallop 2,000th Base Hit," *Bellingham (WA) Herald*, October 30, 1952.
26. Associated Press, "Johnny Mize Will Get Chance."

22. How to Hit

1. Jimmy Cannon, Jimmy Cannon Says, *Newsday* (New York), December 17, 1958.
2. John Fox, "Mize Turns Author: Sense, Characters Cram 'How to Hit,'" *Press & Sun-Bulletin* (Binghamton NY), March 29, 1953.
3. George K. Leonard, "Five on Baseball Are Reviewed," Sports Book Corner, *Nashville Banner*, April 23, 1953.
4. Joe Reichler, "Mize, a College Player at 14, Authors Book on 'How to Hit,'" *Miami Herald*, March 23, 1953.
5. Brown, in discussion with the author, May 2001.
6. Cannon, Jimmy Cannon Says.
7. Brown, discussion.
8. Reichler, "Mize, a College Player at 14."
9. Reichler, "Mize, a College Player at 14."
10. Mize and Kaufman, *How to Hit*, 86.
11. Mize and Kaufman, *How to Hit*, 104–5.
12. Byron Hollingsworth, The Morning After, *Tampa Tribune*, May 28, 1953.
13. Joe McGuff, "A's Hire Johnny Mize to Tutor Hitters," *Kansas City Star*, July 2, 1961.
14. Brown, discussion.
15. Joe Trimble, "Last of 4 Yank Holdouts Sign; Rizzuto Gets 42G," *Daily News* (New York), March 3, 1953.
16. Golenbock, *Dynasty*, 137.
17. Joseph Sheehan, "Mize's 2000th Hit Wasted in 3–1 Loss," *New York Times*, June 17, 1953.

18. "Not Bad for over 40!" *Daily Mail* (Hagerstown MD), March 27, 1953.

19. Whitey Ford, in discussion with the author, May 2001.

20. Joe Trimble, "Mize to Quit," *Daily News* (New York), September 6, 1953.

21. Trimble, "Mize to Quit."

22. "Mize May Quit but It Depends," *Sioux City Journal*, September 6, 1953.

23. Rizzuto and Horton, *October Twelve*, 234.

24. Cannon, Jimmy Cannon Says.

25. Erskine, in discussion with the author, February 2021.

26. Erskine, discussion.

27. Golenbock, *Dynasty*, 163.

28. Dave Anderson, "Campy Has Last Laugh on Stengel," *Brooklyn Eagle*, October 3, 1953.

29. Erskine, discussion.

30. Erskine, discussion.

31. Ford, discussion.

32. Erskine, *Tales from the Dodgers Dugout*, 93.

33. Ford, discussion.

34. Tommy Holmes, "Afterthoughts on the Series," *Brooklyn Eagle*, October 7, 1953.

35. United Press International, "Big John Quits Baseball after Fifteen Years," *San Bernardino County Sun*, October 7, 1953.

36. United Press International, "Big John Quits."

37. United Press International, "Big John Quits."

38. United Press International, "Big John Quits."

39. United Press International, "Big John Quits."

40. Oscar Ruhl, From the Ruhl Book, *Sporting News*, December 23, 1953, 14.

23. Out to Pasture

1. Al Thomy, "Big Jawn Sits by the Sea . . . Forgotten by Baseball," *Atlanta Constitution*, July 10, 1970.

2. Oscar Ruhl, From the Ruhl Book, *Sporting News*, November 4, 1953, 16.

3. Sid Shalit, "Mize Becomes Sportscaster . . . ," Looking and Listening, *Daily News* (New York), January 12, 1954.

4. Shelley Rolfe, Reviewing Sports, *Richmond Times-Dispatch*, February 16, 1954.

5. George Beahon, In This Corner, *Democrat and Chronicle*, April 1, 1954.

6. Al Del Greco, For the Record, *The Record* (Hackensack NJ), April 6, 1955.

7. "Gophers Hurting Erskine," Diamond Diggings, *Jersey Journal*, May 28, 1955.

8. Joe Trimble and Jim McCulley, "Offer Mize Job as Miller Pilot," *Daily News* (New York), October 2, 1955.

9. "Miller Job to Mize? Ryan Hasn't Heard," *Star Tribune* (Saint Paul MN), October 2, 1955.

10. "'Stanky Best Possible Choice,' Claims Ryan," *Star Tribune* (Saint Paul MN), October 3, 1955.

11. "Ewell Blackwell," in Honig, *Baseball between the Lines*, 5:23.

12. "Ewell Blackwell," in Honig, *Baseball between the Lines*, 5:34.

13. "Mize's Wife Dies of Burns," *Orlando Sentinel*, July 15, 1957.

14. "Ex-Slugger Mize Off on Honeymoon," *Dothan (AL) Eagle*, October 24, 1957.

15. Jim Mize, in discussion with the author, March 2022.

16. Mize and Kaufman, *How to Hit*, 3–4.

17. Jim Mize, discussion.

18. Jim Mize, discussion.

19. Dick Young, "Mize Finds Mick's Flaw," *Daily News* (New York), August 7, 1959.

20. Joe McGuff, "A's Hire Johnny Mize to Tutor Hitters," *Kansas City Star*, July 2, 1961.

21. McGuff, "A's Hire Johnny."

22. Young, "Mize Finds Mick's Flaw."

23. McGuff, "A's Hire Johnny."

24. Jim Mize, discussion.

25. Judi Mize, in discussion with the author, March 1999.

26. Lew Krausse Jr., in discussion with the author, February 2000.

27. Krausse, discussion.

28. Judi Mize, discussion.

29. Jim Mize, discussion.

30. "Ex-Pros Travel South," *Brownsville (TX) Herald*, February 22, 1965.

31. Corbett, "Global Fiasco."

32. Corbett, "Global Fiasco."

33. Jimmy Mann, "Mize Finds a New—and Confusing—Home," *Tampa Bay Times*, April 22, 1969.

34. Mann, "Mize Finds."

35. Corbett, "Global Fiasco."

36. "Global League Team Held in Venezuela," *Los Angeles Times*, July 29, 1969.

37. Corbett, "Global Fiasco."

38. Al Mallette, "Baseball Opinions," Change of Pace, *Elmira (NY) Advertiser*, July 29, 1961.

39. Posnanski, *Baseball 100*, 235.

40. Posnanski, *Baseball 100*, 235.

41. Posnanski, *Baseball 100*, 235.

42. Al Thomy, "Too Soon They Forget—Johnny Mize," *Atlanta Constitution*, June 17, 1971.

43. Robert Paynter, "Johnny Mize, Baseball Great Still Outside of Hall of Fame," *Anderson (SC) Independent-Mail*, July 6, 1975.

24. Going Home

1. Hal Bock, "'I Wasn't Invited,' Mize Says," Associated Press, *Capital Times* (Madison WI), August 10, 1977.

2. Bob Broeg, "Doubting Writer Hopes Mize Is All Through as Hitter," *St. Louis Post-Dispatch*, August 14, 1977.

3. Broeg, "Doubting Writer Hopes Mize."

4. Charlie Roberts, "Hall Sees New Mize," *Atlanta Constitution*, February 17, 1947.

5. Roberts, "Hall Sees New Mize."

6. Donald Honig, in discussion with the author, September 2022.

7. Honig, discussion.

8. Zell Miller, in discussion with the author, February 2000.

9. Miller, discussion.

10. Miller, discussion.

11. John Foster, in discussion with the author, April 2000.

12. Foster, discussion.

13. Foster, discussion.

14. Foster, discussion.

15. Ken Picking, "It's Mize's Moment," *Atlanta Constitution*, Marcy 12, 1981.

16. Picking, "It's Mize's Moment."

17. Picking, "It's Mize's Moment."

18. Picking, "It's Mize's Moment."

19. Larry Eldridge, "There's Finally a Niche for the Big Cat," *Christian Science Monitor* (Boston), August 6, 1981.

20. Hal Bock, "Mize Stirs Memories," Associated Press, *Herald-Palladium* (Benton Harbor–Saint Joseph MI), August 3, 1981.

21. Steve Wulf, "The Stuff of Legend," *Sports Illustrated*, June 12, 1989, https://vault .si.com/vault/1989/06/12/the-stuff-of-legend-the-hall-of-fame-was-built-in -cooperstown-upon-a-foundation-of-fable-based-on-a-letter-from-a-madman -and-a-dirty-ball-found-in-an-attic-but-from-such-bogus-beginnings-has-come -a-nearly-sacred-shrine-in-an-alm.

22. Judi Mize, in discussion with the author, March 1999.

23. Judi Mize, discussion.

24. Furman Bisher, "Mize Was a Mountain of a Man," *Atlanta Constitution*, June 6, 1993.

25. Richard Erwin, in discussion with the author, September 2021.

26. Stephanie Chitwood, in discussion with the author, September 2021.

27. Rizzuto and Horton, *October Twelve*, 234.

28. "Mize Expects to Be Active," *Atlanta Constitution*, December 31, 1982.

29. Tom Mewborn, in discussion with the author, February 2000.

30. Mewborn, discussion.

31. Mewborn, discussion.

32. Foster, discussion.

33. Mike Eisenbath, "Mize Is Recalled by Former Mates as a Great Hitter," *St. Louis Post-Dispatch*, June 3, 1993.

34. Joe Strauss, "Mize: From Small Town to 'Big Cat,'" *Atlanta Constitution*, June 3, 1993.

35. Strauss, "Mize: From Small Town."

36. Eisenbath, "Mize Is Recalled."

Epilogue

1. Jimmy Powers, The Powerhouse, *Daily News* (New York), April 25, 1951.
2. Julia Ruth Stephens to Mr. Marcus, May 27, 1980, "Babe Ruth's Wife Claire Was Mize's Second Cousin," Cooperstown Expert, https://www.cooperstownexpert.com/player/johnny-mize/.
3. Mike Eisenbath, "Mize Is Recalled by Former Mates as a Great Hitter," *St. Louis Post-Dispatch*, June 3, 1993.
4. James, *New Bill James Historical Baseball Abstract*, 434–35.
5. Birnbaum, "Guide to Sabermetric Research."
6. Bill James, email message to author, May 14, 2021.
7. Jim Mize, in discussion with the author, March 2022.
8. Jim Mize, discussion.
9. Jim Mize, discussion.
10. Jim Mize, discussion.
11. Jim Mize, discussion.
12. Judi Mize, in discussion with the author, March 1999.
13. Judi Mize, discussion.
14. Joe Frisaro, "Mize Entertains Fans at Baseball Card Show," *Tampa Tribune*, June 25, 1989.
15. Frisaro, "Mize Entertains Fans."
16. Honig, *Fifth Season*, 15.
17. Honig, *Fifth Season*, 15.
18. Donald Honig, in discussion with the author, September 2000.

BIBLIOGRAPHY

Appel, Marty. *Pinstripe Empire: The New York Yankees from before the Babe to after the Boss*. New York: Bloomsbury Publishing, 2012.

Bedingfield, Gary. "Baseball in World War II." Baseball in Wartime, accessed February 14, 2023. https://www.baseballinwartime.com/baseball_in_wwii/baseball_in_wwii.htm.

———. *Wartime Baseball in Hawaii 1944: Here Come the Big Leaguers. Baseball in Wartime Newsletter*, September 2020. https://www.baseballinwartime.com /BIWNewsletterVol12No53Sept2020.pdf.

———. *Wartime Baseball in Hawaii 1945: The End in Sight. Baseball in Wartime Newsletter*, October 2020. https://www.baseballinwartime.com /BIWNewsletterVol12No54Oct2020.pdf.

Birnbaum, Phil. "A Guide to Sabermetric Research." Society for American Baseball Research, accessed November 3, 2022. https://sabr.org/sabermetrics.

Bjarkman, Peter. *Baseball with a Latin Beat: A History of the Latin American Game*. Jefferson NC: McFarland, 1994.

Byrd, J. W. Thomas. "Femoroacetabular Impingement in Athletes, Part 1: Cause and Assessment." *Sports Health* 2, no. 4 (2010): 321–33. https://doi.org/10.1177 /1941738110368392.

Cahn, Steven D. *Sid Gordon: An American Baseball Story*. Self-published, 2022. https:// americanbaseballstories.com/.

Christensen, Will. "Take Me Out to the (Minor League) Ballpark." *National Pastime*, 2022. https://sabr.org/journal/article/take-me-out-to-the-minor-league-ballpark/.

Clifford, Matthew. "Silas K. Johnson: An Illinois Farm Boy Who Made Baseball History." *National Pastime*, 2015. https://sabr.org/journal/article/silas-k-johnson-an -illinois-farm-boy-who-made-baseball-history/.

Cohen, Robert. *The 50 Greatest Players in St. Louis Cardinals History*. Toronto: Scarecrow Press, 2013.

Cora, Sundae Yvette. Prologue to *My Father Martin Dihigo, "The Immortal,"* by Gilberto Dihigo, 11–12. Self-published, Plaza Editorial, 2018.

Corbett, Warren. "A Global Fiasco: Walter Dilbeck's Third Major League." *Baseball Research Journal*, Spring 2020. https://sabr.org/journal/article/a-global-fiasco -walter-dilbecks-third-major-league/.

Cramer, Richard Ben. *Joe DiMaggio: The Hero's Life*. New York: Simon & Schuster, 2000.

Creamer, Robert. *Babe: The Legend Comes to Life*. New York: Simon & Schuster, 1974.

De Kever, Peter. *Freddie Fitzsimmons: A Baseball Life*. Bloomington IN: AuthorHouse, 2013.

Dihigo, Gilberto. *My Father Martin Dihigo, "The Immortal."* Self-published, Plaza Editorial, 2018.

Durocher, Leo, and Ed Linn. *Nice Guys Finish Last*. New York: Simon & Schuster, 1975.

Erskine, Carl. *Tales from the Dodgers Dugout*. New York: Sports Publishing, 2017.

Gay, Timothy. *Satch, Dizzy & Rapid Robert: The Wild Saga of Interracial Baseball before Jackie Robinson*. New York: Simon & Schuster, 2010.

Golenbock, Peter. *Bums: An Oral History of the Brooklyn Dodgers*. New York: Putnam, 1984.

———. *Dynasty: The New York Yankees, 1949–1964*. Chicago: Contemporary Books, 2000.

———. *The Spirit of St. Louis: A History of the St. Louis Cardinals and Browns*. New York: Avon Books, 2000.

Gómez, Miguel Dupouy. "Tetelo Vargas en Venezuela." *Beisból Inmortal* (blog), June 11, 2020. https://beisbolinmortal.blogspot.com/search?q=Concordia.

Greenberg, Hank, and Ira Berkow. *Hank Greenberg: The Story of My Life*. New York: Times Books, 1989.

Grillo, Jerry. "Johnny Mize." Society for American Baseball Research, accessed April 1, 2023. https://sabr.org/bioproj/person/johnny-mize/.

Guilfoyle, Bill, ed. *National Baseball Hall of Fame and Museum Yearbook, 50th Anniversary, 1939–1989*. Cooperstown NY: National Baseball Hall of Fame, 1989.

Halberstam, David. *Summer of '49*. New York: William Morrow, 1989.

Hennessey, Shawn. "Johnny 'Big Jawn' Mize, WWII Service and His Elusive Signature." *Chevrons and Diamonds* (blog), September 12, 2019. https://chevronsanddiamonds.wordpress.com/2019/09/12/johnny-big-jawn-mize-wwii-service-and-his-elusive-signature/.

———. "Morrie Arnovich: Breaking Ground for Branch Rickey's Bold Move." *Chevrons and Diamonds* (blog), May 15, 2020. https://chevronsanddiamonds.wordpress.com/2020/05/15/morrie-arnovich-breaking-ground-for-branch-rickeys-bold-move/.

———. "Struck Out Swinging: Pee Wee Reese, Johnny Mize and Fred Hutchinson on Tinian." *Chevrons and Diamonds* (blog), February 26, 2018. https://chevronsanddiamonds.wordpress.com/2018/02/26/struck-out-swinging-pee-wee-reese-johnny-mize-and-fred-hutchinson-on-tinian/.

Henrich, Tommy. Foreword to *How to Hit*, by Johnny Mize and Murray Kaufman, v–vi. New York: Henry Holt, 1953.

Honig, Donald. *Baseball between the Lines*. Read by Ben Bartolone. Newark NJ: Audible Studios, 2014, 7 hr., 42 min.

———. *Baseball When the Grass Was Real*. New York: Berkley Medallion Books, 1975.

———. *The Fifth Season: Tales of My Life in Baseball*. Chicago: Ivan R. Dee, 2009.

Hynd, Noel. *The Giants of the Polo Grounds: The Glorious Times of Baseball's New York Giants.* Dallas TX: Taylor Publishing Company, 1995.

James, Bill. *The New Bill James Historical Baseball Abstract.* New York: Free Press, 2001.

James, Bill, and Jim Henzler. *Win Shares.* Morton Grove IL: STATS Publishing, 2002.

Kahn, Roger. *The Era, 1947–1957: When the Yankees, the Giants, and the Dodgers Ruled the World.* New York: Ticknor & Fields, 1993.

Lally, Richard. *Bombers: An Oral History of the New York Yankees.* New York: Three Rivers Press, 2002.

Lane, Mary C. *History of Piedmont College, 1897–1990.* Demorest GA: Piedmont College Press, 1993.

Leavy, Jane. *The Big Fella: Babe Ruth and the World He Created.* New York: HarperCollins, 2018.

Mantle, Mickey, and Herb Gluck. *The Mick.* New York: Doubleday, 1985.

McNeil, William F. *Black Baseball out of Season: Pay for Play Outside of the Negro Leagues.* Jefferson NC: McFarland, 2012.

Mead, William B. "The Surgeon General of Baseball." *National Pastime: A Review of Baseball History* 22 (2002): 95–98.

Mize, Johnny, and Murray Kaufman. *How to Hit.* New York: Henry Holt, 1953.

O'Neil, Buck, Steve Wulf, and David Conrads. *I Was Right on Time: My Journey from the Negro Leagues to the Majors.* New York: Simon & Schuster, 1996.

Peary, Danny. *We Played the Game: 65 Players Remember Baseball's Greatest Era, 1947–1964.* New York: Hyperion, 1994.

Peterson, Robert. *Only the Ball Was White: A History of Legendary Black Players and All-Black Professional Teams.* New York: Oxford University Press, 1992.

Posnanski, Joe. *The Baseball 100.* New York: Avid Reader Press, 2021.

Revel, Layton, and Luis Munoz. *Forgotten Heroes: Juan "Tetelo" Vargas.* Carrollton TX: Center for Negro League Baseball Research, 2014. http://www.cnlbr.org/Portals/0/Hero/Juan-Tetelo-Vargas.pdf.

Riley, James. *The Biographical Encyclopedia of the Negro Baseball Leagues.* New York: Carrol & Graf, 1994.

Ritter, Lawrence. *The Glory of Their Times: The Story of the Early Days of Baseball Told by the Men Who Played It.* New York: MacMillan and Company, 1966.

Ritter, Lawrence, and Donald Honig. *The Image of Their Greatness: An Illustrated History of Baseball from 1900 to the Present.* New York: Crown Publishing, 1979.

———. *The 100 Greatest Baseball Players of All Time.* New York: Crown Publishers, 1981.

Rizzuto, Phil, and Tom Horton. *The October Twelve.* New York: Tom Doherty Associates, 1999.

Roorda, Eric Paul. "The Wreck of the USS *Memphis* in the Dominican Republic." *Oxford Research Encylopedias,* February 25, 2019. https://doi.org/10.1093/acrefore/9780199366439.013.488.

Vecsey, George. *Stan Musial: An American Life.* New York: Ballantine Books, 2012.

Weiner, Steven. "September 13, 1953: Johnny Mize's Final Home Run Beats Indians." Society for American Baseball Research, accessed April 23, 2023. https://sabr .org/gamesproj/game/september-13-1953-johnny-mizes-final-home-run-beats -indians/.

Werber, Bill, and C. Paul Rogers III. *Memories of a Ballplayer: Bill Werber and Baseball in the 1930s*. Cleveland: Society for American Baseball Research, 2001.

Zachofsky, Dan. *Idols of the Spring: Baseball Interviews about Preseason Training*. Jefferson NC: McFarland & Company, 2001.

INDEX